AF444097

A LIFE OF GRATITUDE

An Autobiography

Kazuyoshi Ikeno

For information:
kaikeno@aol.com

Production and creative:
jonathangullery.design@gmail.com

FIRST EDITION
ISBN Print: 979-8-218-53222-2
Printed in the United States of America

Contents

PART I

Chapter 1: A Chronological Outline of Key Events … … … … … … … … 106

Chapter 2: The First Five Years of U.S. Pioneering (1972-1977) … … … 110

Chapter 3: The Providence of Home Church and Hoon Dok Hae

(Reading-Study) Church … … … … … … … … … … … … … … … 123

Chapter 4: IOWC Commander (1983-1984)… … … … … … … … … … 134

Chapter 5: The Minnesota and Wisconsin Period (1984-1991) … … … 144

PART I

Introduction

Since I reached 70 years old, I have felt that I should leave some kind of record of my own history. This is because I am convinced that the record of the joys, sorrows, and happiness I shared on earth with my most beloved and respected Rev. and Mrs. Moon will be an irreplaceable treasure in the distant future. They are as precious as God to me, and I call them True Parents; in my faith, they are the Messiah.

Because of misunderstandings, Rev. Moon was subjected to various slanders around this world, causing him to be imprisoned six times. But despite these adversities, he was able to fly up like a phoenix, bigger and better than before. The reason why this was possible is because there is God—God who created the universe has crawled up, step by step, from the depths of sorrow caused by the Fall of the first human beings and is finally embracing the light of hope. Even though Jesus Christ went down the miserable path of crucifixion, the subsequent resurrection formed Christianity, the largest religious cultural sphere in the world. Whenever Rev. Moon was in prison, his enemies were convinced that this was the end of his destiny, but after his release from prison, he became more vigorous than ever before and finally established a global influence in his own lifetime.

Recently, in Japan, a group of people are saying the Family Federation for World Peace and Unification (FFWPU) should be ordered to dissolve.

Rev. and Mrs. Moon are not trying to change themselves into God, but rather, they have been teaching us disciples to respect God more than anyone else. When I look around, tyrannical dictators like Sun Wukong (the fictional Monkey King character who thought he reached the highest point in the universe, but actually he flew in the Buddha's finger) are popping up all over the place, and it is so ridiculous to see dictators' ignorance and arrogance! The fate of materialists (communists) who do not fear God the Creator is limited. The

Soviet Union, which once dominated the world, was destroyed in less than 70 years. When communists or secularists attack a religion, they may think they have temporarily won, but in the end, the one who attacks collapses. This is the law of history.

Most of the people who are now denouncing and slandering the Unification Church are either communists or God-denying secularists. Since they cannot make Japan a communist state or a vassal state of China with the presence of the God-fearing Family Federation in Japan, they must think it's time to pursue a religious obliteration by ordering the dissolution of the FFWPU and stripping away its power.

However, the Family Federation has twice saved Japan from communist take-over attempts. History proves it. If you are humbled and know the reality of the Unification Church, you will not be able to tell stories without tears. The marrow of the Family Federation—its most essential part—is that it is called the "Church of Tears." Church members have long walked the path of hardship with tears for the salvation of humankind without being seen or understood by others.

My 78 years of life have been a journey of searching for God and meeting True Parents and the Messiah. It was also a journey to find my true self. In writing this autobiography, I would like to thank God for guiding my spiritual growth in a way that I could not see, and I would like to apologize for the worries I have caused. I would also like to express my deepest gratitude to True Parents, who knew me from before I was born, as well as God, and who have guided me with their fervent prayers behind my back, sometimes worrying that I was walking on too dangerous a path.

I would also like to express my deepest gratitude to my grandparents, who loved me so much, and to my deceased parents, who raised me desperately after I was born weighing only 850 grams (1.87 pounds) and worried about whether I would live. I am grateful for the sacrificial love of my parents, who listened to my selfishness and allowed me to study in the U.S. despite their financial difficulties. I can only wonder how hard it was for them to live a life of poverty for me. I could never have come to the U.S. if it were not for my relatives, who appeared like guardian angels to help me financially during the most difficult times while I was living in Japan and the U.S. If it were not for my ancestors who came to San Francisco from Kumamoto, my birthplace, 120 years ago, I would not have been able to come to the United States so easily. I needed a guarantor to study abroad.

My sister took good care of my parents until they became old and died, and I am deeply grateful to her. I would also like to express my sincere gratitude to my teachers who have guided me through elementary, junior high, and high school, and who have influenced me throughout my life.

Finally, I am deeply grateful for the guidance I received from many of my seniors in the Unification Church of Japan, and I am grateful that I have somehow made it this far. I would like to express my appreciation to all my friends at Waseda University's CARP (Collegiate Association for the Research of Principles) who organized the school festival called "CARP Fair" in the midst of the campus violence; we rejoiced together in the success of the event. Thanks to our members, my university life became an unforgettable treasure.

Last but not least, it has been 45 years since Rev. and Mrs. Moon introduced my wife and me to each other and married us. As we approach our golden wedding anniversary, our hair is graying and our legs and hips are no longer as mobile as they used to be. Many of the people we knew have passed on to the other side of the world, and I feel a sense of sadness. My wife is now the only one who understands me and is my eternal companion. We have six children (one prematurely died) and 15 beautiful grandchildren. I am deeply ashamed that I have neglected my children and not cared for them meticulously, and left them feeling lonely. I believe that it is my duty to watch over them from behind while praying for their growth for the rest of my life.

I would also like to thank Mr. Fumio Fukatsu, president of Good Time Publishing, for his kindness in helping me write my autobiography during my stay in Japan. It's been almost a year since the publication in Japanese, and this English version is now finished.

It's been almost a year since the publication of my autobiography in Japanese, and the English version is tracked to publish October. I would like to express my deepest gratitude to the four individuals on English version publication. Mr. Sam Nishio :without his strong encouragement, I would not have published the English version. Mrs. Cheryl Wetstein who has worked at *The Washington Times* for 33 years. Her review breathed new life into every chapter of the manuscript. Mr. Jonathan Gullery, who worked at our National Church Headquarters for 40 years. I am really grateful for his careful work. And finally, Mr. Takashi Takenaka, the president of Japan Market Place in Ohio: he has always appeared like a guardian angel, offering indispensable fanatical suppor. I appreciate his generous support. In terms of the title of the book" A Life of Gratitude." In my 80 of years life, I had passed through many hardship, but as our beloved True Parents teach us, no matter what kinds of difficulties surge, if you have the heart of gratitude, you can overcome any difficulties. I deeply appreciate this precious teaching.

October 20, 2024
Milwaukee, Wisconsin,
United State of America
Kazuyoshi Ikeno

CHAPTER 1

A Chronicle of My Life

1. Spiritual Climate of the Uto Region

A. The Kyushu People's Particular Character

The Uto region, located on the island of Kyushu in southwest Japan, is a fertile plain suitable for agriculture. It has a triangular peninsula jutting into the Ariake Sea, which has abundant resources.

The area is said to be a treasure trove of ancient ruins. The early Jomon people settled here 5,000 to 6,000 years ago, and the Sobata shell mound in Iwako-so-cho, Uto City, is a valuable archaeological site. In the middle Jomon period, there are shell middens, such as the Adaka shell mound, and in the late Jomon period, the Kurohashi Shell Mound, which is a designated historic site. The various types of burial mounds (tumuli) in the Tumulus period have been excavated.

The number of kofun (ancient graves) in Kumamoto Prefecture is about 130, accounting for more than 20% of all kofun in Japan. A study of these archaeological tombs shows that the Uto region in ancient times was a rich land where several powerful families could prosper at the same time. The front-recessed circular mounds are associated with the Yamato regime, and the Tsukahara tumulus cluster—one of the largest square ditch tombs in Japan—is thought to be a "common cemetery" for the local powerful people and their entire clans.

However, the struggle between the powerful families under the influence of the central government and the local powerful families who maintained their own sphere of influence over the central government remained unchanged from the Middle Ages to the Early Modern Period and into the modern era.

Kyushu, far from the center of Japan, was considered a "frontier" from the nation's capital. This sense of remoteness is embedded in the depths of the Kyushu people and sometimes manifests as pride in being country dwellers and anti-centralization. Rebellions were common throughout the region's history. The frontier character of Kyushu also served as a place of exile for those who were defeated in power struggles in the central government (e.g., Sugawara no Michizane) and a place of refuge (e.g., Prince Knenaga of the Southern Court).

Through these historical changes, certain characteristics came to be associated with the Kumamoto people: They were thought to have a stubborn temperament, a twisted and dishonest way of looking at things, a disposition of being uncompromising in everything, and a passion to follow one's own beliefs. The word "mokkosu" is used in the Kumamoto region to describe this character. In most cases, the people of Kumamoto have been on the frontlines of history. They took a back seat to other parties during the Meiji Restoration, but on other occasions, as in the case of the Shimabara Rebellion, they have rushed forward with their convictions without thinking about the future. The "Shinpuren Rebellion" that broke out in Kumamoto during the Meiji Restoration was also along these lines.

B. The Kikuchi Clan that Ruled Higo

The emergence of warriors in the Kumamoto region happened early, and in 1019, when the Toui (pirates led by a faction of the Joshin clan) ravaged the Kyushu area, a group of Higo warriors fought under the command of the Dazaifu. The commander-in-chief of the Japanese forces at that time was Dazai General Fujiwara no Takaie (nephew of Fujiwara no Michinaga. The Kikuchi clan was a blood relative of the Takaie clan that defeated the Toui.

In the Kamakura period (1185-1333) in feudal Japan, the Kikuchi clan sided with Emperor Go-Toba in the Jokyu Rebellion, so their territory was reduced, and they were brought under the control of a group of warriors from the eastern part of Japan. However, the Genko Incursion (Mongol invasion of Japan in 274-1281) gave the Kikuchi clan a once-in-a-lifetime opportunity to redeem themselves.

When I was a child, there were many pictures of Kamakura warriors fighting bravely against the Mongolian tribes in the precincts of the Shrine in my hometown. Of course, the pictures were copies of the famous "The Mongol Invasion," but among them was a heroic picture of Takezaki Hidenaga (Takezaki is a branch of the Kikuchi clan) on horseback, knocking down Mongolian soldiers with a sword.

The Kikuchi family was both highly praised and later disgraced, but when the Mongols attacked Japan, Kikuchi Takemoto took credit for the success of the attack and was called to serve as a retainer. He was later appointed as a governor of Higo Province. At the end of the Kamakura period, Emperor Go-Daigo raised an army to defeat the shogunate. Kikuchi Takemoto responded to the order of Emperor Go-Daigo's son, Prince Moriyoshi, and attacked Chinzei Tentaku, but the Kikuchi clan was defeated to the verge of extinction.

C. Lord Kiyomasa Kato and Lord Yukinaga Konishi

In Kumamoto, there is a somewhat violent festival called "Boshita Matsuri." In this festival, riders whip their horses and control them as they ride down the main street, chanting, "Boshita! Boshita! Boshita!" Sometimes the horses are given alcohol to make them more violent, and this is a vulgar festival that excites the onlookers. Nowadays, due to opposition from the Humane Society of Japan, it is not allowed to hit the horses with a rope. The crowd cheers loudly when a gigantic man resembling Lord Kiyomasa Kato (he was 190 cm (6 feet, 2 inches) tall), wearing armor and holding a large spear, pushes a stuffed tiger high into the air behind the horse, cutting it off. What "boshita" means is that he destroyed Korea. In Kumamoto, Kiyomasa Kato is called "Sei Shouko sana" as a term of respect. In Kumamoto, the name "Kato Kiyomasa" is used in honor of him, and a Kato Shrine has been built and is dedicated to him as a god. However, in Amakusa, there are few people who speak well of Kiyomasa.

Lord Kiyomasa Kato, a Buddhist

This is because, in 1589, Yukinaga Konishi was appointed by Hideyoshi Toyotomi (who ruled Japan between 1583-1598) as the new lord of Uto and Amakusa, but the powerful clans known as the Amakusa Five rebelled against the land survey in Amakusa. Seeing that his own forces would not be sufficient to suppress the rebellion of the Amakusa Five, Lord Yukinaga Konishi asked Lord Kiyomasa Kato, who controlled the northern half of Higo, to support him. Kiyomasa showed no mercy to the islanders, especially the Christian peasants, and killed them all. These rumors persist in the region, making Kiyomasa unpopular there.

Before and after warlord Toyotomi Hideyoshi's conquest of Kyushu in 1587, Higo warriors, who had sided with the Shimazu clan, rebelled against Hideyoshi through the Higo People Uprising and other means, many of which were destroyed. With the pacification of Kyushu, Hideyoshi's unification of the whole country was almost accomplished. As Imperial Regent of Japan, Hideyoshi entrusted the northern half of Kumamoto to Kiyomasa Kato and the southern half to Yukinaga Konishi, with the Kase River-Midori River as the border. The two men created two unique cultures due to their different personalities, different visions of nation building, and especially their different beliefs. In particular, the difference in faith between Kiyomasa, a devout Nichiren Shoshu Buddhism follower, and Yukinaga Konishi, a Christian feudal lord, had a great impact on the subsequent strained relations between the two.

Christian Lord Yukinaga Konishi

Kiyomasa Kato was one of the leading generals under the Toyotomi clan and the leader of the Budan (militarist) faction. His relationship with Ishida Mitsunari (fought against Ieyasu Tokugawa after Toyotomi's death) deteriorated as the Bunji (civilian) factions were formed under the Toyotomi regime. He and Yukinaga Konishi constantly quarreled over the boundaries of their respective territories, including a disagreement during the invasion of Korea. Kiyomasa devoted himself to flood control and the promotion of agriculture, and for this, he was revered by the people of Higo. He was also a master castle builder and was involved in the construction of numerous fortresses, including the magnificent Kumamoto Castle and Nagoya Castle. He was prepared to bring Hideyori Toyotomi, the late leader's son, to Kumamoto and challenge the Tokugawa forces in a line of retreat. So, he built a castle that was efficient from both an offensive and a defensive standpoint, and prepared a house and grounds for Hideyori in the castle.

Ieyasu Tokugawa (his family members ruled Japan over 250 years), knowing Kiyomasa's intentions, discouraged him from participating in the Battle of Sekigahara (the most significant of battles in feudal Japan), and he returned to Kumamoto from Osaka with a broken heart. Kiyomasa attacked Uto Castle, the residence of Yukinaga Konishi, when he learned that the western forces were defeated, and drove Yukinaga's brother, who was staying at the castle, to commit suicide. After Kiyomasa's death, however, his heir apparent was forced to resign and the Kato family fell into decline. After the Kato family was exiled, the Hosokawa family entered Kumamoto Castle.

In my birthplace, there is a huge irrigation dike (Tachioka no Tsutsumi) that Kiyomasa had built. A large mountain was created behind it with earth and sand that was dug up from the soil. Thanks to this dike, most of the rice paddies in Hanazono Village are well watered. Kiyomasa was also a genius in river improvement. He took part in the renovation of Kumamoto's four major rivers, protecting Kumamoto from flooding.

Lord Yukinaga Konishi entered Uto Castle in June 1588. For the next 13 years, he ruled Uto, Yatsushiro, and Amakusa. However, due to the invasion of Korea and other reasons, he was in Uto for less than five years. Yukinaga was born and raised as the son of a wealthy merchant in the free trade city of Sakai, and under Hideyoshi, he took possession of Shodo Island (Kagawa Prefecture) and served as naval commander in the Seto Inland Sea. For him, the Ariake Sea was similar to the Seto Inland Sea, and he must have felt a rush of excitement as he recalled the days when he used to manipulate his navy and play an active role in every direction.

Yukinaga's town planning may have been to make Yatsushiro a commercial city like Sakai, and Amakusa a naval base like Shodoshima. Yukinaga also had the privilege of being a Christian feudal lord. He had learned about world affairs from Portuguese missionaries and wanted to make Uto, Misumi, Yatsushiro, and the Amakusa Islands a major base for world trade. It is not difficult to imagine that Yukinaga was thinking of trading with Europe, which was located on the opposite side of the Pacific from Japan, by making full use of maritime transportation.

In his own territory, Yukinaga encouraged Portuguese missionaries to witness in order to gain followers, and taught Bible lessons and baptized people himself. Father Bariniano, a missionary in Amakusa, wrote a letter to Don Luis Serqueira, bishop of the Diocese of Japan, describing Yukinaga's active missionary work in his territory. Mr. Mimasaka (referring to Yukinaga), with wisdom and gentleness, spoke of salvation to the principal citizens of the region, and about 25,000 people were baptized in the land under his rule. This religious fervor spread to Uto. Uto was the main castle of Agos Niinyo (baptismal name of Yukinaga), and another priest went there and baptized about 4,000 people in a few days, and later another 2,000 people became believers. Another priest went to a place called Yabe and baptized 2,500 people. Thus, the mission spread like wildfire throughout Uto, Yatsushiro, and all the islands of Amakusa.

Yukinaga then established an organization of mutual cooperation, called the "Mercy Group" (shinshinkai no kumi) among the baptized fiefdom, so that they could maintain their faith on their own. This was in case Hideyoshi issued a prohibition order in the future and there were no missionaries left.

The doctrinal book, "Dochirina, Kirishitan" (11 chapters), was printed in 1591 by a metal type printing press brought back by the Tensho mission* to Europe. It had stories from the Old Testament, and in the preface to the doctrinal book, Jesus Christ preached and taught his disciples during his life. The main contents of the doctrine were: one, to believe in God Zeus; two, to desire salvation by Zeus, and three, practice the same love of neighbor that they had for Zeus. This "belief, hope, and love" was the fundamental teaching of God Zeus, and was said to be the principle for obtaining salvation of the spirit in the next life. A number of seminaries, called "colegios," were built in the Amakusa

Islands, and their priests and missionaries were sent to Yukinaga's territory to instruct new believers who were baptized.

*During the Azuchi-Momoyama period, feudal lords in western Japan embraced Christianity. In 1582, four young men were sent as Tensho envoys to Rome, seeking support for missionary work and showcasing their efforts in Japan. Despite a warm reception in Europe, their return to Japan in 1590 was met with the harsh reality of Toyotomi Hideyoshi's anti-Christian policies.

Shiro Amakusa Flag

The creation of this "Mercy Group" by Lord Yukinaga ultimately led to their martyrdom. They were devout to God and to each other; they rubbed each other to keep warm in the cold in the middle of winter during the Shimabara Rebellion, which was a powerful incident that shook the shogunate. Lord Yukinaga upheld the teachings of the Mercy Group and protected his adopted Korean daughter, Julia Otaa, near Pyongyang during his war campaign in Korea (during the Bunroku era); he raised her under the care of Mr. and Mrs. Konishi from an early age. Influenced by them, Julia also took the Christian path. In particular, she is said to have developed a deep knowledge of medicinal herbs, which were closely related to the Konishi family's original business.

Later, after Yukinaga was executed in defeat at the Battle of Sekigahara and the Konishi family fell, Tokugawa Ieyasu, who saw Julia Otaa's talent, took her into the inner palace of Sunpu Castle and favored her. However, she refused Ieyasu's request to apostatize from Christianity and refused to be chosen as Ieyasu's official concubine. Thus in 1612, she was exiled to Hachijojima, then Niijima, and finally to Kozushima in the Izu Islands, where the conditions were most severe.

In such circumstances, Julia Otaa's attitude was to practice the teachings of the Mercy Group (shinshinkai no kumiai). She devoted herself to the daily lives of the islanders, even on a barren island with sharp, rocky mountains, and gave hope and joy of life to the exiled people who were cast away. She knew firsthand that there is joy in supporting one another. Joy is born when we live for others, and God's love is felt when we serve others. Although life on the island of Kozushima was hard, Julia is said to have said: "Here I am happier than when I was in the inner palace. I can pray freely and always receive God's love when I live for Him." Even after her death, the islanders to whom she devoted herself with all her sincerity have held a permanent memorial service, called the "Otaa Festival," to honor her.

After Yukinaga Konishi was defeated in the Battle of Sekigahara (1600) and disappeared into the dew at Shijo-Kawara, the survivors and the former Christian believers, while reorganizing the Mercy Group according to the teachings of Yukinaga and the priests, continued to gather several times a week. They held meetings to give testimonies, listen to consultations, solve problems, and pray. This way, they kept the fire of faith burning. They were the so-called hidden Christians, and among them were 37,000 Christian peasants from the Amakusa Islands, Shimabara, Uto, and vassals of Yukinaga. They holed up in Shimabara's castle and rose up against the heavy taxation of the feudal lord at the time, which led to the Shimabara Rebellion (1637-1638).

Few documents remain concerning Amakusa Shiro, the chieftain. There are two theories concerning his place of birth: One is that he was born in Ebe Village, Uto District, and the other is that he was born in Oyano Village, Amakusa District. Amakusa Shiro's father was a retainer of Yukinaga Konishi. After the death of his lord, he returned to farming and lived in Ebe Village in Uto County, where Shiro was born. Some people call him "Ebe Shiro." I recently came across a theory that blends the two theories of Amakusa Shiro's birthplace in a good way, and I would like to write about it. "His real name was Tokisada Masuda, and his baptismal name was Jeronimo. His father Jinbei (Yoshitsugu) was a surviving retainer of the Konishi family, and after the fall of the Konishi family in the Battle of Sekigahara, he lived in Uto, Higo Province (Kumamoto Prefecture), and later moved to Amakusa" (see "History of the Christians in Amakusa," by Norio Kitano). It is said that he later went to Nagasaki to study Christianity and was baptized. I am sorry to be presumptuous, but I was born in the same village of Uto, and Hanazono Village is a neighbor of Ebe Village. When I was a child, I was told many times about Amakusa Shiro. Each time, I felt I had to fulfill the grudge of the 37,000 Christian peasants who died trying to create a heaven ("paraíso") in this land.

Shiro Amakusa Statue at Hara Castle Park

The Uto region was ruled by the Hosokawa clan until the Meiji Restoration, but the strong impression left by Kiyomasa Kato and Yukinaga Konishi's human charm, achievements in flood control and irrigation, and religious lessons are still alive in the hearts of the people.

2. Birth and Childhood

My clan lived in the neighboring villages of Hanazono Village, Uto. They have always known each other with a kindred spirit, a kind of kinship. My paternal grandfather was a close friend of my mother's father. One day, when my grandfather, Kaichi Ikeno, went to visit my mother's father, Yoshiki Kinoshita, he saw Yoshiki's eldest daughter, Yoshiko, who was still very young, polishing a large pot until it shone. My grandfather decided to choose this girl must be my eldest son's bride.

My aunt told me that my father, Kazuo, was the most brilliant person in the village—his talent was the kind that may or may not appear once every 50 years—and he used to stand in for the principal at the morning assembly and give the morning greetings and orders to all the students on the school ground stage. My father's ambition was to go to Kyushu Imperial University, but since his family was poor and he was the eldest son, his destiny was to take over farming. When my father foresaw that my grandfather was going to take him farming, he would climb to the top of a large persimmon tree in the garden and read a book there. When he went to farm, he would not work but would lie down and look up at the sky. My grandfather eventually gave up the idea of having my father become a farmer and instead chose his second son, Akio, to take over the farm, as well as the head of the family.

My mother was the most beautiful girl in the village and was the object of admiration of all the boys. If her younger sister was bullied by a boy, she would chase him around with a stick and beat him until he apologized, sometimes causing him to cry.

My father entered the telegraph department of the Moji Training School of Japan National Railways, which was exempt from tuition fees, and after two years of training, he went to work for Kumamoto Nippon Telegraph and Telephone Corporation. Later, he began working in the communications section of the Japanese National Railways. Meanwhile, my mother lived in China; she worked as a nurse at the Nanjing Army Hospital as her father was a military attaché in Nanjing.

My parents got married on March 15, 1944

My paternal grandfather was also in Manchuria, working for the Kwantung Army, when one day he suddenly received a revelation that his eldest son had to marry Kinoshita's eldest daughter. He, therefore, rushed back to Japan. As soon as my mother received the news, she rushed back to Kumamoto from China.

On March 15, 1944, a wedding ceremony was held. My father had already received a call-up notice, so they had a very short honeymoon, during which time they conceived me. In my hometown, it was customary for the husband-to-be to go to his wife's family home for their honeymoon.

I was born on November 20, 1944, at my mother's family home and later moved to my father's family home in the next village. The name given to me at birth was "Kazuyoshi," after one of my grandfathers' names.

My father's unit was located in Saga, and he was in charge of sending various communication messages from the Imperial Headquarters to the various war zones. For the next three years, from the end of the war until he returned home, my mother had to endure a very hard time raising me by herself.

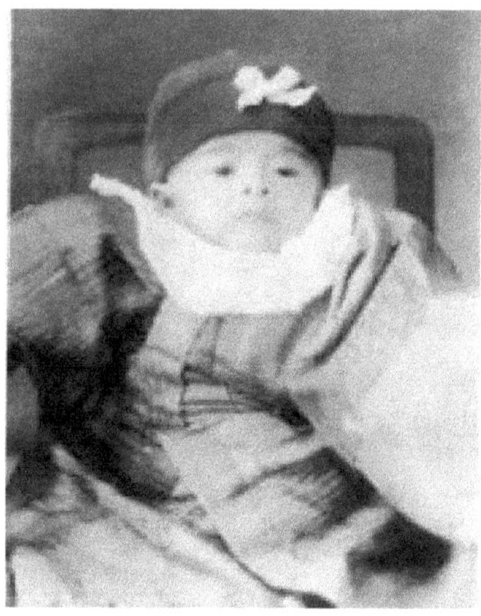

My picture of third day after birth

When air raids during World War II became severe, the air-raid shelter dug in the hill behind my parents' house became the stage of their lives. There were no major facilities in my hometown that the U.S. military would have had to destroy, but there was a dried-up fertilizer plant called Uto Gosei, and it became a target for the U.S. military. At times, B-29 bombers would fly over the roof of my parents' house in a swarm so closely lined up in the sky that people could not see the light. Their bombs would make a booming noise as they flew over the roof of Uto Gosei. My mother was malnourished because she did not have enough food to eat even when she was pregnant. After I was born, she could not produce enough milk, so even though there were dangerous air raids, she risked her life to go to the city to milk the only goat in town. My grandmother always said that I weighed less than 850 grams (less than 2 pounds) when I was born, and I was so small that I could fit into both of her hands.

My mother and grandmother told me that since I was a child, I was a crier. I cried a lot whenever I did not like something, and I would also cry until I got what I wanted. At that time, there was a shortage of goods throughout our countryside, and we rarely went to Uto City to buy anything. However, once a month, a lady peddler called "Omitsu-san" would come with a cart and sell goods. She would go from house to house in the village carrying inexpensive groceries such as candy and string products.

Both my mother and grandmother looked forward to the visits of Omitsu-san. This was partly because they did not have to travel far to buy food, but also because they enjoyed hearing all kinds of rumors. My eyes lit up at the sweets that Omitsu-san brought. The quantity and quality of the sweets differed depending on the price. Some were as high as five yen ($0.03), but in our poor state, my parents really couldn't afford to buy me the five-yen ones even if I really wanted them.

One day, I became determined to eat the five-yen pastries, so when I saw Omitsu-san, I peeked into the cart to see what kind of pastries were available and begged my mother to buy me a five-yen one. She strongly reprimanded me, saying, "No!" I still challenged her, "No, I want the five-yen one," and the argument with my mother began.

Finally, I said, "I want to have the five-yen candy" and began to cry loudly, first in the garden, then on the street outside, and then on the outward bound road (the road in the center of the countryside). The villagers laughed and said, "Kazuyoshi-san is crying all the way around the village again." By the time I finally made it around the village, my grandmother cringed at the sight of me and commented, "Yoshiko-san, why don't you buy him a five-yen candy?" My mother had to give in, and soon I was hiccupping and chewing on a five-yen piece of candy with tears in my eyes.

My Fishing

To help feed our family, I fished a lot. I took dirt and stones from the banks of the river to block the water flow of the small river and then used buckets to empty out the water from morning until night. This exposed the trapped fish, and I caught many of them—large catfish, loaches, eels, carp, crabs, and Formosan loaches—and brought them home in large buckets. The catfish were boiled in miso (soybean paste), and the rest were boiled in sugar and soy sauce. My grandparents and aunts and uncles would eat the fish, exclaiming in admiration, "Kazuyoshi, this is really good!"

One day, I decided to dry out the base of the stream around the levee and river bridge. I worked from morning to evening, as this was a major undertaking. However, I knew that a large catfish, which could be called the master of that river, was hiding and living between the rocks at the base of the bridge. The water became so low that I could see the head and beard of the big catfish. After about an hour of deadly fighting, I was able to catch the catfish, which was about 68 cm (26 inches) long. The shepherd dog Kuma that was with me started barking at the big catfish.

It was getting close to dusk, and as I walked from the bank along the footpath to the street with a small Buddha statue, I saw a small figure standing in the distance. It was my grandmother. "Kazuyoshi, you're late. I was worried about you, so I came to see you." My grandmother waited for me at the Jizo statue on the corner until I returned. Behind us, the sun was setting with its bright light giving way to darkness. With my grandmother, Kuma, and a big catfish hanging out, we hurried home, bragging about our great catch of the day. First, I took a bath in the already boiling bath (it was called "Goemon-buro Japanese bath tub" in those days). As she washed my muddy body, my grandmother said to me, "Kazuyoshi has much darker skin than a black boy," and happily laughed as she washed my tanned back, assuring me that I was sure to win first prize if I participated in a dark-skin boy competition at the end of the summer vacation.

When I arrived at the dining table, there was miso soup with fresh clams and various kinds of fish that I had picked up the previous day. There was a square fireplace with a large pot hanging from the ceiling in the living room. Everyone sat around the fireplace, with my grandparents in the center, each eating a meal over the cauldron.

3. Elementary School Years

Minamata City

Because of my father's work, we moved about an hour's drive south, from Uto City to Minamata City, and then later, north of Uto City to Omuta City, so I had to experience elementary school twice. When I entered Minamata Elementary School, I attended the entrance ceremony with my mother. A large cherry tree in the middle of the schoolyard was in full bloom, and I remember walking to the ceremony with my mother with cherry petals on my shoulders and head. My classroom teacher was a beautiful, young woman named Ms. Tae Kusano. She made a strong impression on me.

I had made a friend at school, but this got me into trouble. I really wanted to have my favorite friend assigned to the seat next to me, but I was too obvious. So, my teacher asked me to stand in the hallway to reflect on that fact. I am still ashamed of this.

I ended up moving far away to Omuta City, so Tae Kusano was my classroom teacher for only six months. But she wrote about my inner potential on my report card. It was hard to say goodbye to her and to the classmates I had finally befriended.

With my sister in Minamata City

Another memory I have of Minamata is that of Mr. A. I became good friends with a classmate, Mr. A who lived below the hill, and we always went to and from school together.

Every morning, I would walk with him from the small hill where the Japan National Railways (JNR) government lodgings was located, through the village of barrack houses, along the bank of a waterway, and arrive at the school.

The Japan National Railways government buildings were located behind Minamata Station. There were two government buildings, with a view of the hillside plaza from the front, a storage shed in the back, and a cliff bank looming behind the shed, with a graveyard on top of it. To get to the government building, one had to pass through a village where Korean people lived. It seems that they made a living by collecting scrap metal and raising pigs. They were forced to live in poverty.

We struggled with poverty too. One day, on the way home from school, Mr. A looked pale and had no energy to walk. When I asked him what was wrong, he replied, "I haven't eaten for the past two days." I took him to my house, went to a wooden rice bin that was wrapped in a quilt in the closet, and held it out to him. He ate most of the rice, which was a mixture of barley, white rice, and sweet potato, while stirring in the miso soup.

That night, there was almost no food in our house, so my sister and I ate the leftover rice with miso soup diluted with hot water. My parents fed us the leftover foods, but they drank only hot water, and all night their stomachs made hungry noises on their bed. My parents did not make any complaint about the fact that I fed the rice in the rice bin to Mr. A.

The drainage canal that flowed by our school always had a strange chemical smell. The mercury flowing out of this drainage channel caused the outbreak of Minamata disease, which has since become a symbol of pollution. If we had lived there another year, we might have become victims of Minamata disease. Fortunately, we moved to Omuta City before Minamata disease spread. However, the Minamata period holds unforgettable memories for me.

Omuta City

During my six years of elementary school in Omuta City, I was blessed with good teachers who guided me while looking at my inner potential. This was the driving force that kept me hopeful for the future.

In September 1951, I entered the first grade at Taisho Elementary School in Omuta City. The teacher, Mrs. Misao Fukuyama, who was in charge of the same homeroom for the first and second grades, valued the children's individuality and, with keen insight, planted seeds deep in our young minds so that even young elementary school students would blossom toward their future potential. In her evaluation of me, she wrote: "He is small in stature, but he is full of vigor and energy, and is very active like a man." In response to the teacher's love, about seven students took turns greeting her every morning, and it became a fun routine to go to school with her surrounded by students laughing and smiling happily.

For the three years from the fourth to the sixth grade, I had another beautiful, young woman as my teacher. Mrs. Emiko Nishida was a graduate of the National University of the Education. Her house was about 30 km (18 miles) away from the school, so she rode a woman's bicycle to school every day. After class, for about two months, except for rainy days, she taught me how to ride a bicycle until I could ride by myself. She told me that I had a talent for painting and guided me to study painting for three years at the Omuta Children's Art Institute. Perhaps that is why my paintings won prizes in various competitions.

Going to second grade classes with my mother in Omuta City

Mrs. Nishida knew that I was concerned about my short stature, so when I entered the fourth grade, she gave me a special homework assignment and told me to research Napoleon and Hideyoshi Toyotomi and report back within a week. I first posed some questions to my father but did not get satisfactory answers, so I went to the library and read every book I could find on the two men. After I reported my research to my teacher, she said, "Although they were very small in stature, they had a high spirit, confidence in themselves, and the fortitude to overcome obstacles toward their vision. They could overcome difficulties."

"You should not be obsessed with external appearance," she advised me. "The inside of a human being is what matters. You will probably have a very turbulent road ahead of you, but don't stop. Become a great person by overcoming difficulties," she said, even though this might have been a little too much encouragement to a fourth grader.

With my former teacher, Ms. Emiko Nishida

Once, when I was in the fifth grade, before Mrs. Nishida came into the classroom, I wrote all over the blackboard, "Why are humans male and female?" She looked at it and asked who had written it. I answered in a small voice, "I did," thinking that she might be offended. She said, "Ask your parents this question." As for myself, I was not trying to ask about the issue of gender but simply ask the question of why there are masculine and feminine characters in the universe. However, I think I was misunderstood. I had to wait until I met the Unification Principle for the true answer.

Graduating to junior high school was hard for me. Tears began to stream down my face as I thought of leaving Mrs. Nishida, who had taken such good care of me. I was supposed to sing "Aogeba Toutoshi" at the graduation ceremony, but I could not sing it because the tears flowed unceasingly. At the end of the graduation ceremony, when I received my certificate, Mrs. Nishida gave me a small piece of colored paper with the words, "Till the day the road grass blooms, endure even if you are stepped on." The teacher explained the meaning of this poem: *No matter how hard your destiny and trials may be, they will all help you to build your character, so do not run away from them, but rather, stand tall and proud in the face of hardship. You should not run away from them, but rather, take them in stride.* These words are still my motto that guide me throughout my life.

Parents Were Passionate About Education

Although my father was the eldest son in his family, he chose to give his agricultural career to his younger brother and study at a railroad technical school. My father was still dissatisfied because this was not the career path he wanted. Therefore, my father probably wanted me, his son, to study hard because he could not study hard enough himself.

From the time I was in elementary school, I was subjected to Spartan education. For example, on hot summer days, my father would put a handmade blackboard inside a mosquito net, write arithmetic problems on it, and ask me to solve them. When I solved a problem, my father would jump up and down, pat me on the head and be happy. However, when I was not able to solve a problem, he got in a bad mood and hit me on the head with his fist. I became more nervous and more afraid of my father's fist than of solving the problem, so, instead of learning how to solve the problems, my head became more and more confused.

My father wanted me to go to an Imperial University. To get from Uto Station to my grandparents' place in Hanazono Sakaime Village, I had to walk along a long, dirt road. In spring, we would hear Mongolian larks peeping in the sky. As my father and I were walking amidst this tranquil scene, he suddenly said in a strong tone, "Kazuyoshi, you are going to go to the Imperial University in the future!" As a young child in the third grade of elementary school, I had no idea what an Imperial University was, and my father's aspiration seemed like a goal far beyond my reach. However, it was imprinted deep within me.

My mother had strong educational desires for me too. When I was in the second grade, I was in bed with a fever after catching a cold. But my mother woke me up and said, "Kazuyoshi, you are going to school!" She wrapped me in a padded kimono and took me to school on her back. She held me on her back until all the classes were over. In this way, I attended all my classes for six years without missing a single day of school. At my graduation ceremony, in front of the entire student body, the principal presented me with an award for perfect attendance. My parents were very proud and happy about the award. My mother kept this award and my Waseda University diploma in a drawer for posterity and was sometimes pleased to see the two certificates. She was fond of saying, "I did not graduate from a university, but you need to go to a university and become a good person for the world."

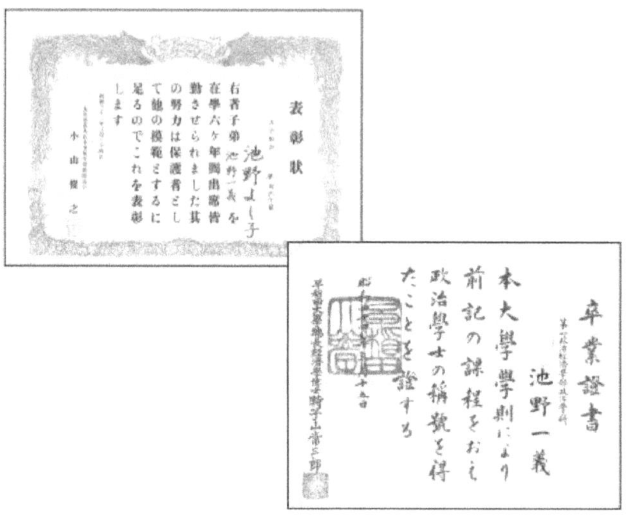

*My mother kept my college diploma and certificate
of perfect attendance commendation*

4. Junior High School

I attended Matsubara Junior High School in Omuta City for two years before my father was transferred to Kumamoto City and I moved to Toen Junior High School in Kumamoto City. Compared to my elementary school days, which had been smooth sailing, my junior high school days were the first stumbling block in my life.

Matsubara Junior High School

This junior high school received students from two different elementary schools. Many of the graduates of Taisho Elementary School, which I attended, came from families employed at the Mitsui Miike Coal Mine; many of these families had parents who held managerial positions. Hence, these students were often dedicated to education, and their grades were good.

Students from Meiji Elementary School, however, typically came from the downtown area of the city, where there were two street gangs.

I was the head of my class for two years at this junior high school, and I had a hard time dealing with this downtown group. Sometimes four or five of them would skip class and hang out in the corner of the schoolyard, smoking cigarettes. I lost my patience and went over and reprimanded them.

However, the boss of one of the gangs said that I was cocky. At first we argued, but finally the other guy started using violence. He hit me as hard as he could with his well-trained fists, and I, being small, was sent flying. The students who were watching from the window told the teacher, and the teacher came running toward us shouting. They ran away as if they had just poked a hornet's nest. The incident did not end there. The next day, I received a private letter of challenge containing a place, date, and time. I could not back out of the deal, so I made my own conditions.

With basketball teammates in Matsubara Junior High School

First, the fight must be one-on-one. No one else is to join in. No witnesses. No teachers were to be notified. So, I went to the assigned place. The boss was not there. There was no need for him to fight, so they had sent the junior boss.

It was after school hours, and there was no one in sight. We had to use the large classroom at the end of the second floor. We put our bags in the corner and started fighting. We went from fisticuffs to fisticuffs for about two hours, until both of us were wobbly with nosebleeds and bumps on our noses. At the time, I was a member of the basketball team and ran about 15 km (9 miles) every day before practice, so I was confident in my physical strength. A gangster messenger came to check on me. Later, the chief of the gang came to me and said, "I want to draw this duel. Hey, chief, what do you want us to do?"

I quickly replied, "As long as you come to school, you must follow the rules at least as much as possible. As long as they come to school, I want them to follow the minimum rules." After that, their behavior improved considerably.

Matsubara Junior High School

In junior high school, there was one very important custom that was different from when I was in elementary school. In junior high school, the results of the midterm and final examinations were announced in the hallway for everyone in the first through third grades. In junior high, the results of the examinations were announced only for the first 50 students out of 270 students in each grade. Thus, school changed from a fairly relaxed place to a harsh, competitive system. My friends from the same elementary school were now my academic rivals. It was a very sad thing. I lost a lot of things in this system—not only myself but also my friends.

I became egoistical, which delayed my development of compassion, pity, and charitable feelings. It was customary for me to prepare for exams by staying up almost all night to study, and when morning came, take a bath to relieve myself of fatigue and nervousness. I later heard that my pride and competitive temperament, combined with my desire not to "lose" to my fellow students, made me look very formidable during the exam period. I was generally always in the top five in all grades. One time, I was at the top. So, I was recommended for class president over the freshmen and sophomores.

What will never be forgotten in Omuta is the Mitsui Miike Coal Mine dispute. It started when a small labor union strike paraded through town, but it later became militant. The discord reached the classroom, and cold confrontation began to develop between the children of management and the children of the general coal-drilling employees. The main reason for this was that the leftist communists worked to portray the labor dispute as a class struggle that could only be resolved by adopting communist thought. Moreover, the character of the labor union changed drastically when Kyushu University Professor Itsuro Sakisaka, a communist economist from Omuta, opened a school for workers. He called it the Sakisaka Classroom and began lecturing on "capital theory" and other subjects.

Standing near Kumamoto Castle

Prof. Sakisaka considered Miike Coal Mine as a base for the coming socialist revolution and sought to train militant activists through education on "capital theory." Some of the teaching staff participated in this educational training, and some even tried to inflame students with communist ideas. For instance, in a social studies class, the vice principal of Matsubara Junior High School blurted out that the ongoing Miike coal mine dispute was a typical class struggle between the capitalists and the working class. Some children took this notion to heart.

Prof. Sakisaka also had hostility toward the U.S. He knew that Japan surrendered in response to the indiscriminate U.S. bombing of Japan and the atomic bombings of Hiroshima and Nagasaki. But he also said the U.S dropped different types of atomic bombs on Hiroshima and Nagasaki to study the effects of the bombs and to secretly study the aftereffects of atomic bomb disease in order to understand the power of the bombs. Prof. Sakisaka had a grudge against President Truman and other leaders, and he imposed it on us students. As I watched the union demonstrations, which were becoming more militant every day, I knew that this communist theory would not lead people to happiness.

Kumamoto City Toen Junior High School

I had to move to Kumamoto because of my father's job transfer. My father had been promoted to ward head of the Kumamoto Administration Bureau. He was aware of my academic records, and arranged with an acquaintance for me to cross the border to an excellent junior high school that competed for the top two places in the city. This school attracted many children from wealthy families in the city center, and even today, when I return to my hometown, my old classmates Mr. Furukawa, Mr. Seto, Mr. Sakakibara, Mr. Megumi, Mr. Komatsu, Ms. Goto (now Mrs. Sakamura), Ms. Kobayakawa (now Mrs. Shimizu) and others gather there. This school was located right under Kumamoto Castle, and during lunch break, I looked forward to sitting on the stone wall with my lunch box and eating it while chatting with my classmates with a view of the castle tower. I made lifelong friends there.

When the entrance examinations approached, those who were going on to higher education had remedial classes in English, mathematics, and Japanese. Sometimes they would return home at 7:00 PM. In any case, it was an enthusiastic preparatory junior high school.

As was customary at this junior high school, after midterm and final exams, the grades for all grades were posted in the hallway at the same time. I was usually within the top 10. Unlike the junior high school in the countryside of Omuta, there were many excellent students in this sophisticated city school. There were three famous high schools in Kumamoto City, and the best students from each junior high school were preparing for entrance exams to Kumamoto

High School, Seiseiko High School, and Daiichi High School, which specialized in girls' education.

Climbing Mount Aso

The First Stumbling Block

One week before the entrance examination, I got a high fever and began to cough badly after getting cold during my customary morning bath. The school was going to have a mock exam that day, so I went out. However, the fever made my head spin, and I hardly had the energy to solve the problems. I abstained from taking the exam and went home, but the fever and cough did not abate, and then the entrance exam arrived. As expected, I could not concentrate on the questions and many of them were not answered, so I finished the entrance exam with a low score. I realized later that I had made a huge mistake in math and Japanese, and that night I could not sleep. Five days later, when the results were announced, my shocking failure caused quite a stir at the junior high school. My homeroom teacher, Mr. Kai, and the vice principal both urgently begged the high school to review my exam papers; however, it was too late to change the result.

The news that "Ikeno failed the entrance examination into Kumamoto High School" caused a commotion. Mr. Kai and the vice principal each called to comfort me. But the person most shocked by this news was my father. He must have thought that his dream of having his son attend a top high school, enter an Imperial University, and eventually become a great man, while he had been giving his son a Spartan education since he was a child, had been shattered.

Indeed, the failure of the high school entrance exam came as a big disappointment for my family.

However, in hindsight, I now see that it was God's plan. My failure to excel in the exam made me realize what a small shell I had been living in. I realized that there were more important things in this world. Quietly, looking back on my three years of junior high school, I realized that my personality had gradually changed. My competitive spirit even drove me to post my report card in the hallway after every exam! My perspective had become narrow, and I had spent the past three years seeking the sweet sense of superiority that came from outshining and outperforming my opponents. As a result, I had transformed from the generous and considerate person I had been in elementary school to a selfish individualist. My spiritual growth had stopped. Had I continued on this path, I might have become a ruthless rationalist who felt no compassion. From that vantage point, I became convinced, even if a bit cynical, that God had created this situation.

While I was thinking about this, a good friend of mine from junior high school, Mr. Jitsuo Sakakibara, motivated my depressed mind by showing me a higher-standard high school to comfort me. He told me that Kagoshima LaSalle was a Catholic high school whose motto was not only to improve students' academic performance but also to promote spiritual growth by deepening their religious understanding.

I went to visit it. The school was a boarding school, with its own rooms and study rooms for the whole school, and a cafeteria next door. I could see smoke from the majestic Sakurajima, Japan's most active volcano, from the schoolyard. There was also a chapel. The principal was a priest, and I asked him many questions. He explained to me that the unique feature of a religious high school is that students can achieve harmony between character and study by studying hard while engaging in spiritual cultivation. I thought I had found the answers I had been seeking for a long time.

I was impressed that a small school with a total enrollment of 200 students could produce 40 to 60 students who were accepted to the University of Tokyo. Three days after taking the entrance examination, I received a letter of acceptance. I tried to convince my parents to send me to that high school, but my father raised an eyebrow when he realized that the tuition would be more expensive than the tuition at a private university in Tokyo. I was temporarily in Taniyama City (where LaSalle High School is located), but due to my parents' strong wish that I return to Kumamoto, I decided to return to Kumamoto and attend a local high school. I felt sorry for my father, thinking that he, too, had given up hope with this kind of feeling.

5. Kumamoto High School

At Kumamoto High School, I decided to shift my focus from the study-oriented life I had led up to this point to focus on my favorite club activities and pay special attention to my spiritual growth over the course of the next three years. At this high school, after the midterm and final exams, all the grade reports were posted in the hallway. Although I did not join the literary club I contributed a novel, titled "Catastrophe," in my freshman year and another one, called "Island with a Monument," in my sophomore year. My work at that time was awarded the Governor's Prize. In the newly established oratory club, my classmate, Mr. Oki, won the top prize at the national contest and was awarded the national Education Department Cup. I also participated in two national competitions and won prizes. In sports, I was a member of the Ekiden (long distance running) club and ran 20 km (12 miles) every day. I ran as an anchor in the annual prefectural race.

Becoming Student Body President

Kumamoto High School was the best preparatory school in the prefecture. As such, remedial classes were frequently held to prepare students for university entrance. However, most of the students failed to qualify for sports-related competitions. I always thought that I should not be satisfied with such a jinx; I thought that I should be able to study well and also be good at sports.

I liked the school's rules. When you enter the school gate, there is a bust of the first principal, Mr. Noda, with the motto "Shikunshi" inscribed on the stand. "Shi" means the self-discipline of a samurai, and "kunshi" means "gentleman" in England. A gentleman in England is said to be a person who, having disciplined himself, wishes for the happiness of others and has "aspirations" for the peace and prosperity of the country. I thought that this school code should be passed down as a tradition. When I was running for student body president, I used the catchphrases "Revive the spirit of Shikunushi!" and "Make a beloved student council!" The specific policy was to enhance the athletic department, which meant that more than half of the budget given to the student council would be distributed to the athletic department.

Becoming student president and chairperson of city student council

The idea was to encourage more students to join the athletic department. I proposed a program to make the athletic festival more fun and family oriented, where all participants could indulge in folk dancing. I also proposed inviting other schools to the Art Festival and awarding the third place prize to the nominees, including those nominated by the other schools and the nominee from my own school. For the student body president elections, the opposing candidate was one of our school's most gifted students, Mr. U. (He later became a professor of mathematics at Kyoto University.) As a candidate for vice president, he chose as his running mate the most beautiful and sharp-witted female student, known as the "Madonna of Kumamoto High School." It is said that the campaign was the most spectacular since the school was founded. Someone spread a rumor that "money was exchanged," and the whole school became absorbed in the election campaign.

At the end, all 1,500 students gathered in the schoolyard, the two camps were introduced, and the presidential candidates gave speeches. I began my speech with the words, "Though my color is black, my blood is red. When the time comes to say 'Kamakura,' I will stand up for the Yamato Spirit of Kyushu!" I dared the participants to be excited. Next, I explained to everyone my motivation for running for office and my concrete plans for the future. As a result, I received 995 votes and won over my opponent by a huge margin with 485 votes. At that moment, I realized that a great invisible force, the "spirit world," was behind me and assisting me. Since then, whenever there was something important to do, I have been able to do my utmost to win with the help of the spiritual world.

The Kumamoto High School student council president was also the chairperson of the "City Council," an organization formed by the student councils of 38 schools in Kumamoto City, and was in charge of planning and directing a sports festival for 34,000 high school students from all over the city.

Spirit-led Mr. Miyagi

When I entered high school, there was a man named Mr. Miyagi who was the chairman of the board of education of Suwa City in Nagano Prefecture. He studied English literature at the graduate school of Waseda University, was an English teacher at a high school in Suwa City for a while, and later became the chairman of the board of education. He was a devoted Christian and had been led by the Spirit. He came to Kumamoto High School after changing jobs. He told us how it happened. One night, in a dream, his grandmother appeared to him and told him that a serious incident was about to occur at Kumamoto High School and that he should go there immediately to prevent it. He told us what had happened one day.

In a dream, the grandmother of his ancestors appeared and told him that from now on she wanted him to believe in what she was asking him to do and be faithful to her without putting his own heart or opinion into it. When he had doubts, she appeared again in his dream and said, "If you still don't believe me, go up to this roof tomorrow and you will find three acorns with leaves on them." So he climbed up the ladder to the roof in the morning and, sure enough, there were three acorns with leaves on it. Since then, he has followed his grandmother's orders with absolute faith, no matter how difficult they may be.

The first thing he did at Kumamoto High School was distribute English-Japanese Bibles published by the Gideon Society to all students. Many students gathered in the gymnasium to receive the free Bibles. It was decided that a Bible study group would meet once a week, using both the English and Japanese translations of the Bible. I also participated. The teacher talked about various items in the Bible and told us about the joy of God's creation and the suffering of His return through the stories of Bible characters.

In his regular classes, he used Lafcadio Hearn's (Koizumi Yakumo) "Ghost Stories" as a textbook, and here, too, he told us various stories of the spirit world.

I eagerly awaited his lessons. The textbook was full of interesting content, but I was fascinated by his stories about his experiences in the spirit world. The other students treated him like a weirdo and mostly ignored his stories of the spirit world. I wondered what kind of serious incident would happen at this high school if the teacher's stories about the spirit behind him were true, and I was secretly afraid that it might involve me.

Suicide of a close friend

Shumei Matsunaga joined the oratorical club I founded when he was a freshman in high school. He joined the club because he wanted to change his passive personality into one that was not shy in front of others. He had been reading a lot of difficult philosophy books. He struggled to find salvation by projecting his own mental problems onto Nietzsche, Hermann Hesse, and others. He wrote more poetry than fiction. His posthumous manuscript, "Night Train," is a full-length work, and it is hard to believe that it was written by a high school student, as it depicts the inner life of a human being and his deep compassion for the passengers who come on and off the train. This collection of his posthumous poems was published in "Reimei," the journal of the oratorical club. His poems were admired by well-known poets.

Shumei was not very enthusiastic about his schoolwork by the time he was in his second year in high school. At the fall festival, the speech club members had to make presentations in front of the students. I wrote a speech, entitled "The Dreams of Youth." The speeches were given in the main hall on the seventh floor of Taiyo Department Store (the largest department store in Kumamoto at that time). All eight members of the club had written their speeches and started practicing. However, Shumei did not seem to want to do that. One day, he stayed over at my house, and I spent the whole night listening to his problems. He was a concerned about the deepest aspects of human existence itself, a concern about love, which was beyond my control. I have never known a high school student who looked so deeply into the human condition, worried so much about its contradictions, and writhed in an attempt to find a solution.

In his senior year of high school, Shumei and other students were under a lot of pressure as they were all preparing for higher education. Although he was smart and capable of getting into any famous university, he stopped coming to school many times in his junior year. His parents were concerned about his long absences.

Mr. Miyagi was also deeply distressed by Shumei's absences and was exhausted because he could foresee how serious things could become. At one point, he told us that he had been used by God to stop two tragedies from happening at the high school, one of which was to "stop [Shumei] from committing suicide," and the other was to "teach [Ikeno] a lesson" so that I would not get into trouble in my relationships with women and make changes now so that these problems would not occur. "Sexual depravity is just as damaging to the soul as suicide. Keep this in mind, overcome Satan's temptations, and live a clean life. That is my desperate wish," Mr. Miyagi pleaded with me.

Very sadly, in the early hours of May 1963, we received word that Shumei Matsunaga had committed suicide near Aso Station on the Hohi Line, overlooking Mount Aso. He died by placing his head over the wheels of the train while gazing up at the majestic Aso. I had been thinking about the cause of his suicide, and after talking with him all night last year, I realized that what he needed most was the love of a mother who could understand and embrace his sensitive, wounded heart. He could not get that at home, so he turned to a woman as compensation. Unfortunately, this could not fulfill his feelings, and he became mentally exhausted and impulsively chose suicide. No one knows how often he felt on the verge of committing suicide. I felt deep regret at my inability to stop his death.

A week later, his funeral was held at his home. I was supposed to read the condolence message as a representative of his friends, but I was so sad from the depths of my heart that I could not read the condolence message but only sobbed. It felt like God was weeping over the loss of His own beloved son. But as a consolation to him, I vowed in my heart, "I will surely live your part too, so watch over me in the afterlife."

We had another shock after this. One day, the vice principal said to me, "Where the hell is this Mr. Miyagi?" When Mr. Miyagi came to our school, he did so suddenly. This time, he disappeared suddenly, without a sound. He was truly a mysterious man. I thought that he must have followed the order of his ancestor's grandmother and left for another job elsewhere.

Years later, in the spring of 1971, I was in Korea. On a small hill in Suten-ri, Rev. Moon turned to me and said, "When you were in high school, something dangerous was about to happen, so I sent someone to stop it." I felt that all the mysteries had finally been solved. Rev. Moon had requested Mr. Miyagi's grandmother to send him to Kumamoto High School.

6. Escape to Tokyo

I had lost hope in school education and was so upset by Matsunaga's suicide that I came to Tokyo with nothing but my clothes and a little money.

As former student body president, I should have read the commencement address. But due to Matsunaga's death and the current biased education system that was greatly affected by it, I did not attend the graduation ceremony and left for Tokyo because I was not comfortable criticizing the education system even if I stood on stage. I wanted to live alone in Tokyo to solve the big problem Matsunaga left behind and to make a plan for my future life. I wanted to think, pray, and find some answers. It was an escape to pursue a dream.

From Tokyo Station, I found lodging with Nariaki Ideta, a former member of the speech club in Shinjuku who was already studying at Waseda University. The Tokyo Newspaper Delivery Office in Tsurumaki-cho was looking for deliverymen, so I applied and decided to make a living by delivering morning and evening newspapers.

At first, I lived with two nihilistic young men at the newspaper dealership. These young men lived as if they were dead. After the morning delivery, they would lie down on their beds and not get up until the evening delivery. I thought I could cheer them up somehow, so I suggested to them that I would replace the wallpaper in their room to make it a little nicer. They agreed, so I went to the store to buy wallpaper and started putting it up that night. The finished product was excellent. The owner of the store was pleased to see it. What pleased him most was that the two nihilistic salespeople began to act more lively.

The job of newspaper delivery was not an easy one. I woke up at 4:30 AM, wove various advertising flyers into the newspaper and delivered the morning edition from 5:30 AM to 8:30 AM. Later, I delivered the evening edition from 5:00 PM to 7:00 PM. In the early days, when I was not used to it, I was so exhausted when I was done with the morning run, I would lay on the floor, falling down with a thud, and sleep until around noon. After lunch, I would start inserting flyers into the newspaper at around 4:00 PM, and then deliver the evening editions. Unlike the Asahi and Yomiuri newspapers, the Tokyo Shimbun was not as popular, so the scope and time of delivery was twice as long. In order to make a living and save some money, we had to distribute at least 300 copies.

In this world, people are forced to make a living and work hard. This is the world and, in society, each person has his or her own role; the whole lives as a cog in a wheel, large and small, connected to the whole. I was young and innocent but naïve. I moved to Tokyo by myself, without the support of my loving grandparents or parents, to find my own life, but poverty relentlessly crushed me and forced me to struggle hard every day to survive.

Then, in the midst of a very precarious life both mentally and financially, I felt a burning pain in my lower abdomen while delivering newspapers. I was taken to a nearby emergency hospital, where I was diagnosed with acute appendicitis. I was told that I needed to have an operation immediately, but I had no money to pay for the surgery, let alone the hospitalization. However, since it was a life-threatening matter, they decided to operate on me.

As I lay on the hard operating table, I was struck by a tremendous sense of emptiness. Around that time, my sister had sent me a letter. In the letter, she told me that my grandparents were really worried about me. She also wrote that my father was crying on the porch looking at my picture.

I felt their great and deep love from my heart. Fortunately, my cousin Masayoshi Seto, who had come to Tokyo from Los Angeles to train in Japanese cuisine, came to visit me at the hospital, and he paid my hospital bill. My friends from Kumamoto High School visited me in Tokyo and advised me to start studying for the entrance examination for Waseda University, as it was not too late to do so.

When I left the hospital and told the owner of the Tokyo newspaper delivery store that I was quitting my job, he was very disappointed. The two young men were finally motivated, the family had become cheerful, and the number of newspapers delivered was increasing rapidly. He gave me a parting gift, saying that although he would have loved to have me stay on, he was happy to hear that I would go to college for my future and become someone who could look at the world from a larger perspective. The two young men sent me off with smiles on their faces, telling me that they would be all right. It was a short stay, but I felt it was worth coming to Tokyo to be able to live with people who were trying to improve themselves.

This all happened in November, and I wrote to my parents that I had an appendectomy and that my cousin Masayoshi paid for the hospital bill. I said I had attended Waseda Entrance Prep School near Waseda University, and that I planned to take an entrance examination for Waseda next year. Therefore, I was sorry to ask, but please send me some money. My parents were surprised that I had acute appendicitis and had to have surgery—but they responded well to my request.

CHAPTER 2

College Days and Encounter with the Unification Principle

1. Introduced to the Principle Study Group

My parents sent money soon after I was discharged from the hospital, so I decided to first go somewhere quiet to devote myself to studying for the entrance examination. I rented a house along the Seibu Shinjuku Line in Shimoigusa, a short distance from Shinjuku and Takadanobaba, where two families can live in a single house. Since I had been diagnosed with mild kidney disease due to overwork from delivering newspapers, I decided to cook for myself. I took English and mathematics classes at a preparatory school and then bought reference books and studied by myself. I had been keeping notes on my life for a long time, but from November 1964, I started to keep a proper diary.

November 20th was around the time of my 20th birthday, and since then, my heart had been somewhat in a state of excitement. I wrote in my diary something like a vow to myself that I would become more than Jesus Christ. I was excited when I wrote such an ostentatious thing, but later I tore up the page because I was embarrassed to have sworn such a shameful thing.

I was admitted to the School of Political Science and Economics at Waseda University on April 1, 1965. Upon entering the university, I first joined the International Studies Association and the Waseda Literature Club. I thought that I could not talk about the world from now on without knowing about the U.S. and China, so I began to attend a private Chinese language school, Zenrin Shoin. There were truly unique people in the Waseda Literature Club. Two of them are now famous writers. One of my acquaintances, a female writer, joked,

"It's a pity that if you had stayed in the club until your third year of college, you would be competing with Haruki Murakami, who is now a successful author." As soon as I joined the club, I was entrusted with the leadership of one section. I guessed that this was probably the result of my showing a novel from my high school days during the interview to join the club.

In my section, there were about 20 literary youths who would gather together and bubble over with excitement every time. After I joined the Collegiate Association for the Research of Principles I continued to be a section leader of this literary group for about six months. I met Mr. Takuo Nagano there. He had a good physique but sensitive nerves and a complicated family background, which made him a good candidate for writing. When he heard that I had joined CARP (the Principle Study Group), he said he wanted to join as well, so he quickly completed his studies from the seven-day to the 40-day workshop and joined the group. I wrote a play, "Cosmic Pencee," at the Waseda Literature Club. It depicted the struggle between God and the devil that lurked within human beings.

The International Situation Study Group had three breakout sessions under the broad theme of how world peace can be built. I was in charge of the "Cold War Structure and UN Reform for Peace" subcommittee. After a fulfilling first year of university life, I returned to Kumamoto for the first time in a long time during the summer vacation of 1966. I felt I had to report to my grandparents and parents, who had worried about me, about what had happened so far. Shortly after returning home, on July 10, I heard a knock at my front door, and when I opened it, I found a tanned, fearless-looking young man wearing a yellowish shirt standing at my doorstep.

The young man, Mr. Y, was from the Kumamoto Unification Church, and he asked if I had any old newspapers or bottles. I had had a hard time delivering newspapers in the past, so the young man looked shining like God to me in the hot weather, wearing a shirt with a stained and darkened collar. He explained to me that he was not a Kumamoto resident but a Wakayama resident, and that he had been sent here on a pioneer missionary mission for the past 40 days to evangelize and collect scrap metal to raise funds for his activities. He asked about me, and when I told him that I was a student at Waseda University and was returning home for summer vacation, he exclaimed loudly, "You are a student of Waseda University?" I did not understand why he was so surprised at that time, but later I found out that Rev. Moon, the founder of the Unification Church and CARP, had studied at Waseda University.

Mr. Y implored me to visit CARP (the Principle Study Group) when I returned to Waseda. I was infinitely interested in the Unification Church for sending such a young man. I told him that I would definitely visit CARP, and we parted ways. I sent him off with a bundle of old newspapers lying around. Unfortunately, I lost touch with Mr. Y for a long time after that, and when I tried to contact him about two years later, he was no longer there. Even now, I fondly remember that tanned, fearless face.

After the summer vacation, I returned to the university in September 1966 and looked for the Principle Study Group. At the time, the university was in the midst of its fall festival, and an exhibition of the Principle Study Group was being held in a large classroom on the third floor of the School of Political Science and Economics. The large classroom was crammed with CARP exhibits. On a large sheet of paper, there was a general introduction, the Creation Principle, the Fall, eschatology, the restoration history of mankind to providence, and finally the Second Coming. Maps of Japan, Korea, and China were drawn to show when and where the Second Coming was to occur.

I was impressed by this logical explanation of the development of human history and especially the four-position foundation of the Principle of Creation. I also thought that he was somehow saying the same thing that Toynbee was saying about the simultaneity of history. This is the time of the apocalypse when the world will change from the sovereignty of evil to the sovereignty of good, and at this time, the world will be in the greatest turmoil. However, God the Creator will send the Savior and the Second Coming of the Lord to this world, and the age of conflict and struggle of mankind will end and the eternal heaven will be ushered in, he concluded. As I looked at the exhibits one by one, the person who explained them to me was Mr. Shinkichi Suzuki, who had just finished his seven-day workshop, and if I had any questions, Mr. Toshiyuki Tsuboi, who was then the head of CARP of Waseda University, would explain them to me in places.

I was urged to write a report after listening to the exhibits, so I first wrote that the Unification Principle is a wonderful, revolutionary theory. I was deeply moved by this exhibition because it gave me the answer to a question that I had been asking myself for a long time and which had not been resolved since my fifth grade homeroom teacher asked me why all things in the universe consisted of pairs of male and female. I was again impressed by the explanation that, according to the Unification Principle, this world is composed of the two sexes of yin and yang (male and female) and the two phases of internal character and external form. He described that I was impressed by the four-position foundation and the Parallel History of Restoration.

In addition, there was a column asking who you admire the most. I wrote Gandhi and Jesus Christ, which elicited sighs and exclamations of admiration from the members present.

2. Participation in Workshop

To reduce the burden on my parents, I moved into the house in Shimoigusa acquired from the Hosokawa family of Kumamoto. They converted it into a two-story dormitory and named it "Yuuhigakusha" (a dormitory for students), and about 100 students attending universities in Tokyo lived there. The dormitory provided a comfortable living environment with two meals a day and was close to Waseda with convenient transportation. Dormitory life was enjoyable because everyone could relax and have honest conversations in the Kumamoto dialect. However, ever since I went to the exhibition of the Principle Study Group, I always received a phone call from Mr. Suzuki at 5:30 in the morning. Each time, the lady who was on meal duty had to call me and said, "I want to rest more, but I am always woken up by your friend's phone call. What is so important that you have to do it every day?"

As the year went on, in 1967, Mr. Suzuki called me and asked me to attend the Tokyo-area Student Conference on May 20 as a part of the May Festival at Tokyo University. When I went there, I found that about 2,000 students had gathered in the Yasuda Auditorium of Tokyo University. The lecturers were Mr. Yoshikazu Komiyama and Mr. Minoru Omori, a well-known reporter from the Mainichi Newspapers. Mr. Komiyama's topic was "The Giant Star of World Liberation." He drew a large diagram and placed it on the side of the stage, and based on it, he spoke in his unique voice about the difficulties in human history. Mr. Omori's lecture was titled "The Fierce Situation in the Far East," in which he spoke about what the world situation would be like in the future, based on his own experience of the Vietnam War. I also listened to his lecture, taking notes. After the conference, students gathered around Sanshiro Pond to celebrate the victory of the convention and began to sing loudly together holding each other's shoulders. It was the first time in a long time that I was moved by the energy of these young people.

In the summer of 1967, Mr. Suzuki said, "I would like you to meet the Giant Star, because he is coming to Japan." When I asked him who he meant, he replied that he could not say at this time, but that I would be able to meet him if I participated in the summer seven-day training session (July 3 to July 10). The training session was held at the headquarters of CARP in Japan, in Nanpeidai, Shibuya. The building was a modern, two-story, Western-style building with a spacious lawn garden that was surprisingly large for the middle of Tokyo. The lecturer was Mr. Takeshi Kamiyama; the facilitator was Mr. Masuda of Tokyo University; and the group leaders were Mr. Yoshioka of Chuo University, and Ms. Tsuboi and Mr. Higashimori of Waseda University. Mr. Takakuwa (Mrs. Nakajima) of Tokyo University of Education was in charge of music. They were all fresh and likable, and about 25 people attended.

During the training session, the facilitator informed us that "only one of those who passed the Principle Test today will be taken to the testimony meeting of Rev. Won Pil Kim at the Shoto-cho Headquarters." The office staff told me that Rev. and Mrs. Moon would be away from Tokyo for a while on a regional tour, but they encouraged me to listen to the testimony of their first disciple, Rev. Won Pil Kim, who was giving a series of testimonies about the pioneering days of the Unification Church. Fortunately, I was able to attend the testimony session because I passed the examination at the top of my class.

In the hall, Rev. Won Pil Kim gave a testimony about Rev. Moon at Hung-nam Prison in a gentle voice. He recalled how one prisoner was (spiritually) visited by an ancestor. When the prisoner asked the ancestor what kind of person would be coming to the prison, the ancestor started walking up the stairs leading to heaven. A divine and shining person stood before him with an everlasting smile on his face. The person was a young but dignified youth. The ancestor told the prisoner, "This is the one who is coming to this prison. Serve him well," and disappeared.

I realized that this person was the "Giant Star" that Mr. Suzuki had mentioned, and I made up my mind to attend the special training sessions that had been recommended to me several times. However, I was also preparing to go on a trip to China to meet Mao Zedong at the time of the Cultural Revolution in China through a private language school called Zenrin Shoin. I was faced with a big choice: If I canceled my trip to China, the money I had spent for the China trip would not be returned, and I would have to work part-time somewhere to make up the expenses.

But I also wondered who in the world would bring peace to this world? I felt that if I could find that person, I was determined to devote my life to that person.

In the end, I did not go to China. I worked the late-night shift at the Japan Printing Company (DNP), where I could easily earn cash to pay for my expenses. The news that I had joined CARP quickly became known to the people in the Kumamoto dormitory. Many of my friends tried to discourage me from joining, saying they could not believe I would join the "CARP Movement that makes parents agonize over their children," which they had recently read in the newspapers. I was also harassed. My newly purchased Bible, which I had bought to participate in the special training program, was taken from my bookshelf. However, when my friends realized I was determined to attend the program, some of them said to me, "Go for it!" and gave me money they had collected through a fundraising campaign as a parting gift.

The 43rd special retreat was held at Nagoya Church (Nagoya Culture Center). Compared to the previous special training sessions held in Okurayama, this one was smaller, attended by fewer than 70 people. The first half of the lectures were given by Kiyoshi Horiguchi and the second half by Takeshi Kamiyama. Lecturer Horiguchi was intelligent and lecturer Kamiyama was emotional, each with his own personality. My group leader was Soichiro Nakamura, and the mother figure of the workshop was Chizuko Joya (now Abe), who was also a graduate of Waseda University and took good care of me. The special lectures were given by President Osami Kuboki and Ken Sudo. The lecturers talked about deep topics directly related to us. I was impressed not only by the content of the lectures, but also by the personalities of the two lecturers.

While I was taking the training session, a storm of intense persecution was brewing outside. Starting with the Asahi Shimbun's "Principle Movement brings agony to parents" (an article in the evening edition of July 7, 1967), various weekly newspapers wrote alarming things about the Unification Church in a barrage of articles. During the training session, the group leaders were very nervous and tried to make sure the participants did not receive any bad influences from the outside.

However, one participant brought in a copy of the "Weekly Post" that featured the Unification Church and proudly explained to the other participants, "This is Rev. Moon." The picture was taken on the occasion of his visit to Japan

(June 12), when Rev. and Mrs. Moon, their children, and some of his disciples, a total of 16 people, arrived at Haneda Airport. Among the many Japanese church members who welcomed them was President Osami Kuboki.

I was a little surprised when I saw Rev. Moon's plump and splendid face in the picture. President Kuboki also had a good face, and I thought that with him, the Unification Church of Japan would be in good hands.

The five group leaders began to investigate who had brought the weekly magazine, and those who had brought it with them were escorted out of the room. I was not affected in any way. Instead, I thought that the more the Unification Church people were beaten up in the press, the more genuine they must be. Even though various persecutions came from then on, I developed the courage and spirit to stand up to it.

I was given two lectures on the Unification Principle at this training session, which deepened my understanding of the Principle. The lecture notes provided me with valuable guidelines for my future activities.

3. Living Together with CARP

The annual 40-day summer pioneering missionary work was carried out from July 20 to August 28, 1967. After the special training, I was assigned to go to Maebashi City in Gunma Prefecture for pioneer missionary work. The district head there was Mr. Kazuo Hoshino, a handsome and manly young man. The mother, Kazuyo Kuramori (now Mrs. Sudo), had a Christian background and knew well about the saints and righteous people in the Bible. Every morning, we would go to a holy ground in a park about 30 minutes away from the church, where we prayed. Sometimes, the district head, Mr. Hoshino, would conduct morning prayers. After breakfast, I went out to evangelize. One day, while I was preaching in downtown Maebashi, a middle-aged woman of refined appearance listened attentively to what I was saying.

Mrs. F's question was from John 5:19, "The Son can do nothing of himself except what he sees the Father do" and also, "Whatever the Father does, that is what the Son also does." "If the Son is to display Jesus, who is the Father?" was her question.

I had just finished a training session a week earlier and could not answer such in-depth questions, so I had to rely on Ms. Kuramoto, a senior member of the group. She opened the Bible and the Principle commentary and explained why

Jesus called Moses "Father." Satan, who had never surrendered to God, had no reason to surrender to Jesus, so God set up Jacob and showed him the symbolic path to bring Satan to his knees. So, Moses was also able to defeat Satan by walking the symbolic route, modeled after Jacob's route, and Jesus was able to bring Satan to his knees by walking the actual route, modeled after Moses' route. Therefore, Jesus called Moses his father. And yet the roles of Jesus and Moses are fundamentally different, she concluded. "Jesus came as the Messiah to liberate mankind, while Moses was the national liberator."

Mrs. F was impressed by this clear explanation. After that, we visited her home several times. One time, the whole family listened to our talk. They were all devout Christians.

CARP members at Fuji Motosu Lake

During the pioneer period, in addition to street preaching, we also collected recyclable waste. We collected old newspapers and bottles while visiting homes with a wheeled cart, and took them to a waste collection company to exchange them for money. It reminded me of Mr. Y, who used to visit my house to collect recyclables for money.

This summer pioneering mission is an annual event in the Unification Church tradition. Although it was difficult to go alone to a place where there was nothing, it was recommended to new members because they could have various spiritual experiences and their faith would be firmly established during the missionary work. The following year (from July to August 1968), I also went to Kawasaki as a pioneer missionary. At first, we worked as a team of about five people, but soon I was assigned to a certain area in Kawasaki to pioneer by myself.

I visited homes and looked for people to evangelize, but it was not an easy task. The frustration of walking around all day with exhausted legs and not finding a single person to take the class was very frustrating. Exhausted and hungry, I was looking for a place to rest when I found a garage with a mini-truck with a canvas (top) attached parked inside. As I was about to enter the truck, a middle-aged man came up to me and said, "You must be hungry. Eat this." He handed me a watermelon and a rice ball. The man explained that he was waiting for me in front of the mini-truck because he had had a dream that a young man would come to him hungry, and he should prepare food and wait for him.

After the summer pioneering activities were over, I returned to the Yuhi dormitory and thought I would go back to the university, which was in the midst of the student revolt movement and noisy as usual. I thanked God that this was also His plan. I believe that the foundation of my faith was nurtured through my stay at CARP. Most of the students who entered the CARP home were university students from Tokyo. Since there were quite a few people in Tokyo who had attended special training sessions and participated in pioneering activities over the past one to two years, the purpose of the CARP home was to educate this group and raise them to be future leaders.

The top leaders of the Unification Church were in charge of education there. For example, Mr. Hideo Oyamada from Tohoku University, a highly respected Christian and a brilliant man, was the head of the school. Mr. Nobuyoshi Hori from the University of Tokyo, a brilliant and theoretical man, was the vice head; Ms. Michiko Kozaki, a graduate of Fukushima Medical University, was the mother position; and Ms. Atsuko Ono, a generous and patient woman, took care of the 20 students with rich personalities in general affairs and food duty. The students were all unique and took good care of each other. It was like embarking from Shokason Juku (school), which produced the key figures of the Meiji Restoration.

However, it was not all smooth sailing. The following year, the CARP home was relocated to Tsurumaki in Setagaya due to economic difficulties that made Nanpeidai in Shibuya unsustainable. It was renamed Seiwa Gakusha, and a new start was made. The area was ideal for running in the mornings, as there was still spacious countryside in front of the school. Living a life of faith while pursuing my studies was the ideal pattern of life I had always envisioned for myself.

I had an unforgettable Holy Spirit experience at Nanpeidai. After listening to a moving sermon by Mr. Sudo, we all went out into the garden, and out of nowhere I heard the hymn, "God is Love." As I began to sing the song, the Holy Spirit suddenly covered my heart. Large tears began to stream down my face, sobs broke out, and a hot ball of fire washed away all my dirt. Only beautiful and pure emotions welled up from the depths of my heart. I was convinced that this was rebirth by the Holy Spirit.

Life at the dormitory was a far cry from life at previous dormitories. We woke up at 5:00 AM and had morning worship and reading of the Word for an hour from 6:00 AM. The main teachers were Oyamada-sensei or Hori-sensei. It was significant that we read through the Bible three times during our stay at the dormitory. Mr. Kuboki, the president, asked for our impressions after reading the Bible three times, and two or three of us reported our impressions. Among them, the late Mr. Hiroshi Matsuzaki commented, "I can only say that the Bible is not a holy book but an unbearably ugly book that describes the ugliness of human beings in its entirety." Mr. Kuboki said, "The Bible is indeed a record of man's evil deeds, and at the same time, the Bible is a record of God's heartache as He watches over them." There were too many memories of my 20 colleagues to describe each one, but only the pleasant ones come to me.

At that time, I was looking forward to evangelizing. Seiwa Gakusha had a lecture room and when I brought students to the school, three lectures were there to help me if any of the brothers were available. During my time at Seiwa Gakusha, I evangelized 19 people. Not all of them were successful, but I will give examples of failures that did not bear fruit. On that reflection, we should keep in mind that in order for evangelism to be successful, it must first transcend death and create love for the other person eternally in order to bear fruit. Then, without incarnating the principles until we are completely memorized, it is not possible to truly resurrect a person to a new birth.

One example of failure is Ms. O, who was student vice president of an evening class associated with a high school. The student councils of the day and evening classes interacted with each other and helped each other. She came from a poor home, so she worked while attending the evening class, and their student council was formed to provide support to those in need among the students. She was not daunted by adversity and devoted herself to helping others, so I first informed her about the Unification Church and the Unification Principle. A short time later, she took a leave of absence from her company and came to

Tokyo. During her month-long stay at Seiwa Gakusha, she attended most of the Principle lectures and special training sessions while living with us.

After that, she returned to Kumamoto and fortunately returned to her former job and was evangelizing with church members. However, I lost contact with her after that, and a year later I found out that she had left the church because she got involved in the troubles in the church. I realized it was necessary to keep in touch and take care of people like her on a long-term basis without letting down our guard.

The next person I attempted to evangelize is someone I met when I was a part-time worker loading and unloading luggage to Sacred Heart University for the new semester. Ms. F was the dorm head at the time and directed the luggage assignments. She showed me the classroom where Princess Michiko had studied. I had not yet joined the Unification Church at the time, so I listened in silence as she explained to me about Jesus and the significance of the Holy Communion.

After that, we corresponded by letter, but something awesome happened to me (I joined the Unification Church), and I was wondering how to tell her about it. One day, I heard that Professor Kentaro Sukeno, who has a personal relationship with the Unification Church, was organizing a symposium on the theme of "Dialogue between the Catholic Church and the Unification Church." Mr. Oyamada gave one lecture and a sister who studied theology gave another, and Professor Sukeno served as the moderator. I thought this was a great opportunity for Ms. F and encouraged her to attend the symposium. She came and later wrote to me about her impressions of the meeting.

I replied that I would make arrangements for her to visit Seiwa Gakusha in the near future, and three days later, she paid us a visit. A student from Sacred Heart University who attended the symposium had a question for Mr. Oyamada, and we listened to her question earnestly. The question was, "The Catholic Church only pursues heaven in the spirit world, but the Unification Church aims to create heaven both on earth and in the spirit world. How can you say that?"

Mr. Oyamada replied, "When Jesus died on the cross, Satan invaded his physical body, so there is only spiritual salvation, but at the Second Coming of the Lord Jesus, both spirit and body have not been violated by Satan, so salvation of both spirit and body will take place. Therefore, in the end, heaven will be established both on earth and in the spirit world."

I gave Ms. F a copy of the Divine Principle, and she began asking me many questions. Whenever she had a difficult question, I asked her to come to Seiwa

Gakusha to answer it, with the help of Mr. Hori as well as Mr. Oyamada. But I soon became puzzled by the thickness of the walls of the Catholic Church.

This failure made me realize that in the future, when evangelizing people of other denominations and religions, I should be patient and focus on emotional relationships rather than pushing doctrine forward.

The third person I attempted to evangelize was Mr. O, a junior at Kumamoto High School, who joined the speech club, later became student body president, and is currently enrolled in the law department of Waseda University. I gave him a brief lecture on the Unification Principle in the university cafeteria and encouraged him to attend a seven-day training session in Nanpeidai, which he did. However, at the time, he was in a romantic relationship with a woman. After hearing about the Fall of Man, he was deeply troubled, but he could not break the relationship and ended up marrying her. I am still friends with him.

He is now a professor at the law school of his alma mater, but he always says, "That retreat was a turning point in my life." When I think of him, my heart aches at my own inadequacy. I realize that we need to have compassion for people's inner suffering and not judge them.

The fourth person was Ms. I, who was also the head of the literature club at Kumamoto High School. She dreamed of becoming a novelist. Her writing was sharp and delicate, and I was overwhelmed by her ability to describe things even though she was a high school student. At the time, she was majoring in German literature at the graduate school of Hiroshima University and was pursuing her dream of studying abroad in Germany and teaching German literature at a university while writing novels. When I told her about the Unification Church and the Principle, she responded positively. So, after the summer pioneering work, I stopped by Hiroshima and showed her around the Hiroshima Church, where she attended a series of lectures on the Principle. After that, she came to Tokyo and participated in the 40-day training session. One day, however, her parents kidnapped her, and after that, I looked for her but could not find her. One day, I received a heartbreaking letter from her, telling me that she was leaving the church; the letter had no return address.

This incident became a painful experience that scarred me for long time. The years passed in vain, as I did not know what to do about a person when I did not know where she was, but I suddenly found out that she was in Germany. I learned through the news that she had recently lost her husband, who had been ill for some time, and was now living alone, studying German literature and writing poems on her own. How to share the Word of God again so close to death would be the most difficult test for me. However, God has a heart to save the worst of us, so He will tell me to tell them without giving up.

During my time at Seiwa Gakusha, I evangelized a considerable number of people, many of whom were excellent people who were truly able to be successful in this world. I realized that babies must be fed with milk constantly, and that if you cut corners even a little, they will die, so we must be patient and keep feeding them with our lives. I haven't written about them here, but my heart tingles when I think of them because so many others died when they were spiritual babies.

At the end of 1967, I returned to Kumamoto to spend New Year's with my family. I knew I had to report to my parents that I had joined the Church and moved from the prefectural dormitory to the church's student dormitory. Fortunately, when my younger sister came to take the entrance examination for Bunka Fashion College in Tokyo, she had stayed at Seiwa Gakusha for a week, so my parents already knew how I was living from my sister and there was no need to explain. My parents gave their tacit approval, which made me feel lighter.

I went to a small mountain called Mount Tatsuda for an all-night prayer to express my resolution to God for the new year. At the foot of the mountain was the grave of Gracia Hosokawa. As I prayed deeply, I was surrounded by the spirits of many Christians related to Kumamoto. There was, of course, Gracia Hosokawa, but also Christian feudal lord Yukinaga Konishi and his wife; Julia Otaa, who was born in Pyeong Yang, Korea; Shiro Amakusa, who was born in the same village as me; and the 37,000 nameless peasants who stood up during the Shimabara Rebellion to create heaven on earth. There were also young men of the Kumamoto Band who vowed to become true Christians at Mount Hanaoka in Kumamoto City in the modern age. They vowed to build a heaven on this land, but they were unable to fulfill their vow, and their voices were heard asking for the release of their grudge. This spiritual experience was deeply embedded in my mind.

CHAPTER 3

Full-Scale Activities Begin in CARP

1. Launching the World Student Times Newspaper

In 1968, upon returning to Seiwa Gakusha after the New Year's break, all members were informed that they should move to their respective university homes and join the members of CARP at those universities, thus graduating as the first class of the Gakusha. All of us moved to our respective CARP centers before the new semester began. I went to the Sosei Ryo (dormitory) in Nogata (this center was named by Rev. Moon who visited the dormitory in Nogata on October 8, 1965).

The Sosei Ryo was located along the Seibu Shinjuku Line, 20 minutes from Takadanobaba. At that time, the president of CARP at Waseda University was Mr. Kunihiro Onishi. He had a rich personality and had the power of the Word; he and I got along well. At the CARP Fair the following year, he was the director of Waseda CARP and I was the chairman of the National Cultural Festival Committee. We worked together to promote the project. As a result, I decided to officially withdraw from the two campus clubs I had been a member of and focus solely on the CARP activities.

Later, Mr. Hideo Oyamada, then dormitory head of Seiwa Gakusha, was appointed president of the National CARP (April 1968), and I was selected to serve as the director of information bureau at the headquarters of the National CARP. The mission of the information bureau was to put together a concrete concept of the CARP Principles and promote them throughout Japan. The goal of the VOC (Victory Over Communism) was to debunk the theories of the leftist communist student movement and present VOC theory as an alternative to communism.

The leftist student movement published a newspaper for each sector to justify its own activities, so there was a strong opinion that we should also publish a journal as soon as possible. We made various flyers for evangelistic purposes, but publishing a newspaper would require trusted human resources.

Waseda University CARP members

Later, Mr. Kazuhiro Horimoto, who had been engaged in information-related work in the Nagoya area, was transferred to CARP headquarters for the publication of a bulletin, and Mr. Horimoto became editor-in-chief. Junichiro Owaki, Yuichiro Watanabe, Yasushi Onoya, Tae Koizumi (now Eitoku), and I joined the editorial team to make various preparations for the publication of the newspaper. The newspaper was named "Sekai Gakusei Shinbun" (World Student Times) by President Kuboki.

After about a month of hard work collecting articles, the first issue was finally published on November 1, 1968. I was in charge of the second and third pages and wrote mainly about how ordinary students (non-radical) had lifted the blockades and normalized the universities that had been closed off by radical activists. My stories were based on my impressions while visiting Hosei University and Tokyo Medical and Dental University and my conversations with the people involved. The headline of the article was "Student Movement of Love and Dialogue against Violence!"

Mr. Watanabe was in charge of the theory section, and Mr. Owaki wrote the editorial. In addition, Mr. Oyamada wrote a serial article, "Eros and Agape," and Mr. Tadashi Ogasawara wrote a serial novel, "Hato no Hashi" (Bridge of Doves).

I also began writing "The President's Story" in the November 1, 1969, (Issue No. 14) until my departure for the U.S. in an effort to stimulate people's interest in the United States. I asked many university professors to write manuscripts in their respective fields, further enhancing the quality of the paper. Through the publication of this bulletin, CARP became a part of the student movement, both in name and in reality. At universities with a large number of CARP members, they published their own CARP newspaper, such as "Waseda Student Times."

2. Formation of the International Federation for Victory Over Communism (IFVOC)

The world was in a state of turmoil in 1968. The Vietnam War was escalating in intensity and, with no sign of a cease-fire, anti-war movements were spreading like wildfire around the world. In China, Mao Zedong instigated the Cultural Revolution against certain parts of Chinese society, and various massacres were carried out. In the U.S., the pessimistic mood of the war spurred a conspicuous decline in the morals of young people.

During these events, on April 5, 1968, Rev. Martin Luther King, Jr. a black minister who was a leading figure in the civil rights movement, was assassinated in Memphis, and New York Sen. Robert Kennedy, a presidential candidate, was assassinated while campaigning in Los Angeles on June 6, 1968.

The tendency to condone violence in the world increased markedly. In particular, the democratic movement of students and intellectuals in Czechoslovakia led to the ouster of the dictator of a country by the power of "speech" of the students and intellectuals. As part of what would be called "Prague Spring," Czech intellectuals issued a 2,000-word declaration in defense of freedom and human rights in their homeland. Antonin Novotny, the first secretary of the Czech dictatorship, was replaced with Alexander Dubcek, who was considered the leader of the progressive camp.

Student demands for democratization and liberalization showed no signs of abating. However, on August 21, 1968, armies from four Warsaw Pact countries—the Soviet Union, Bulgaria, Poland and Hungary—invaded Czech Socialist Republic. The armies took over a major airport and conducted crowd control.

Dubcek was eventually forced to resign and was replaced by the Soviet-approved Husák regime. From then on, a harsh purge of Czech liberalists began.

I had watched the "Prague Spring" with hope since it involved students standing up for democracy and liberalization, but I was outraged by the Soviet army that cruelly put them under tanks. Together with my fellow student Shinkichi Suzuki, I wrote this message on a long banner: "Tokyo University students, it's time to wake up now! The Soviet Union, which suppressed the democratic movement in the Czech Republic in a barbaric manner, is indeed a follower of violent revolution, equally common to all communists, who are willing to use violence for the sake of their cause. This is the true nature of the violent revolution that JCP (Japan Communist Party) and Minsei (Japan Youth Communist group) are vigilantly seeking to achieve in Japan!"

We went to the red gate of the University of Tokyo at 4:30 in the morning to paste the long roll. The reason was that the University of Tokyo was a stronghold of the JCP and Minsei.

The onslaught of world communism began to affect Japan as well. Using the anti-Vietnam War campaign as a background, the anti-war, anti-U.S. movement of left-wing forces agitated for a communist revolution in Japan. The situation in Japan was reminiscent of the eve of a revolution. Molotov cocktail wars were being waged across the country in anticipation of a Japan-U.S. Security Treaty. University campuses were becoming havens for leftist students. There were eight Revolutionary Marxist factions, and they would dominate particular campuses. Waseda University, for instance, was dominated by the Kakumaru faction.

Even local socialist governments arose, such as Tokyo's Governor Ryokichi Minobe. Given these circumstances, the only way to save Japan and save the world from a violent communist revolution was to form the International Federation for Victory Over Communism (IFVOC), which was armed with anti-communist theory.

First, the Japanese edition of "New Critique of Communism," written by Dr. Sang Hun Lee to overcome the communist ideology, was published on March 2, 1968. Although we were completely ignorant of communism, this book helped us understand the errors of communism and gave us the idea of building a better world. The VOC in Japan was founded, with Mr. Ryoichi Sasagawa as honorary president and Osami Kuboki as president, on April 1 of the same year. The IFVOC movement was also launched simultaneously throughout Japan. Lectures on VOC theory were given in front of train stations in major cities and on the campuses of major universities to educate the Japanese people about the errors of communism.

National VOC students meeting at Tokyo University (May 31, 1970)

The CARP group was formed and proclaimed the study and service that would establish a tradition of youth who would rebuild and save their country and the world in July 1964. Meanwhile, as the movement of students for Victory Over Communism ideology was growing in Japan, the All-Japan CARP adopted the following statement in Section 3 of its Platform of Action: "We are convinced that we can establish a unified philosophy that can unify all principles, ideas and religions, by absorbing materialistic ideology, and we stand on the anti-communist front to establish the philosophy of victory over communism."

From this platform, CARP inherited the guiding principle of the IFVOC and—in addition to the existing activities of CARP—organized a "Victory Over Communism Study Group" with 3,000 full-time students and 40,000 members in 120 universities throughout Japan.

One of the problems for those of us who cry anti-communism was that Japanese people had never experienced communism and were completely ignorant of the actual state of the communist world. On June 14, I went to Seoul to participate in the "Japan-Korea University Students' Victory Over Communism Convention." We visited the 38th parallel in South Korea to hear the experiences of the Korean uprising and the stories of North Korean defectors from North Korea. Before the revision of the Japan-U.S. Security Treaty in 1969, the campus was in an uproar. The national convention to promote the Japan-U.S. Security Treaty was held at Hibiya Public Hall on March 8 of the same year; we formed a united front with other anti-communist groups to hold the "Victory Over Communism National Convention." On that day, 3,000 VOC members from all over Japan gathered at the Tokyo Sankei Hall, and we students participated as active promoters of this convention.

Meanwhile, on the campus of Waseda University, a student movement called the First Waseda University Struggle, which began at the end of 1965 as a campaign against tuition hikes and the management of student halls, took the name of Zenkyoto (radical communism student movements against authority). It involved not only radical students but also a wide range of students from Waseda University. The movement later became the forerunner of the Zenkyoto movement—nationwide student struggles that included the blockade of university-wide barricades. For the last two years, students were hardly able to attend classes. Mid-term and final examinations were held at a nearby high school, but even these could not be taken due to obstruction by Revolutionary Marxist (Kakumaru faction) students.

The main cause of the student movement was the current skeleton of the university, which had been greatly distorted from its original form, i.e., a university centered on truth. Sensitive students, aware of the contradiction, saw communism as a means of relieving their resentment. This was a common problem not only in Japan but around the world, as seen in the May Revolution in France and the Strawberry Statement student protest that originated at Columbia University in the United States. However, the current state of student conflicts today is that they are struggling to find a solution to their problems.

Around 1967, the anti-war coalition (non-sectarian radicals) took the lead in a struggle to occupy the student hall at Waseda University. They made a blockade of the office of the Dean of the Faculty of Political Science and Economics, and violent incidents occurred. However, sensible students and professors confronted them and removed the blockade. This is known as the Second Waseda University Struggle.

It became clear that the communist group was going to refuse to leave the campus and continue to occupy the building illegally. Their goal was to destroy the school and authority.

As a student of the Faculty of Political Science and Economics, I, too, confronted the Marxist Kakumaru faction with two demands from the podium to the 3,500 students gathered. First, I asked that the Kakumaru faction remove the blockade of the dean's office immediately. We ordinary students had not done anything that resembled studying for the past two years, and we could not tolerate any more obstruction of our studies. If the blockade was not lifted, we would immediately recruit student volunteers and remove the blockade ourselves.

Second, we demanded that the university immediately turn off the gas, electricity, and water in response to the continued occupation of the student hall by the Kakumaru faction.

We formed a coalition of about 30 outstanding and unique students. We discussed our demands and wrote them out for the leader of the Kakumaru faction (Revolutionary Marxist Party). I handed it to him and waited for his reply in the Okuma Garden Hall. The other request (about temporarily shutting off the utilities) was given to the university authorities in writing, also forcing them to respond by 9:00 PM.

Responses were given to our demands, but they were not satisfactory. For instance, the university authorities said that cutting off the gas, electricity, and water services was not permissible from a humanitarian standpoint.

However, the situation moved quickly after that. Former Vice President Sakaguchi took the initiative, and together with us ordinary students who opposed to the Revolutionary Movement, the blockade was lifted through the use of force. The coalition of 30 volunteers was named the "Sensuikai," and afterwards, it became a powerful group of general students for the normalization of the campus.

The Third Waseda University Struggle began with the kidnapping and vicious murder of Waseda CARP member Daizaburo Kawaguchi on November 8, 1972, by men associated with the Kakumaru-ha Revolutionary Marxist faction. I am still angry at the lack of foresight of the university authorities; I believe that if they had temporarily cut off the water, gas, and electricity as we had demanded, such a murder would not have occurred.

The situation with Kawaguchi went like this. In April 1971, Kawaguchi entered Waseda University's First Faculty of Letters, Arts, and Sciences (humanities program) to study literature. He participated in Buraku liberation movements (to reconnect outcast Japanese citizens to society).

However, he also associated with Marxist organizations on campus. One of these was the Kakumaru-ha group, which controlled the executive committee of the neighborhood association (civil society group) of Waseda's First Faculty of Letters section.

Kawaguchi became disappointed with the Kakumaru-ha group, and in 1972, he joined a rival Marxist group, the Chukaku-ha, and began participating in their meetings. But he became disenchanted with them as well, according to his classmates and mother.

Later that year, Kawaguchi, age 20, joined the Waseda CARP after showing interest in our Waseda Student Times newspaper.

On November 8, 1972, according to later investigations, activists with Kakumaru-ha grabbed Kawaguchi and took him into the Student Government Association room on the Waseda University Faculty of Letters campus. The activists were enraged with Kawaguchi for going with their bitter rivals, the Chukaku-ha group, and spent several hours torturing him before killing him. Kawaguchi's body was found the next day on the campus of the University of Tokyo and University of Tokyo Hospital. A medical report said Kawaguchi's body showed signs of being tied on his wrists, waist, and neck, and that he died after being "severely beaten with logs and square timbers."

The Marxist assailants were arrested and convicted, and the murder caused great turmoil on the Waseda University campus for many years.

However, this tragic incident has an important ending.

The university authorities agreed to pay 6 million yen to his mother, Sato Kawaguchi, as a sympathy payment for the incident that occurred on campus. Mrs. Kawaguchi, however, overcame her angry and sad feelings and donated the entire amount for a beautiful guest house. She wanted to establish a place for prayers for Waseda students so that they would never again experience a tragedy like her son's. Her idea came into reality with the completion ceremony of the Kawaguchi Memorial Izu Seminar House Foundation in the scenic mountains of Izu on June 20, 1975. The people who helped bring this to fruition were CARP President Michio Fujii and his wife, as well as Masuo Oe and Yasuo Inoguchi, members of the Waseda University CARP group.

The following September, after the completion ceremony, President Murai of Waseda University and his wife came to the U.S. on a business trip, and I met them in Boston together with Mr. and Mrs. Fujii, former president of CARP, who was working in the U.S. at the time. After hearing the story of the hardships that led to the completion of the seminar house, I was convinced that a new student movement based on love and cooperation would take the place of the communist student movement, which had brought only hatred and confrontational struggle.

3. Publicizing CARP,
Overseeing College Festivals Nationwide

Autumn is the time of the University Festivals. These events were the occasion for the formation of the All-University CARP Festival Executive Committee. I and seven other executive committee members (Ikeno, Tsurugaya, Yamada, Maeda, Fukatsu, Onoya, Kimura, and Sato) were elected. As the head of the National University Festival Executive Committee, I developed a plan for the festival, wrote a draft, and presented it to the CARP chairpersons at each university. If the draft was approved, it would be distributed nationwide, and exhibits would be created according to the scale of each university.

We had to address the aftermath of the previous two years of mayhem when the campuses of all universities were barricaded and the university festivals were generally sluggish. Large plywood boards were still up on the campuses, and their contents were all about the "The year of 1970 struggle," "Japan-U.S. Security Treaty," "Textbook Trial," and "Okinawa," all in the propagandas of the Zengakuren (Federation of Radical Student Groups).

In contrast to the unpopular leftist political rallies, the CARP group was asking questions such as "What is the goal of life? What is love? Is God really dead?" CARP delved into the marginalized issues of human beings through philosophical, religious, and existential questions. Many students sympathized with the exhibition of Divine Principle teachings. It offered relief and hope to the ordinary students who had suffered when their schools were ravaged by the leftist student movement and its brutal violence.

A. Waseda CARP Fair

By 1969, the campus seemed to have regained some semblance of normal life. That year we decided to launch a nationwide "CARP Fair" to create a bright atmosphere by our own hands, replacing the dark images of the left-wing student movement. Among the many CARP fairs scheduled and planned at various universities, the University of Tokyo's 20th Komaba Festival (Tokyo University Campus) and the 16th Waseda Festival caught our attention. The plans for the "CARP Fair" at the 16th Waseda Festival were almost finalized and announced by the Waseda University CARP, the VOC Study Group, and others. The entire building of the Faculty of Law, which is said to be a stronghold of the Minsei, was rented out and plans were made for a large-scale event with seven sections.

Asian VOC conference at Waseda University (November 30, 1969)

One of them was the "Asian Students' VOC Conference," a high-profile conference for Asian solidarity organized by the VOC Study Group, which was held from 1:00 PM on November 30 in Room 31 of Building No. 4, the only base of the JCP and their Youth Organization at Waseda. The convention was attended by about 1,500 participants, including representatives of students from Korea and the Republic of China (Taiwan), as well as alumni of the VOC members from all over Japan. The conference began at 1:00 PM with a performance by the

Waseda University brass band, followed by a powerful opening declaration. Mr. Masatoshi Matsushita, a member of the House of Councilors, stated, "The VOC movement is a movement for the purification of thought." Mr. Masatoshi Abe, Secretary General of the IFVOC movement, stated that "there is no true peace movement except the VOC movement."

Mr. An from the Korea Foreign Language University and Mr. Lee from the Taiwan University of the Republic of China (Taiwan) stood up to deliver remarks from their respective countries. Their passionate anti-communist cries, which emanated from their respective experiences, were met with particularly loud applause. From Japan, Ms. Akiyo Takahashi (Waseda University literature student), a courageous woman who worked with VOC, quietly reported the current situation of street activities, deeply moving the participants. The convention was opened with the declaration of the event by Mr. Tetsuo Kasai, which was adopted with thunderous applause. Following the pledge, at 4:00 PM, most of the participants took part in a victory march. The demonstration was a magnificent one, with 1,500 people marching 3 kilometers (1.8 miles) from the Waseda University headquarters to the Faculty of Science and Engineering. The people on the street and in the shopping district applauded generously for this demonstration, which was different from the usual leftist demonstrations.

The second project was "Waseda Crusade" on December 2, with a choir chorus and testimonies in the background, followed by a sermon by Hideo Oyamada on "Why God is Sought Now" and by Pastor Shinichi Nakamura of Union Church on "Jesus is Still Sorrowful." The content of their sermons made the desolate wilderness bloom with beautiful flowers. The third program was "Why is God Sought in Our Time?" Professor Erlin Hagen of Sophia University, Pastor Shinichi Nakamura, and Hideo Oyamada, president of the All-University CARP, spoke at the symposium, which was followed by a question-and-answer session.

The fourth project was the "VOC Symposium," which was chaired by Professor Tadao Ishikawa of Keio University, Professor Yoshio Imadate of Chuo Gakuin University, Associate Professor Kenji Nomura of the Japan Institute of Technology, and me (Ikeno). Leftist students also participated, and after the three professors presented their themes, the question-and-answer session covered a wide range of topics, including the differences between Mao Zedong's ideology and Stalin, Japanese diplomacy in the Cold War era, and its direction during the Cultural Revolution in China. The discussion went on and on, including whether there is a compromise between state power and the student movement.

The fifth program was a lecture by Professor Emeritus Kiyoshi Oka of Nara Women's University on "The Future of Japan and the Role of Youth." About 600 students gathered to listen to the renowned professor. In his aged but resonant voice, he expressed his concern for modern Japan and said, "Now is the time for the youth, whether male or female, to stand up and rebuild Japan. If things continue as they are, Japan will perish in the first half of the year 2000 due to the communist revolution and moral decadence." He sounded the alarm.

In addition to the lectures, various exhibitions were held in four rooms during the university festival. In Room 201, there were panel exhibitions on "The New Order of Love: From Eros to Agape Love"; in Room 202, "The Way Forward for Japan: Beyond the 1970s, Where Should We Go"; and in Room 203, "The Hidden Historical Revelations of the Japanese Communist Party and Their Youth Movement." In Room 205, slide lectures on the Bible, the Unification Principle, and VOC theory were presented.

Finally, a coffee shop called Juju was opened as a place for relaxation. Everyone felt a sense of accomplishment after five days of comprehensive planning. The fact that we were able to present our principles and arguments so openly in the midst of the devastated Zenkyoto movement set the direction for the future of our organization. The total number of participants reached 5,600.

B. University Festival for Academic Year 1970

The University Festival of 1970 was more peaceful, cultural, and "human" than in previous years. The left-wing forces, which had been promoting a movement to turn the university festivals into a political tool under the slogan to prevent Japan-U.S. Security Treaty, were on the wane due to setbacks and factional splits. Since the original call was "How can we live as human beings?" the activities of CARP and VOC were expected to help humanity as a "post-political" movement.

An executive committee was formed with 16 members representing universities throughout Japan, and I was chosen as the chairperson of the National University Festival Executive Committee. The committee met twice a week for both the Principle and VOC divisions, and presented the general outline of the festival.

The VOC section's bold approach to the specific problem of "the unification of a divided nation" drew attention from all quarters. While previous projects of this kind had been conducted mainly in Tokyo, this year's conference was expected to be successful in that it was the start of nationwide research activities, with each section and subcommittee sharing the responsibility for collecting materials and holding discussions.

In the Principle division, the plan was to exhibit the fundamental principle, the Unification Principle itself. There was also a research presentation, prepared by four subcommittees, on the theme of "Establishment of the Order of Love."

The theme of the first session was "Sociality of Love." The responsible schools (Kyoto University, Hiroshima Women's University, and Yasuda Women's University) discussed how love must be a part of human relationships in order to overcome the spiritual starvation caused by urbanization.

The theme of the second session was "The Acquisition of Love," and the responsible schools were Waseda University, Meiji Gakuin University, Okayama University of the Sacred Heart, and Hiroshima University. The presentations were about how we must search for the conditions under which we can love, and we will find that these conditions are not money, power, or position but the love that strikes us at the end. Then how to acquire that love?

The theme of the third sectional meeting considered the issue of the two loves that move mankind, Eros and Agape. The former love developed with Marx, Freud, and Marcuse, and became the support of the whole communist movement. Religious love, on the other hand, which is the sublimation of the human spirit, has become a major force in the formation of a new order of love.

The theme of the fourth session was "Conditions of Marriage," and the schools in charge were Aoyama Gakuin, Keio, Senshu University, Meiji University. This session examined the conditions for love and marriage, which can be both a hope for modern youth and a dangerous trap if it is misused.

C. VOC Division

The theme was "The Korean Peninsula Reunification and Japan," focusing on the 38th parallel issue on the Korean Peninsula as a representative example of the East-West problem in the world and approaching the reunification.

The theme of the first session was a general analysis of international affairs and studying the contemporary international situation and the Far Eastern issues within it. The schools in charge were Keio, Meiji Gakuin University, Tohoku University, and Shimonoseki City University.

The second session was on "What is the problem of unification in a divided country?" The schools in charge were Tokyo University, Kyoto University, and Waseda University. The seminar explored the possibility of unification by reviewing the similarities and differences among the divided nations of Germany, Korea, Vietnam, China, and other countries.

Session three was on "The 6.25 uprising" (Korean War) and the contemporary world. Schools in charge were Tohoku University, Niigata University, Waseda University, and Meiji University. The 6.25 uprising (Korean War) was strongly suspected to have been primed by a 1950 statement by Secretary of State Dean G. Acheson. The Nixon Doctrine was also viewed as a factor.

Session four's theme was Japan's 38th Parallel. The schools in charge were Chuo University, Taku University, Toyo University, and Meiji University. Two Korean resident groups in Japan could be called the second 38th parallel: North Korea's Chosoren (General Association of Korean Residents in Japan) acted in accord with the wishes of North Korean Chairman Kim Il Sung, while Koreans who opposed communism joined South Korea's Mindan (Korean Residents Union in Japan.) The Chongryon established the Korean University, and its influence had been increasing as the issue of the Immigration Control Bill had become more publicized.

The theme of the fifth session was "Approaches to the Unification of North and South Korea." The schools in charge were Hiroshima University, Meiji Gakuin University, and Waseda University. The discussion was that the Korean Peninsula needed a unification philosophy that went beyond democracy versus communism. The principle that could transcend the differences were interdependence, mutual prosperity and universally shared values, as these could support prosperity after the unification of the Korean Peninsula as a coalition of Asian nations.

We also considered the position of Japan, which has 600,000 Korean residents.

After the national university festival, we published a book titled, "The Unification of the Korean Peninsula is the Keystone of World Peace." Rev. Moon read this book and added it to his library.

4. Entering Graduate School at Waseda University

As the new year of 1969 arrived, I had to think about my career path. I was tempted by two options. But when I asked myself what I had learned during my four years of college, I realized that when the school building was barricaded and there were no classes, I was able to learn only about one year net— and I had no time to study. So, I wondered what I had learned during my four years of college. In that respect, I had regrets about my university life.

It was Professor Tadao Horie who helped me make the decision to stay at the university and study a little longer. In order to work with influential people in the future, I had to develop my character through learning about the big picture at a young age. I decided to think of my studies as a 20-year span in which I would gain insight into myself. Professor Horie's opinion, that the true meaning of study lies in the fact that my university studies become my insight and are incarnated as a part of my personality, had a tremendous impact on my subsequent career path.

Since I decided to go to graduate school, I first had to submit my bachelor's thesis, so I submitted it under the title "The Origins of Democracy." This was based on the materials I had collected in "Presidential Tales," which I had contributed to the World Student Times. I received a compliment from my professor, Professor Mikio Shimoda, who said that I had done a good job in my research and that I had hit the essence of the subject.

The entrance examination for graduate school was to be held in late February, and I had less than two months to prepare. Some of the students were from other schools, but I somehow passed the entrance examination and began to enter the Graduate School of Political Science in April.

I had two research projects in graduate school. One was the question of whether it is possible to establish a union of Asian nations similar to the European Union in the field of international politics, and the other was to study the interrelationship between religion and economic politics in the context of American history to see how politics can be a factor in harmonizing religion and economics.

On January 25, 1971, I finished my master's thesis, "The Relevance of Economy and Religion in Political Communication," as a result of about two months of research at my parents' house. Three examiners complimented me, saying that it was a novel thesis on a large scale.

The scope of my activities grew rapidly after becoming a graduate student. I visited the Republic of China (Taiwan) as a member of the Japan-China goodwill delegation for two weeks from March 29, 1970. The Taiwanese side wanted to invite representatives from the IFVOC and the Liberal Democratic Party to participate in the "Youth Festival." I and Takashi Sugiyama from VOC in Japan and 10 representatives from the Liberal Democratic Party participated in this project. We had a "Youth Festival" and other events, a meeting with the government leaders, and a meeting with President Chiang Kai-shek. President Chiang's voice was full of energy despite his advanced age. He encouraged us to join hands with the youth of Japan and Taiwan to build peace and prosperity in Asia since it is the youth who will carry the burden of the next era.

The next day, we had a meeting with the former Red Guards (from the Cultural Revolution in China) who had fled for their lives from the mainland. We had a meaningful meeting as we learned the reality of the Cultural Revolution led by Mao Zedong. I was deeply chilled when I heard their testimonies because I had been scheduled to go to China in the summer of 1967 through Zenrin Shoin. I was shocked to hear their testimonies and learn that 90% of the Red Guards were anti-Mao.

In the latter stages of the Cultural Revolution, even the most innocent Red Guards found out that Mao Zedong had spurred young people to start the Cultural Revolution for his own purposes. Mao had used them to kick out Liu Shaoqi, who had become an obstacle to him, and as a result 90% of the Red Guards became anti-Mao. Some of these former Red Guards, such as Mr. Chen Yongsheng and Ms. Yuan, visited Japan to explain the situation in China. This was at a time when the United Nations was about to recognize mainland China as the representative to the UN instead of Taiwan.

The executive committee meeting was held at Kawana Hotel in Ito City to prepare for the WACL (World Anti-Communism League) Japan Congress on May 12, 1970. I participated in the preparatory committee of the WYACL (World Youth Anti-Communism League), a student youth organization under the WACL, as the Japanese student representative. Thirty student representatives from 12 countries, including the U.S., the U.K., France, and West Germany, also participated in the meeting, which was held to prepare for the WYACL's participation in the WACL Japan Congress to be held in September.

The 4th WACL General Conference was held at the Kyoto International Conference Hall in Kyoto from September 15, 1970, and the WYACL General

Conference was held at the same time. On September 20, the WACL World Congress was held at the Budokan in Tokyo with 25,000 participants, including 250 representatives from 53 countries. Guest speakers at the convention included U.S. Senator Strom Thurmond and Ms. Juanita Castro, sister of Cuban Prime Minister Fidel Castro, who was in exile in the United States. After the convention, a "World Student Friendship Symposium" was held jointly with 30 students from 12 countries who participated in the WACL and WYACL at the University of Tokyo (September 22) and Waseda University (September 24), where professors and others had lively discussions on the theme of "Japan's Position from the World Perspective."

Mr. Henry Blancher, a representative of France (Sorbonne University), spoke about the current crisis and the way to overcome it from the standpoint of France, which has passed through many revolutions. He emphasized that France, unable to overcome its materialistic universalism, is now facing moral decadence and the expansion of communist forces, and that its civilization is collapsing and it is looking to the spiritual civilization of the East for the path to a new revival. This was our first international student conference.

5. Goodwill Exchanges Begin With Professors and Students from Japan, Korea, and China (Taiwan)

A. Communist Forces Surrounding Japan and Korea

The Chinese Communist Party and North Korea, which had been unable to take a clear direction since 1959 due to the outbreak of the Sino-Soviet conflict, began to make concrete moves from the talks between Zhou Enlai and Kim Il Sung and between Zhou Enlai and Park Sung Chul in 1970. In other words, they shifted their emphasis from crying out against "U.S. imperialism" to condemning "Japanese militarism." They called for the "formation of a united anti-Japanese militarist front" while solidifying a system of "mutual full support for the liberation of Taiwan and the struggle for the unification of Korea."

Inevitably, the policies of the Chinese Communist Party and North Korea toward Japan came to be aligned through the Immigration Control Bill and other issues. As a result, leftist forces in Japan began to form a broad united front that included the Chosoren. This trend developed further and could have influenced the fate of Japan. Meanwhile, in South Korea, the policy of "construction on one side and defense on the other" had been successful, defeating the North Korean armed guerrillas' intention to invade the country, and, to a certain extent, establishing domestic security. However, since it was directly confronting communist forces at the 38th parallel, it could not let its guard down, and it was also struggling with countermeasures against rear distraction and espionage through the Chosoren. Moreover, if Japan were to establish a communist government, Korea would be caught in the crossfire, and there was a danger that it would be converted to communism without a moment's respite.

Despite the fact that the destinies of Japan and Korea are truly one, the gap between the two countries remains deep due to the Japanese contempt for Koreans and anti-Japanese sentiment among Koreans. This reality is alarming when one considers that the unity of Japan and Korea is the key to preventing aggression by communist powers and to ensuring peace in Asia.

Goodwill exchanges between Japan and Korea are not merely a matter of politics and economics. It is the goodwill exchanges in the private sector, especially among youth and students, that will establish a new relationship. This is because young students are the driving force that overcomes past enmities and revenge and builds the future. The friendships between the youth and students of the two countries that are fostered in these exchanges will create true friendship between Japan and Korea and lead to the establishment of a united front to prevent the aggression of the communist forces. This will bring true peace to Asia and the world.

B. Korean Students' Goodwill Mission to Japan

The first group of Korean students arrived in Shimonoseki on March 3, 1971. The second group arrived two days later. They were leaders of the student movement, such as the president of the student association at the university or the editor-in-chief of a newspaper. Most of them were visiting Japan for the first time and were surprised at the economic development of Japan. However, they shared the common view that such economic development in Japan was due to the special demand benefits of the Korean War. They did not have such a bad impression of Japan, partly due to generational differences. However, some of the students said that their parents had been killed by the Japanese military. For some, Japan was seen as a country they could truly fit in with; for others, every single thing about the Japanese seemed to be repugnant. However, the kindness and sincerity of the Japanese students who accompanied them for more than 10 days softened their hearts, and through sightseeing and seminars, they began to develop friendships that transcended national barriers.

The first group of joint seminars consisting of students from Japan and Korea was held on March 9 at Tozanso in Gotemba, and the second group was held on March 12 at Oiso Academy House. The common theme was the "International Situation in the Far East and Future Challenges," and I gave a report as a representative of the Japanese side. A representative from the Korean side also presented a report. The reports from both countries were well written, and the Japanese side's report had already been published in a booklet and distributed to all the participants.

It was at this time that I first put forth the idea of an " the Union of Asian Nations." I stated that Japan and Korea, which are currently surrounded by the Communist bloc, including the Chinese Communist Party, North Korea, and the Soviet Union, cannot avoid the problem of communism and achieve any solution to it. I also called for a "nucleus of a coalition of Asian nations" that "must transcend nationalism and join together in solidarity with countries in Asia that share the same values of freedom and democracy." As a concrete proposal, I examined the process of establishing the European Economic Community (EEC) in Western Europe. While most of the countries in the world have formed some kind of national federation and joined it, Far East Asia alone has not yet formed anything that can be called a national federation. This situation may lead to an economic and political lag behind the world trend, which in turn may lead to communization.

Considering that the ECC was originally formed from the three Benelux countries, we believe that an Asian federation of states should start with the central states of Japan, Korea, and Taiwan, and we should make efforts to unify them economically, politically, militarily, and culturally as soon as possible.

In response, Seoul National University's Hsu Deok-gil, a reporter from South Korea, ridiculed the idea, saying, "I support the idea, but unless the deep enmity between Japan and South Korea, aside from Japan and Taiwan, is first resolved, the coalition of Japan, South Korea, and Taiwan is a figment of the imagination."

Some of the Korean participants spoke of how their relatives had been cruelly killed by Japanese imperialist soldiers. These words made the Japanese students' hearts ache, and they were surprised that such deep scars were still evident in both countries. The atmosphere changed dramatically when the Japanese representative answered Mr. Hsu's question, saying he believed that young people should not look at the past as revenge—the past is a lesson for the present and the future, so let us exchange ideas for the next stage of construction. From then on, heated and constructive discussions continued until 3:00 in the morning.

Korean students were welcomed overwhelming by Japanese members

C. Goodwill Visit to Korea by 120 Japanese Students (March 19-April 2, 1971)

The Japan-Korea Student Friendship Seminar held in Japan was successfully concluded, and the mistrust and misunderstandings were cleared up, and an inseparable emotional bond was formed.

I soon went to Korea as the head of the delegation. Exchange meetings and seminars were held one after another at Seoul National University, Kyunghee University, Yonsei University, Korea University, Dongguk University, Chung-Ang University, Sungkyunkwan University, and Konkuk University. The exchange between Japan and Korea, based on the emotional foundation established in Japan, was further advanced and brought about great results. We met with the presidents of the universities and the heads of student affairs departments, had friendly discussions, and selected good reporters from among the students for us, making for a very productive seminar. The schedule for most of the seminars was the result of the best efforts of the students who had visited Japan in the past.

Some 120 Japanese students visited the 26th and 25th Division of Korean Army frontlines that day at the 38th parallel.

One of the students asked one of the young leaders on the frontline (25th Division), "What do you think of the fight between comrades of the same ethnic group?" He immediately replied, "I think this is not a fight between comrades of the same ethnic group, but a fight between communism and democracy." We were all struck by his reply.

D. Visit to Korea by 100 Representatives of Japanese VOC Students (October 18-November 3, 1971)

Following the March meeting, 100 Japanese students of VOC visited Korea to study the VOC philosophy and interact with Korean students. They also took to the streets to appeal for the achievements of the VOC movement in Japan and to promote goodwill between Japan and Korea. In Korea, the student movement was ignited at Korea University, Yonsei University, Sungkyunkwan University, and Seoul National University. On October 15, martial law was declared, and most universities were closed.

The students from Japan appealed to the Korean people to join with them in defending Asia from the communist revolution. In particular, people in their 40s or older who could speak Japanese were deeply moved and asked about the actual situation in Japan. They asked pointed questions about the movements of leftist students in Japan, whether Japanese militarism is really making a comeback, and what the current economic situation in Japan is like.

We also tried to understand the lives of students in Korea through street visits, university visits, and seminars. On October 30 and November 1, we held sports events with 100 members of the Korean Association for the Study of VOC, playing volleyball, football, tug-of-war, and mock cavalry battles. In the evenings, the students held talks and deepened their friendship. It was significant that the youth of both countries were able to pledge to each other to build peace in East Asia and the world in the future through such cross-border competitions.

E. Japan-China (Taiwan) Student Joint Seminar (April 7-13, 1971)

After the joint seminar in Korea, we (President Komiyama, Director Ikeno, and Tomiko Nojima) traveled to Taiwan with the consensus of opinion in Korea. We held a joint seminar in Taiwan to convey the viewpoints we had reached in Korea—that students from Japan, Korea, and China (Taiwan) should create a strong movement for VOC together.

We held seminars at major universities in Taipei to discuss what the common ideals of the future should be, and if there was an ideology and system that fully encompasses the three countries, what form of state should it take. We learned that they had sharp criticisms of the current Japanese Constitution. At the same time, they wanted to know if we Japanese students were interested in a continental counteroffensive. However, students from both countries were creative and active in exchanging opinions on the anti-communist point. They reaffirmed the urgent need for solidarity among students and professors from the three countries, both at the five universities and in the anti-communist salvation of the country.

These are the events:

- April 8: Seminar at Taiwan University. The most important issue for them was the current Japanese Constitution and the level of interest of Japanese students in the counteroffensive on the mainland.
- April 8: Meeting at the Youth Anti-Communism movement. The topic was future exchanges between Chinese and Japanese students. A consensus was reached to promote solidarity among students from Japan, Korea, and China.
- April 12: Seminar at Fu-Jen University. This was a Catholic university and 30% of the students were Christians. However, there was a stronger sense of continental anti-offensive than at other universities.
- April 13: Seminar at the Chinese Culture Institute. This university was purely Chinese in appearance from the school building and made extraordinary efforts to preserve Chinese culture. They were also interested in Japanese culture and Japanese political awareness.

F. The First Japan-Korea Professors' Friendship Seminar (August 3, 1971)

On August 3, 1971, the first Japan-Korea Professors' Friendship Seminar was held under the theme of "Current Situation and Prospects of the Student Movement" with the participation of 17 Japanese professors and 12 student section chiefs from Korea. Shortly after 9:00 AM, following the declaration of opening remarks by Mr. Hiroo Suzuki, lecturer at the University of Education, Mr. Osami Kuboki, president of the International VOC, delivered the host address in which he stressed the need for unity and exchange between Japan and Korea and the importance of the unification of the two countries amid the turbulent international situation.

Next, a message from the Minister of Education was read by Mr. Kazuho Tanigawa, former Parliamentary Vice Minister of Education. After the introduction of the Japanese and Korean professors, Mr. Tanigawa gave an invited lecture on "Problems and Measures for Students in Japan." In his lecture, Mr. Tanigawa criticized the ideological coloration of the Japanese student movement and the university conflicts caused by the inability of the universities themselves to manage their own affairs. At the same time, he pointed out that the Japan Teachers' Union viewpoint, which had been consistently drilled into students from their secondary education, is "a class warfare approach that says power is all evil and must be overthrown. The purpose of education is to create warriors to defeat this evil." This education is an indirect cause of the university conflict, and he exposed the sophisticated tactics of the communist student movement.

In order to move from such a violent and destructive student movement to a true student movement, he said, "I hope that a vigorous leadership philosophy will be established that will win the hearts and minds of the youth, and that new activities will take place that will be at the forefront of the de-ideological era, infused with the energy of completely new ideas."

Next, the theme lecture was given by Choi Yeol-Shin, director of the Student Affairs Division at Seoul National University, on the theme of "The Current State of the Student Movement in Korea and Proposals for Fostering VOC Student Movement." In his lecture, Choi stated, "The collective work of students has existed in all ages and cultures, but it is a product of the complexities of modern society."

The student movement of the 1960s has emerged as a political, social, and global issue. He described the background of the student movement in Korea, saying that the April 19 Uprising in Korea (Popular demonstrations by students and citizens against the massive rigging by Syngman Rhee in the fourth presidential election in March 1960) led the student movement in the world. Choi, who had been a leader of the student movement since his days at Sungkyunkwan University, gave a powerful presentation on the history of the student movement in Korea up to the vivid April 19 Incident, and stated that the Korean student movement was characterized by anti-communism and based on patriotic nationalism.

In response to the question, "How should the reformist Korean student movement be guided and nurtured in order to realize democratic values from a nationalist standpoint?" Choi concluded, "I would like to strengthen the student movement from a victory over communist standpoint in Korea."

From the Japanese side, Professor Tadao Horie of Waseda University gave a lecture on the theme of "The Student Movement and Marxism in Japan." Based on his direct contact with students at Waseda University as the executive director in charge of students at the time of the second conflict at Waseda University in 1969, Professor Horie clarified the destructive path followed by communist student activists, citing many examples, and criticized Marx's "dialectical worldview" as the guiding philosophy of the movement. He also stressed that the philosophy on which the student movement must be based in the future must first rigorously demonstrate the 19th century antiquity and defects of the Marxist ideas of "the law inherent in society" and "historical necessity," and then establish such an idea that man must take responsibility for history.

After the thematic lectures by both countries, a panel discussion was held, moderated by Mr. Shoben Choi and Mr. Hiroo Suzuki. During the panel discussion, the most concentrated points of discussion were the issues of nationalism and the student movement from the Japanese side and how academic criticism of communism is linked to the anti-communist movement from the Korean side. The seminar concluded with a discussion on the development of future exchanges between Japanese and Korean professors and cultural figures. I planned the invitation of Japanese professors for the first and second seminars and the overall schedule for the goodwill seminar.

G. The Second Japan-Korea Professors' Friendship Seminar (December 12-21, 1971)

Building on the success of the Japan-Korea Professors' Friendship Seminar held in August, a delegation of 33 heads of student affairs departments from major Korean universities visited Japan on December 12. As deans of student affairs at Japanese universities, the delegation was particularly interested in student affairs in Japan.

After visiting Keio University, the University of Tokyo, and Waseda University and receiving a warm welcome, the group participated in the Central Conference organized by the IFVOC on November 14, and stood on the stage surrounded by 3,000 young people. The group was deeply moved to see so many young people participating in the movement in Japan, which they had assumed to be lukewarm to communism.

On the following day, the "Second Japan-Korea Professor Seminar," which was the main purpose of this visit to Japan, was held at the Japan Business Federation

International Conference Hall under the theme of "Values and Future Vision of Modern Students" with the participation of 33 from Korea and 36 from Japan.

Following a message from Japanese Minister of Education Takami, Lee Kyung-gu, head of the Korean faculty delegation (Sungkyunkwan University), and Tomoo Miwa, head of the Japanese faculty delegation (former president of the University of Education), delivered opening remarks, which were followed by the theme speeches. The Japanese lecturer, Hiroo Suzuki (lecturer at the University of Education), spoke of the negative effects of postwar democracy in Japan, citing (1) the influence of teachers, (2) the mass media, (3) the poor ideological formation of students, and (4) the lack of appropriate instructors as the major causes. These trends indicated that today's students, despite their various problems, have the potential to grow into students suitable for a democratic society in the long run.

Next, Chuo University Professor Park Sang Hui raised issues from the perspective of the domestic and international political situation in Korea, and examined the values of today's Korean students in terms of (1) traditional family values, (2) political attitudes, (3) attitudes toward foreign countries, (4) values toward leaders, (5) attitudes toward war, (6) goals in life, and so on. The study also examined "Korean students' nationalistic views." He concluded, "Korean students' conception of the nation is based on the idea that 'I am with the nation.'" However, young people, including students, are currently in a very difficult position. "But if they want and enjoy freedom, they must know that they must defend that freedom with the nation," he concluded. After lunch, the afternoon moved on to a panel discussion. The focus of the issue was Marxism and its impact on students.

From the Korean side, questions were particularly focused on the state of thought in Japan. In response, Professor Suzuki said, "In the unscrambled questionnaire, I am convinced that there are more liberal scholars. However, the mood of the majority is leaning left. This is due to the relative strength of the leadership of leftist professors." Professor Tadao Horie of Waseda University also commented, "The economic principles of Marxism are losing their power as it has become clear that they are completely unrealistic. However, its historical philosophy, materialist historical perspective, based on dialectics, still has strong support." He stated the need for an alternative value system and view of history.

In response to a question from Japan about anti-communist education in South Korea, the Korean side responded that communism was taught as a form of fascism. In Japan, anti-communist education has focused on the actual situation rather than theory, but recently there has been a qualitative shift to comprehensive anti-communist education, or so-called VOC education.

The three-hour discussion concluded with a summary by moderator Hideo Oyamada and confirmation of the third seminar.

After the seminar, the professors visited Nippon Steel Corporation's Kimitsu Plants and Mitsui Engineering & Shipbuilding's Goi Plants, and after sightseeing in Kyushu, they were given an enthusiastic welcome by VOC students before returning to Korea on February 21. This seminar was a further development of the July seminar and established the foundation for future exchanges between Japanese and Korean academics.

Visiting Korea Marks a Turning Point in My Life (1971-1972)

1. First meeting with Rev. and Mrs. Moon

I met Rev. and Mrs. Moon for the first time when I visited Korea as the leader of a delegation of 120 university graduates on March 19, 1971.

We held a seminar on Victory Over Communism (VOC) at a dozen universities in Korea. At that time, a storm of communism was raging in Korea, especially in university circles. I first sincerely apologized for the various inhumane acts committed by our Japanese ancestors on the Korean Peninsula. Then, I proceeded to lecture the communism-obsessed students about the errors of communism. I stressed that world peace begins with the recognition of human dignity, that human beings need freedom and a system of democracy to protect it, and that an economy based on free competition will lead humanity to a prosperous world.

As soon as the seminar and the touring lectures were over, the 11th Parents' Day was held at the Sutaek-ri training center. As Rev. Moon spoke his sermon, he referred to the "Marriage of the Lamb" in Revelation 19:7, saying, this becomes the origin of Parents' Day. April 11, 1960, the day when a bride without original sin, prepared as the only begotten son and a radiant only begotten daughter among the white-clad people (the nickname of Korean people) whom God has long cultivated and nurtured , was blessed in holy matrimony, has become the most important day in human history. From this point, direct descendants were born to True Parents, and by receiving the "Blessing" from True Parents, humanity is liberated from the original sin that has been continuously transmitted through Satan's lineage, undergoes a linage change, and connects to God's lineage, thereby creating heaven on earth and in heaven, and forming one great global family. He delivered a sermon filled with dream and hopes.

11th Parents' Day (March 22, 1971, at Sutaek-ri, Korea)

After his sermon was over, Rev. Moon asked me to share my testimony in front of the leaders and members who participated in the festivities. I spoke my own testimony as well as on the theme of "The Path to World Peace." When I finished speaking, Rev. Moon encouraged me, "You will become a man among men." During that time, we visited many places, especially Gyeongbokgung Palace, and played with their children. They also took me to the movies.

One day, we decided to go to a holy place in Namsan, with me riding next to the driver and Rev. and Mrs. Moon in the back seat. Since I was a little boy, I had one thought that I had kept in my heart. It was the thought, "I have a real father somewhere in this world." As the car drove through a small hill away from Gyeonggi village and the fields came into view ahead, Rev. Moon turned to me and asked, "What is your father doing?" I answered, "Yes, he is an engineer for the Japanese National Railways." He meditated for a while and then said in a solemn voice, "I am your real father." At that moment, I was deeply moved by his words.

I spoke about the path to world peace and gave a testimony

I was finally able to meet my true father, whom I had sought for so long. Moreover, the Messiah said to me, "I am your true father." Tears flowed freely until we arrived at the holy place in Namsan. The story did not end there. During my stay next to Rev. Moon's room at the training center in Sutaek-ri, God gave me the revelation that Rev. Moon had gone to the United States and he taught me all kinds of strategies to save America—which was now dying—and told me each and every one of them.

For example, he told me enthusiastically that we would make a mobile team in the U.S. and go around to each state, meeting with state governors, mayors, and university presidents to share our teachings. I was told that I would also participate in this providence, and at that moment it was decided that I would go to the United States. The conversation in Rev. Moon's room at the former headquarters in Cheongpa-dong is still deeply etched in my mind.

One day, I was invited to the headquarters church and was eating lunch in the first-floor cafeteria when Mrs. Won Bok Choi came and asked me, "Father asked why did you not receive the 777-Couples Blessing?" I answered, "I think some indemnity condition was lacking. In particular, I think that the foundation of the substance could not be built." After I answered, Mrs. Choi went upstairs to Rev. Moon's room to tell him what I had just said. I could see that the hundreds of thousands of spirits behind me were very saddened that I had missed last year's Blessing Ceremony, and my heart was deeply depressed.

I thought that Rev. Moon had understood this through his psychic sense. He told me to come to his room immediately, and I was ushered into that room. He grabbed a marble vase with both hands, turned it around on his feet, and said, "I heard you missed the Blessing, but don't worry. You just didn't happen to have the right person. In a little while, there will be a woman tough enough. Even [if she is] getting stabbed by your sharp tongue, she will not die and come back to life. By the way, I know you [would] like a woman with an open nose and eyes extended long sideways, but with such a woman you will both go down." He comforted me by advising me.

He then asked me, "How do you feel about the Unification Church?" I immediately replied, "I love the Unification Church with all my heart." He continued to tell me about what had happened in his old lodgings at the Mitsuhashi family and his many memories of Waseda University. He then spoke again about the program for the restoration of the United States.

During a subsequent visit to Korea (May 1972), we traveled by bus with students of World International Collegiate Association for the Research of Principles (W-CARP) from 10 countries to various cities to participate in the VOC student convention. When we returned to our lodgings after giving a lecture at Korea University, Rev. and Mrs. Moon had just returned from the Third World Tour and took us (student delegates) to a clothing store, where they individually selected and bought new clothes for each of us. He had a hard time finding the right color for me, but he chose a light blue suit.

We were to wear our new clothes and attend the Holy Day service, where we were introduced in front of the Korean church members. After the service, we were taken to Rev. Moon's room, where a meal was being prepared for us and where Hyo Jin, Ye Jin, and senior 36 families were also waiting for us. Afterward, we were asked to sing a song, and I joined the other two Japanese brothers in loudly singing "The Tree of Youth" while shaking my fist. Rev. and Mrs. Moon and their children also sang at the end.

When I was leaving for Japan, we took a commemorative photo at Gimpo Airport with Rev. and Mrs. Moon, their children, and the 36 Couples Blessed

Family members, and bid them a fond farewell. Rev. Moon clasped my hand with his thick, warm hand and said in a gentle voice with a smile, "Thank you for your hard work." I replied, "Yes, I will see you in the U.S. next time," and returned his strong handshake. I had to walk to the plane, and True Family and the senior disciples were waving to us on the deck until we boarded the plane.

2. Appointed Waseda Regional Director by Rev. Moon

During my visit to Korea in March 1971, I was asked by Rev. and Mrs. Moon to carry out two important missions. First, I was told that I must play a role in the revival of Christianity and the spiritual renewal movement in the U.S.—especially among the youth—to save the U.S., which was now on the verge of death. Rev. Moon had been receiving frequent revelations from God about the restoration of the U.S. since March 1971. He had a detailed plan for the restoration of America.

With Waseda CARP members during my time as regional director

I was able to prepare for my going to the U.S. without any hindrance. The president of All-University Japan CARP had been informed that any obstacles to my going to the U.S. would be Satan's work, so everyone helped me.

Since it would take some time to complete the procedures and travel to the U.S., Rev. Moon directly appointed me to the new position of "Waseda Regional Director" and told me to work hard until I traveled to the U.S. He encouraged me to become the King of Waseda. This was my second mission. The Waseda region was a large block of three universities in the Waseda University area, and the regional director was to supervise the CARP members at those universities.

The Sosei dormitory was moved from Nogata to Mejirodai. In addition to the two-story, Western-style main house, a two-story, prefabricated building was added as a study room, providing enough space for 30 students to study. The members of the institute were very busy with campus evangelism, running various branch clubs, and studying. When I was appointed as Waseda Regional Director, Mr. Mitsunori Nakagawa was appointed as Vice Regional Director. He was an open-minded person and easy to work with. The group of more than 30 members was led by Mr. Kenei Miyamoto, director of the Waseda University CARP, with Ms. Akiyo Takahashi (now Mrs. Tsunoda) serving as the mother figure of the group. In the 18 months before I left for the U.S., I was determined to complete everything in Japan and go to the U.S. for my next mission without any regrets, so I worked feverishly to complete projects in all areas of my life.

I went to Jogashima Island for all-night prayer with the members of the Waseda CARP group, watched and guided them in their daily lives and established a lifelong emotional bond with them, which became an irreplaceable treasure. During this period, eight students went to the 40-day special training program and joined the Waseda University CARP as dedicated members. They are still working hard on the frontlines.

3. Achievements in the Waseda Region

A. VOC Student Movement Expanded Worldwide

The VOC movement of students in Japan entered a new phase in April 1972. In response to the desire for an international united front against international communism, VOC students from around the world gathered in Tokyo and Seoul to confirm their solidarity with each other. Of course, international solidarity had already taken place at the World Anti-Communist League (WACL) World Congress, but this was the first time students gathered for such an international conference.

Our attitude was that the world is moving in the direction of unity, despite its many conflicts. It is the cry of human history and the trend of the times to unify the world through frequent exchanges in economic, political, and cultural issues. However, the last obstacle to unification still exists in the world—the ideological struggle between communism and democracy. Unless humanity ends this internal ideological struggle now, it will not be able to achieve peace forever. Under these circumstances, it was very meaningful for VOC students from around the world to gather together to affirm our solidarity and unity.

It was also a great benefit to have our eyes opened to the world beyond the Japanese dimension. In the course of these exchanges, it was proposed that an intelligence organization and an international research institute, among others, be established in the future as an expression of international solidarity. The participants also agreed to form the United Front for Democracy against Communism to focus attention on the 38th parallel—where communism is fighting its fiercest battle—and to provide concrete support for South Korea. In this way, the rich internationality of the VOC student movement would continue to be achieved through frequent international exchanges.

B. Protesting UN Recognition of the People's Republic of China (PRC) Over Taiwan

The topic of the People's Republic of China (PRC), which was formed in 1949, joining the UN came into the spotlight as soon as 1971 began. The Republic of China (Taiwan), under Chiang Kai-shek, had been a UN member state since 1945 and had a seat as a permanent member of the Security Council. Admitting the PRC (and its insistence on a one-China policy) meant expelling Taiwan.

The free world countries were having difficulty making accurate judgments when it came to the China problem, and they were confused by the situation left and right. VOC immediately established the "Institute for Chinese Communist Studies" to promote correct understanding of the Chinese problem among alumni and the general public, and to promote research activities. On May 23, 1971, Japanese VOC members began the "Seven-Day Fasting National Assembly Against Recognition of the CCP" at Sukiyabashi and 13 other locations throughout Japan. We fasted at the main gate of Waseda University and appealed against the CCP (Chinese Communist Party) to be a member of the UN. However, on October 25, 1971, a two-thirds majority of the UN General Assembly passed resolution No. 2758, which admitted the PRC.

The world was undergoing major changes centering on the China issue as a result of the ping-pong diplomacy between the U.S. and China, the announcement of U.S. President Richard Nixon's visit to China, and China's accession to the United Nations. Under these circumstances, in order to appeal to alumni and citizens for the path that Japan and Asia should take, we proposed "The Chinese Communist Problem and the Vision of an Asian National Coalition" as the unifying theme of the VOC study group at the Fall University Festival and presented a vision for the future of Asia.

C. Lecture by Ms. Yuan

On May 24, 1971, our VOC group hosted an important lecture at Waseda University that was called "On Escape from the Chinese Communist Party and True Freedom."

Ms. Yuan's speech at Waseda University (May 24, 1971)

The speaker, Ms. Yuan, was the daughter of a physician and part of a family of doctors in Chongqing, in the Sichuan province of mainland China. In 1958, when the Chinese Communist Party began its occupation of the Chinese main-land, she was a second-year student in the mechanical engineering department of Chongqing University. She was identified as a rightist by the Seifu Movement (Chinese Communist movement of re-education and self-criticism) and sent to the Nanxiang coal mine in Sichuan to work for over three years. During the Cultural Revolution, her parents were killed and all of her family's property was plundered on the pretext that she was a rightist.

Ms. Yuan said she began to think seriously about escaping from China from that moment on, and one night she escaped from the factory by climbing over the barbed wire fence. She reached Burma on May 1, 1970, after walking for more than 10 days and overcoming the long road through the mountains of Chongqing, Guiyang, Kunming, and Baoshan. Unfortunately, she was caught as an illegal entry and deported to China, where she was sent again to a labor refor-matory and a suffering life. She escaped again and finally succeeded in reaching Mandalay in Burma and then crossed the Burmese border into Thailand in July 1970. Soon after, she moved to America, where her sister was living.

Ms. Yuan's lecture was based on her vivid, real-life experiences of the most turbulent period in China, the re-education movement to the end of the Cul-tural Revolution. About 300 students and many professors attended the lecture.

D. Waseda University School Normalization Movement

Waseda University has long been considered a stronghold of the Kakuma-ru-ha, a Revolutionary Marxist faction. They had been extorting from Waseda University more than 200 million yen per year (the amount at that time) collected from all 40,000 students as student council fees under the guise of managing most of Waseda's faculties (except the Faculty of Law) and more than 250 clubs. This source of funds was the lifeline supporting the nationwide activities of the Revolutionary Marxist faction. The leftist faction's true intention was to destroy the universities, defeat the government, and establish a communist regime in Japan.

In order to cut off this source of funding, we decided to recruit circles that sympathized with us. Tetsuo Kasai, president of Waseda University CARP, worked hard to bring together about 90 circles that wanted to leave the jurisdic-tion of the Revolutionary Marxist Movement and formed a new circle coalition on the main campus.

As a result, one-third of the First Student Hall came under the jurisdiction of our new circle group, and a certain amount of the community association fees were passed on to us. Mr. Kasai was appointed as the chairman of the standing committee, and four of the other six members of the standing committee were elected from the CARP.

The next battle was to retake the main leftist circle group. If the proposal of the leftist Revolutionary Marxist faction were to pass, the students would go on strike again the next day and would be without classes indefinitely.

We used the name "United Volunteers" to submit a counterproposal completely different from those of the Revolutionary Marxist Movement and the Communist Youth League; our message to the general students was the slogan "No student strike! Normalization of the campus!" The chairperson of the United Volunteers had to make a speech before the election, so everyone worked out a draft and the members playing the role of chairperson practiced hard to prepare for the day of the election.

The student rallies began at the law school on Nov 11. They moved to the Faculty of Political Science and Economics, and the first and the second literature school, on Nov 17. Next was a rally at the Faculty of Sociology and the Faculty of Science and Technology on Nov 18, and finally at the Faculty of Education on Nov 30.

We put forward a counterproposal to all the faculties. Our members had been trained through summer pioneering, door-to-door donation solicitation, and street speeches during evangelistic activities, so we were confident that we could defeat the left-wing students and Revolutionary Movement groups with the "United Volunteers" in each department.

When the voting began and the votes were being counted, the gymnasium was filled with surprised shouts of "Wow!" Our votes outnumbered the votes of the Kakumaru faction and the Communist Youth League (Minsei) in some departments. The left-wing revolutionary faction rose up and said, "We cannot allow opportunism in a situation like this," and invalidated the ballots.

The next day, the Marxist faction stormed into the clubroom of the Waseda Student Times Newspaper Association (CARP newspaper publishing office) and seized the draft of the newspaper that had reported on the reckless outrages of the Revolutionary Marxists. I immediately reported this illegal act to the office of the dean of Students and the director and also sent a letter to the Waseda University president. Our view was that there would be no normalization of the school unless the financial resources of the left-wing Revolutionary Movement were cut off. In order to cut down this source of funding, we had formed a coalition of circles and were risking our lives to present a counterproposal in the name of "United Volunteers" at student rallies in each department. We demanded that the university consider more serious countermeasures. The university's response was, "We will not allow the Kakumaru-ha to manage Second Student Hall. Our plan will give some improvement to normalize the school."

An academic institution is vulnerable to violence. Even at the University of Tokyo, the authorities were unable to do anything due to the long-term barricades and guerrilla tactics of the communist factions. Waseda University was no different. The university officials might talk tough, but in the end, they were afraid, and so they compromised with the radical students in the face of the guerrillas and group demands.

I thought that the normalization of the school would be successful when the university authorities, faculty, and representatives of the general student body were strongly united, incorporating the wishes of the general student body. However, the tension between us and the leftist student activists continued to simmer.

E. Asian Victory Convention (May 22, 1971, Tokyo)

On May 22, 1971, the Asian VOC Convention was held at the Japan City Center Hall. Following messages from the heads of Japan, Korea, and Taiwan, the movie "Forward to Victory" of the previous year's WACL convention was shown.

Next was a special testimony by Mr. Xinchao Kim, a captured North Korean spy who spoke about the realities of North Korea, followed by a talk by Ms. Yuan, who had escaped from mainland China and knew the realities of the Chinese Communist mainland. Next, Mr. Jin of the Japan-China Cooperation Committee gave a lecture on the future direction of free Asia, followed by the adoption of a resolution and a 1,500-member march against the approval of the CCP.

F. Visit to Waseda University, Yeungnam University, Korea

Yeungnam University merged two universities in Daegu, an educational city in Korea's ancient capital, and the government purchased a 1,000,000-square-meter plot of land. There, the new master plan called for an up-and-coming faculty to build a model university, and Dr. Lee Seon Geun, former Secretary of the Ministry of Education, was appointed president.

President Lee had graduated from Waseda University with a doctorate degree in literature and history. He and Waseda University President Murai held a meeting at first, and Waseda University agreed to cooperate in the development of Yeungnam University. The dean of Student Affairs, the president of Student Affairs, and eight editors-in-chief of the university newspaper were invited.

Three members of the Waseda University CARP Group (Ikeno, Miyamoto, and Tsunoda) were assigned to accompany the eight students as they toured famous universities throughout Japan and prepared a schedule that included seminars with Japanese students. In Tokyo, 35 Tokyo-area university students and a student representative from Yeungnam University held a heated discussion on "Peace in Asia and the Mission of Japan and Korea" at the Waseda Service Center.

Meeting with President Lee of Yeungnam University
and President Murai of Waseda University

They also visited the University of Tokyo, Keio University, Kyoto University, Osaka University, Nara Women's University, and Hiroshima University. After visiting the Atomic Bomb Memorial in Hiroshima, they joined Hiroshima University and three other universities in a discussion titled "Asian Peace and the Mission of Japan and Korea." There I advocated the concept of an Asian Nation

Alliance. After visiting Kyushu University, the group flew to Busan by Korea Air Lines.

Later, during a visit to Korea, I had an opportunity to visit Yeungnam University and meet President Lee. He expressed his gratitude, saying, "The university has grown to an amazing degree by taking advantage of the university reform policy I learned during my visit to Japan in September of 1971."

G. World Student Conference (April 27, 1972, Tokyo)

In late April, 15 students from nine foreign countries, including the U.S., France, and Germany, visited Japan. A "World Student Conference" was held by a total of 35 students, including foreign students living in Japan.

After the opening remarks by the chair, Mr. Michio Fujii (president of all Japan CARP), and the introduction of representatives from each country, Mr. Yasushi Onoya, a fourth-year student at the University of Tokyo, gave a lecture on the theme "Challenges and Missions of Students from East and West for the Promotion of World Peace." He emphasized that students are the pioneers of a new era with such a mission.

After a question-and-answer session and lunch, each country presented its report, which was followed by an enthusiastic discussion. A communiqué was adopted, pledging to hold the next meeting in the hope that this conference would develop into such an event. This was the first event in which an international united front of VOC students was confirmed, and it subsequently became a conference of historic significance. I served as the moderator of this meeting.

H. World Congress of Students for Victory Over Communism
(May 1, 1972, Seoul Civic Center)

The conference was held in the main hall of the Seoul Civic Center with about 3,000 students from Seoul. As soon as I entered the hall, I could feel the enthusiasm of the young people.

It stressed the need for greater cooperation among students in the democratic camp to overcome communism. It also called for stronger unity of the free world and protested the aggression and barbarism of the Kim Il Sung regime.

The communiqué was adopted. Messages were then read to Korean President Park Chung Hee; H.E. Stanislaw Trepczynski, Secretary-General of the United Nations; and heads of state and government, bringing the event to a successful conclusion. The conference was broadcast live on Seoul Broadcasting Corporation and other TV and radio stations.

I. First World Student Symposium (May 2, 1972)

On May 2, an international conference was held at the Cosmos Hall of the Walker Hill Hotel, attended by 25 representatives of various countries, 30 representatives of Korea, and 80 observers.

Professor Shin Dong Ok of Konkuk University gave a lecture on the "Rapidly Changing International Situation and Mission of University Students," followed by a question-and-answer session, and after a general discussion, a joint communiqué was prepared and adopted.

This communiqué, called the "Seoul Declaration," had five main points: (1) to support the creation of new ideals and new cultures, (2) to strengthen international solidarity for VOC activities, (3) to establish all kinds of cooperation and support systems for liberal countries, (4) to designate May 2 as "World Peace Day," and (5) to inform student organizations around the world of this statement. The statement was a highly elegant one.

The declaration thus issued in Seoul, Korea, was carried around the world and kept burning as the ideal fire of the VOC student front in each country.

After the conference at Konkuk University, the 25 foreign students who had completed the conference toured the country according to a new schedule, holding seven conferences and 14 seminars at 21 universities in six cities. They received a great welcome in each location, and lively discussions and in-depth pursuits took place, especially at Seoul National University, Dankook University, and Korea University.

During these three weeks of activities, the foreign students came to the following realization. First of all, the problems that students face are common to all countries, and solutions must be pursued together since shared contemporary issues transcend national boundaries. It was concluded that the university structure should be reformed in order to allow the university to deeply pursue and obtain answers to the more essential questions like "what is life?" "what is truth?" and "what is study?" For this purpose, a joint proposal was made to build a research organization based on international solidarity.

The First World Student Symposium and touring Korea

From another perspective, the participants shared the common understanding that the issue of the 38th parallel was a symbol of all the contemporary contradictions in the world—thus, the people of the world should not turn away from the 38th parallel but should do everything they could to provide mental and material support to South Korea. The foreign students realized the seriousness of the 38th parallel for the first time during their visit to Korea, and they promised to appeal to the public about this situation after returning to their home countries.

The contact between young souls from around the world that took place in Korea would eventually permeate the youth of each country and be of great use for a united front of the world's youth. In this sense, this event was a historical event of great significance.

J. Second World Student Symposium (May 22-23, 1972 ,Tokyo)

On May 22, foreign students who stopped by Japan on their way back from Korea attended the World Student Symposium held at the University of Tokyo. The symposium was held at the invitation of the University Problem Research Group of the University of Tokyo and had the theme of "How Universities Can Contribute to World Peace." After a lecture by a professor, speeches were given by representatives from the U.S., Germany, Italy, and Japan on May 23, followed by questions and answers from students from each country. The relationship between universities and world peace was seriously discussed.

What emerged was the image of students as subjects who transcend nationalism, as subjects who construct ideals, and as subjects who overcome obstacles and put them into practice in order to realize their ideals. The meeting ended with a successful conclusion, with a strong appeal for students to work together in solidarity to establish a new philosophy that transcends communism.

Until now, in developed countries, the university issue was an excellent source of struggle for the communists. But once the VOC camp seriously tackled the university issue and did more for the university than the communists, universities could surely free themselves from the hands of the communists.

4. Preparation for Travel to the U.S.

A. My Relatives Came to the U.S. 120 Years Ago

When I came to the U.S. in 1972, my relatives, who came to Ukiah in northern California 120 years ago, played a major role for me.

The family's name is Onomiya. My maternal grandfather was adopted into the Kinoshita family from a branch of the Onomiya family. I have heard from my grandfather that there were various merits in this area that led this family to be awarded the 8th degree of the Order from the government. The Onomiya family was the guarantor for my study in the U.S. I was especially grateful to Etsuko Seto, who was a member of the Onomiya family. In particular, my Aunt Etsuko, who loved me more than her own children, was my guarantor for my study in the United States.

My relatives in the U.S. (Aunt Etsuko Seto and her children)

She is the daughter of an enterprising young man named Suematsu Onomiya, who traveled alone to San Francisco in 1896. However, Suematsu's beloved wife died when their daughter was 3 years old. They were placed under the care of my grandfather, Yoshiki Kinoshita, who was a nephew to Suematsu. My mother and Aunt Etsuko were raised like sisters. My mother called Aunt Etsuko "big sister," and Aunt Etsuko loved my mother as if she were her own sister. Takeichi Onomiya, a nephew of Suematsu and an elder brother of my grandfather, saw his uncle's success in the United States, so he moved to the U.S. by himself, even though he was the eldest son. He chose a career in agriculture in the United States. Driven by a sense of nostalgia, he wanted to farm in a place similar to his hometown, so he looked for a place north of San Francisco and ended up in Ukiah.

This place was the basis of the "International Ideal City Project" that Mr. Nishikawa first established in the U.S. and was called "Boonville." Aunt Etsuko soon returned to her father's place, where she married an elite engineer who graduated from the University of California, Berkeley. Sadly, her husband died of illness, leaving her with two young children. When the persecution of Japanese in the U.S. began after the outbreak of World War II, Aunt Etsuko returned to Japan with her children. After the war was over, the brother of Aunt Etsuko's late husband came to visit her in Uto, and she and Uncle Toshiro returned to the U.S. again.

Aunt Etsuko went to San Francisco to see the vinyl factory her late husband had built, but it had already been confiscated and was in someone else's name. She worked hard to build a Japanese restaurant called Otemo. Before I was born, there was war after war, and some of my relatives died in the war (my mother's brother was killed in Leyte, Philippines). I cannot help but cry when I think of the hardships my Aunt Etsuko must have gone through to escape persecution from the Americans, crossing the border left and right with her young children.

B. Rev. and Mrs. Moon Visit Japan to Form the One World Crusade

Rev. and Mrs. Moon, who had formed the One World Crusade in the U.S., stopped by Japan on April 22, 1972, and formed the Twelve Crusades in Japan as well. They gathered 2,000 members from all over Japan in Sayama Park and organized them into the Twelve Crusades. After that, all members of the Crusades participated in a two-week training session at Moriyama Training Center in Nagoya from April 30. The instructor at that time was Rev. Yeong-hui Kim, the head of the Korean Church. Rev. Ken Sudo was appointed as the general leader of the group.

At the time, I was taking care of 15 students from nine countries who were visiting Japan to participate in the VOC student conventions in Japan and Korea. They had to attend various conventions (the April 25 World VOC Congress and April 27 World Student Conference) and were also very busy preparing materials for the Korean convention. Rev. and Mrs. Moon returned to Tokyo from Nagoya, gathered the Japanese delegates who would visit Korea in May, took them to the Ueno Zoo during the day, and took them to see the movie "The Story of a Great Life" at night.

Jesus' life up to the cross in the movie was so tragic that I wept in my heart. I thought that the restoration of the Christian nation of the U.S. depended on the ability of its citizens to understand the heart of Jesus. I was grateful to have been shown such a film before I came to the U.S., as it taught me what is most necessary for the restoration of the U.S. Finally, we went to Tokyo Tower at night and enjoyed my last night in Tokyo with Rev. and Mrs. Moon.

C. Leaving My Homeland

After the month-long tour in Korea, I began to communicate with Professor Reischauer of Harvard University and President McGill of Columbia University through the "Sekai Gakusei Shinbun" (World Student Times) and notified them of my application to study in the United States. Before my departure for the U.S., I learned that Professor Reischauer happened to be in Tokyo, and when I asked him for his opinion on university issues as editor-in-chief of World Student Times, he readily accepted my offer, and we conducted an interview in the lobby of the hotel where he was staying. The article appeared on the front page of the World Student Times. This led to my acquaintance with the professor, and I often asked him for his academic insights in his courses at Harvard University.

When I asked President McGill of Columbia University to write an article for the World Student Times on how he viewed the origins of university conflicts and his proposal for university reform, he immediately sent me a copy of the article in English. Reading the article, I was impressed by his sincere attitude toward how to reform the university while addressing the wishes of the students.

I sent him a vase I had bought in Korea as a thank you gift, and he was very pleased. Later, when I visited his office after I started attending Columbia University, I was delighted to see the vase on display. These two people are very important people with whom I need to have a deeper emotional exchange, so I contacted them in advance, and it worked out well.

In early June, I received a phone call from President Kuboki. He said, "Rev. Moon called me from Korea and told me to tell Mr. Ikeno to go to the U.S. immediately. Is your trip to the U.S. going well?" I told him that since the U.S. immigration bureau required a guarantee from someone with a certain amount of assets who can provide financial support in case of emergency to study at an American university, I had asked my aunt, who lives in Los Angeles, to be my guarantor, and I would be able to go as soon as I had that paperwork. Mr. Kuboki said, "Rev. Moon knew you well and told me, 'Mr. Ikeno suffered a lot but overcame all his difficulties.' I would have had the opportunity to study in the U.S. at any time, but this is significant the Messiah is telling you to go."

He also gave me some fine fabric to make a suit and gave me a parting gift. At the same time, the 12 men selected by Happy World to be sent to the U.S. (Katsue Shinba, Takeshi Ito, Ryoji Sawamukai, Hiroshi Matsuzaki, Zenichiro Hayashi, Kazuo Sato, Takashi Takenaka, Tetsuaki Izukawa, Kiyoshi Nishi, Toshiaki Watanabe, Kazuro Ono, and Rikio Yamamoto) left for New York on June 23, 1972.

I flew from Haneda Airport to Boston via Los Angeles on a Pan American Airlines on June 29. At Haneda, I received a grand send-off from my brothers and sisters, relatives, friends from junior high school, friends from high school, staff members of the CARP Headquarters, members of the editorial board of the World Student Times, members of the Waseda CARP, my teachers at Waseda University, and about 40 peoples' gathering . I was leaving for an unknown country, but one that I had longed for, the United States of America. I decided to leave everything that would happen to me in God's hands, just as the Pilgrim father once left their fate in God's hands when they set out for the unknown country of America.

PART II

Introduction

While Part I covered my personal life, Part II will cover my 50-year history of U.S. pioneer witnessing and overseas missionary activities.

Part II has a somewhat different format from Part I, which is based on the author's memories of his time in Japan. In the second part, the tone is much more casual, and the language is more like that of an interview.

Part II took shape after I was asked to give a testimony about my history of 50 years of missionary activities in the U.S. and abroad to the Japanese members living in the U.S. I had two opportunities to give this testimony in front of about 500 Japanese members.

Afterward, in 2021, I met with an organization called "Kodan group" (mission group) that unites Japanese living in the U.S. Mr. Hiroshi Inose, president of the Kodan organization, and his wife said, "I think it is necessary to leave for posterity the history of Mr. Ikeno's 50-year pioneering work in the U.S. We will record it once a week, so please make a PowerPoint presentation and use that as a basis for your explanation." The 2021 recordings, which started on March 8 and ended on May 14, took about two and a half months.

Fumio Fukatsu, president of Good Time Publishing Company, suggested I rewrite this video in spoken language as Part II of my memories of my time in the U.S. I agreed, and this presentation, "History of the 50th Anniversary of the Pioneering and Overseas Missions to the United States," constituted the second part of my autobiography.

I have to admit that there are some parts that I repeat from time to time. I sometimes have to explain them again when PowerPoint pictures or other information appear, which makes it difficult for readers to understand. However, I would like to express my gratitude to the late Mr. Inose of the Kodan group for his foresight, which enabled me to write my history about my years in America and other countries.

This was the time when Rev. and Mrs. Moon were devoting all their passion to the American pioneering. Their start was smooth, but then came severe persecution. In 1981, Rev. Moon was accused of tax evasion. During his New York trial, he launched *The Washington Times* newspaper on May 17, 1982. Sadly, Rev. Moon was convicted and imprisoned in the Federal Correctional Institution in Danbury, Connecticut. The members, his wife, and their children were all heartbroken. But during his time in U.S. prison (July 20, 1984 to July 4, 1985), Rev. Moon made plans to launch a weekly magazine and monthly magazine by the end of 1985. He also sent 400,000 cassette tapes of the *Divine Principle* to pastors across the country and sent 7,000 pastors to Korea for pilgrimages to deepen their understanding of the Holy Land and the *Divine Principle*.

In addition to the 50 years of pioneering in the U.S., I traveled to Russia, China, Belgium, and South America and was active on five continents. Strictly speaking, I should add that the history of the U.S. Pioneer Movement is a history of missionary activities spanning four continents other than the United States. That is why I titled my autobiography, "My Life on Five Continents."

This Part II is a testimony to church members, and since it is the practice within the church to refer to Rev. Sun Myung Moon as True Father and Mrs. Hak Ja Han Moon as True Mother, I may happen to use those titles. Please understand this.

A 50-YEAR HISTORY OF PIONEERING IN THE UNITED STATES AND OVERSEAS

20 YEAR JOURNEY TO PIONEER: THE EARLY DAYS IN THE UNITED STATES

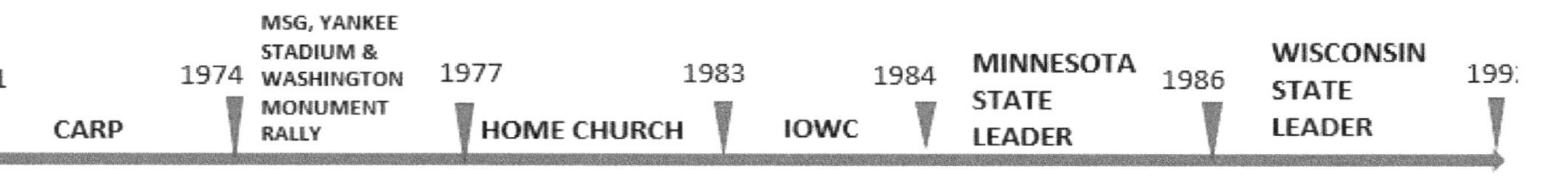

10 YEAR OVERSEAS MISSION

20 YEARS OF CHURCH OUTREACH / HEAVENLY TRIBAL MESSIAH ACTIVITIES

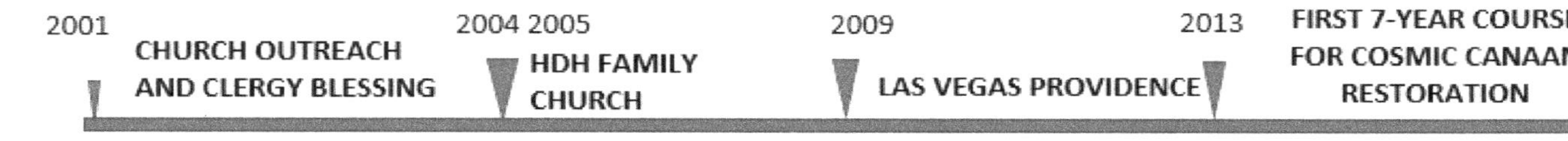

CHAPTER 1

A Chronological Outline
of Key Events

1. Outline of the history of the 50th anniversary of the pioneering in the U.S. and overseas missions

In 2021, I accepted the invitation from Mr. Inose, president of the Kodan group, who asked me to give a testimony of my 50-year history of the pioneering work in the U.S. I was called by heaven to go to the U.S. in 1971. Looking back today, I realize that half a century has already passed, and I have been preparing for it and running selflessly. I looked through my diaries, the speeches that Rev. Moon gave every Sunday for about 12 years, the reading sessions in Las Vegas, and the notes from the conferences in Korea. I found 218 notebooks in total.

I was very worried about how I would be able to put it all together in such a short period of time. However, I thought that if I lost this opportunity, I might end up leaving all these materials behind and going to the other side of life. I did not want to die without knowing who would organize these materials, so I decided to collect them and put them into a record of what I had done in the U.S. As it turned out, the record turned out to be a 15-meter long roll of paper.

Next, I was struggled with how to put this 15-meter roll of paper into a PowerPoint presentation. With the help of my wife, we managed to put it all together.

The first section, "Pioneering in the United States," covers a period of 20 years. Next is the "overseas missionary period," which lasts 10 years. The "Minister Witnessing, Tribal Messianic Activities, and the First Seven-Year Course of the Heavenly Cosmic Canaan Restoration" is a 20-year journey. In total, the period is 50 years.

First of all, among the many providences, I will choose only two to talk about this week.

Then on the following Monday, "Home Church," "Meeting of Studying and Reading of Scriptures," and finally, "Heavenly Parents Holy Community," which Mrs. Hak Ja Han Moon recommended.

I believe that this final providence will focus mainly on this Holy Community. As we look at this trend of the past half-century, we can see that Rev. Moon has always emphasized the "restoration of people and witnessing."

In addition to evangelizing on the streets, Rev. Moon also hoped we would evangelize our own clan, neighbors, and friends at the university. If it is possible, we can read in the recent words of Mrs. Hak Ja Han Moon that she is hoping for the restoration of people in the community. She uses a Korean word, *Topangepa*, which means "defeat and break through community," but what this means is to penetrate into the community.

Rev. Moon said that it is necessary to restore the people of the local community. The reason for this is that communism is, after all, the greatest enemy of us believers in God. Because Satan is in charge of the Earth, he uses various kinds of wiles and sneaky ways to infiltrate human life. The current Chinese Communist Party is just like that. If you study their methods, you will find that they have already invaded and violated us without our knowing it, and when we try to get out of their infiltration, they will try to keep us in their grip through threats, actual murder, and other such methods.

It is not only individuals but also companies, governments, and lawyers that are targeted, with universities the most important places to penetrate. Therefore, when I led a group of 120 graduates to Korea in 1971, we had Victory Over Communism rallies at 12 major universities there. South Korea was also really infiltrated by communist activities from the North. Rev. Moon was really worried about that.

Rev. Moon met with Prof. Reischauer (at his home March 23, 1973)

That's why he said that the Collegiate Association for the Research of Principles (CARP) is so important. He said communism always comes from universities. On the East Coast, it is Columbia University in New York City. On the West Coast, it is University of California, Berkeley in California. CARP must take full control of this. Otherwise, communism will always use professors to brainwash students from there. In fact, when I was at Columbia University, it had a journalism department, and most of the students joined *The Washington Post* or *The New York Times*.

When I spoke with the students, I was stunned. I wondered if they were brainwashed. They would go to *The New York Times* and make a pro-communist editorial. Or they would go to NBC or CNN. This is exactly the strategy of communism. We have to be very sensitive to that. How much has communism penetrated the United States today? When I think about that, I realize that the CARP movement is very important.

At the same time, from the very beginning, Rev. Moon expected the restoration of the Christian church in the United States to take place. When Rev. Moon went to Danbury prison, he told us state leaders that he would send 7,000 pastors to Korea to undergo training in Korea and that he would take them on the pilgrimage to understand what he had been going through in Korea. He said he would guide them all the way. He encouraged us to love these pastors and encourage them to do the same with us. As a state leader, I had to inform the pastors there about the CAUSA (Confederation of Associations for the Unity of the Societies of the Americas) ministry and the issue of communism, so I have been doing such activities in two states for about seven years. (Minnesota and Wisconsin).

International Leadership Seminar visit to Columbia University

Next, Rev. Moon said that we must bless 144,000 pastors in this pastoral outreach. Rev. Moon himself, in spite of his 80-odd years of age, went on a 50-day tour of the 50 states to give a lecture. When I saw his activities, I realized no one other than Rev. Moon understood what was really needed to restore the United States.

So, during this period of 50 years, Rev. Moon has been working for the revival of Christianity by witnessing through community activities. His belief was that the UPF (Universal Peace Federation) and CARP movement were bulwarks to protect human rights, democracy, freedom, and the foundations of Christianity, which the founders of various cultures and Christianity in the United States wished to preserve. He told us of his belief that we cannot save America unless we study communism and become more sensitive to it.

He also said that world peace starts from families where true love dwells, and that it begins with young people taking the initiative and seeking international marriages that transcend race and national borders.

CHAPTER 2

The First Five Years of U.S. Pioneering (1972-1977)

1. Studying in the U.S. and Meeting Professor Reischauer

On June 29, 1972, I left for the United States to study abroad. The reason why I had to register at Harvard University was that there was a righteous man there. Prof. Edwin Reischauer, former Ambassador to Japan, is that person. His parents came to Japan as missionaries of the Presbyterian Church and founded Tokyo Women's University. Born in Japan, he had a deep knowledge of Oriental culture and was the perfect person to serve as a bridge between the East and the West.

At the time, President Park Chung Hee of South Korea enacted the Restoration Constitution. This paved the way for a dictatorship comparable to that of President Kim Il Sung of the North, and U.S. President Richard Nixon responded by withdrawing U.S. forces from Korea. Indeed, the U.S.-South Korea relationship was becoming increasingly strained.

Prof. Reischauer met with Rev. Moon and Mrs. Choi Won Bok at his home in Boston on March 23, 1973. He opened the meeting by saying, "Mr. Ikeno, he is an excellent student." He knew what was going on in North and South Korea, even though not many of his students were interested in the Korean Penninsula issue.

Prof. Reischauer, who came from a family of missionaries, listened to Rev. Moon's explanation of what the Unification Church was and was deeply impressed by what he heard about salvation and the Messiah. The conversation turned to the tense Korean Peninsula, and five days after the meeting, Prof. Reischauer wrote two articles in *The New York Times Magazine* opposing the withdrawal of U.S. forces in Korea. After that, President Nixon stopped talking about the withdrawal of U.S. forces in Korea.

Prof. Reischauer also promised to speak at Harvard University to 120 graduate students attending an international leadership from Japan. In addition, his wife became the honorary president for the return of Japanese wives from North Korea.

With Prof. Reischauer and his wife

2. Establishment of CARP at Columbia University

My main intention was to establish CARP at Columbia University. Meanwhile, I was studying at the Graduate School of International Studies in New York City, where I would not only witness but also engage in various other activities. On February 1, 1973, I met with President McGill of Columbia University, with whom I had had several exchanges in Japan, and when I told him of my intention to enroll at Columbia and establish CARP, he graciously offered his cooperation. After several public hearings, CARP was officially established in Columbia on September 24, 1973.

For international students, the amount of reading in graduate school in the U.S. was five to six times more than in Japan each week. Moreover, in seminars, students frequently had to write essays about their opinions, hand in the papers to the professor and all the participants, explain the contents of the papers, and receive criticism not only from their classmates but also from the professor—a big challenge for those whose English was not so fluent. It was a difficult time for me. The classes, church activities, and fundraising kept me overworked to the point that I would urinate blood. My research question was how "international integration theory" could be applied to the Asian region. One day, Rev. Moon told me that "without centering on God's deep heart, there can be no world integration," and that I should theorize about it. Even though the study at Columbia was so hard for me, several worldwide renowned professors opened my eyes to the world. I want to recognize those professors: Professor James Morley, my guiding professor, (East Asian Studies), Professor Zbigniew Brzezinski (Soviet Studies), Professor Louis Henkin (International Law and Human Rights Law), Professor Gerald Curtis, (Japan Reseach). They give me tremendous intellectual assets.

Rev. Moon met with President Nixon at the White House

Outside of campus, major events were swirling around us. Protests against the Vietnam War had started in the 1960s, and by the early 1970s, these began to inflame the campus atmosphere, and students became emotionally confused and fell into a state of decadence. Then in 1972, the Watergate scandal broke, and the movement to remove President Nixon from office gained momentum on a daily basis. I often participated in the debates held in the lounge and expressed my opinions. Rev. Moon placed an ad in leading national newspapers offering an alternative solution to Watergate: "Forgive, Love, Unite." Rev. Moon met with

President Nixon on February 1, 1974, and encouraged him to publicly repent and seek the American people's forgiveness. However, the President resigned on August 9, 1974. That was 40 days before Rev. Moon's big rally at Madison Square Garden.

Meanwhile, Columbia CARP was busy. Campus evangelists gathered in the rotunda every day during lunch, gave speeches, handed out flyers, and invited students and others to listen to lectures in the small center we had rented. Gradually, the students connected, and finally eight students joined the club, and Fred and Ken began living in our center together. The first Sunday service was a memorable day, though it was just the five of us: three American students, a Japanese language student, and me. Later, Columbia CARP expanded to five major universities in New York by sending personnel to five universities in New York. The number of students grew to 75, and many events were now held jointly.

For example, on June 25, 1974, a symposium to commemorate the 24th anniversary of the start of the Korean War was to be held at Columbia University with 1,000 participants. But 40 to 50 Communist League students scrambled into the venue and struggled with people at the entrance. We somehow managed to block their way, and the event was a great success. After hearing the report of the conference, Rev. Moon gathered CARP members in New York on September 29, 1974, to talk about CARP's role in preventing communism in the U.S. He said, "There may not be a Communist Party in the U.S., but tenured liberal professors are brainwashing students with communist ideas, and they are spreading communist ideas centrally in important sectors of society, and society is moving further and further away from God-centered thinking. First, the communists are focusing their activities on Columbia University on the East Coast and the University of California, Berkeley on the West Coast, and CARP must also expand its influence on these two universities."

After that, international leadership seminars consisting of graduate students from Japan, England, and other countries were held frequently. The first leadership seminar was held at the Belvedere Estate from July 18 to September 1, 1973. I also made an arduous effort to invite professors from the most prestigious Ivy League schools on the East Coast. Around 120 students from the U.K. and 120 from Japan participated. The Japanese students attended lectures at the Unification Theological Seminary (UTS), where I also gave a lecture on "The Founding of the United States and the Development of Democracy." Both groups attended a joint seminar in Boulder, Colorado. In addition, Japanese graduate students visited Harvard University and Columbia University to listen to lectures by renowned professors. Many of the staff members were old friends who had worked together on CARP activities in Japan and renewed their friendships.

In March 1975, Japanese blessed wives (women married in our church) who had come to the U.S. were sent to the 50 states and asked to create CARP in each state. We published "Sekai Gakusei Shinbun" (World Student Times) to assist them. This was distributed monthly to states that requested it. By the following year, CARP was established in 48 states.

Prof. Anderson and two others from Columbia University participated in the Third International Conference on the Unity of the Sciences (ICUS) on November 27, 1975. It featured Sir John Eccles, professor of physiology and biophysics at the State University of New York and Nobel Prize Laureate in Physiology and Medicine. He had been connected to ICUS through Prof. Anderson.

3. Carnegie Hall Rally and Madison Square Garden Rally

I was on campus selling tickets to the Carnegie Hall rally. The convention lasted three days (October 1-3, 1973) and consisted of "The Hope of Man," "God's Hope for America," and "The Future of Christianity." The rally was a success, overcoming fierce opposition from fundamentalists in front of Carnegie Hall.

At the 1974 Madison Square Garden rally, Columbia CARP served northern Manhattan, including Harlem, and was able to hire 20 buses and mobilize 1,841 people. I rode the last bus leaving Harlem to Madison Square Garden, but the venue was already packed, and many people were hanging out outside the venue because they could not get in. I happened to be able to enter the venue in exchange for someone coming out of the venue.

What was noteworthy about this 1974 rally was that about 300,000 posters were put up in all areas of New York City and Manhattan five days before the rally. When the Madison Square Garden event was over, our members immediately went into Manhattan and removed all the posters. This stunned New Yorkers.

The goal was set to gain 3,000 new members to ensure victory at the Madison Square Garden rally. It is regrettable that this goal wasn't fully realized. Had this goal been achieved, the subsequent providence would have been very different.

4. Movement for the Return of Japanese Wives Trapped in North Korea

On October 2, 1974, a movement was launched in the United States to bring home over 6,000 Japanese wives who had been deceived, taken to North Korea, and not allowed to come back to Japan. The representative was Fumiko Ikeda (real name: Yasue Erikawa), whose own sister had fallen for the lies of the Chongryon (a pro-North Korea group in Japan) and had gone to North Korea with her Korean husband. Ms. Erikawa was a bold and decisive activist. At the same time, we handed copies of the signatures to the UN Human Rights Commission and the International Red Cross Society in Geneva, Switzerland, and asked for their cooperation in realizing their return to Japan.

Yasue Erikawa and I met with Mr. Solzhenitsyn requesting his support for the return of Japanese wives trapped in North Korea. (Zurich, Switzerland)

We also met with Aleksandr Solzhenitsyn in Zurich, Switzerland, and asked for his support. Mr. Solzhenitsyn, who himself had experienced a harsh life in prison in the Soviet Union, expressed deep sympathy for the Japanese wives and immediately expressed his support for the movement. He recommended attending a human rights conference in London, which we did. We then visited Amnesty International in London, England, and requested cooperation in the return of Japanese wives. We gave a copy of 4,500 signatures to the headquarters of the International Women's Federation in Paris, France, and requested cooperation in their return.

On the issue of the return of Japanese wives, on May 25, 1975, we participated in the General Assembly of the United Nations Women's Year in Mexico City and appealed to women representatives from all over the world about the devastating situation of Japanese women taken to North Korea and the efforts to bring them home.

5. Yankee Stadium Rally (June 1, 1976)

Mr. Ethan Brown, a follower of Father Divine, was so moved when he saw us CARP members doing early morning street cleaning along Broadway that he donated his five-story brownstone house (worth $1.8 million at the time) for $1.00. Later, on September 14, 1975, this building became the center of activities for student rallies, Sunday services, the Yankee Stadium rally, and the Washington Monument rally. Rev. and Mrs. Moon visited on January 21, 1976, and were pleased to hear how the building was dedicated. They told us that if it was such a precious gift from heaven, we should carpet the entire staircase with red carpet. Unfortunately, the building was later sold due to CARP's financial difficulties.

Mr. Osami Kuboki, president of the Unification Church of Japan, paid a surprise visit to the Columbia CARP Center on January 19, 1976. During this visit, he informed us of Rev. Moon's message about the historical significance of the upcoming Yankee Stadium rally—officially called the Bicentennial God Bless America Festival at Yankee Stadium—and encouraged us to do our best because he had great expectations for me and for CARP. Around 200 Columbia alumni attended the banquet andchanged our gloomy atmosphere drastically.

Two days later, Rev. and Mrs. Moon visited the CARP center and spoke about the significance of the Yankee Stadium rally and the Washington Monument rally (date undetermined at the time). Twenty-five CARP members attended. First, the couple interacted with each member individually and then told them that the relationship between the three rallies was that the 1974 Madison Square Garden rally was from Adam's perspective, the upcoming Yankee Stadium rally was from Jesus' perspective, and the upcoming Washington Monument rally was from the perspective of the Second Coming of the Lord. Therefore, the Yankee Stadium rally was in the second position, and in this most difficult rally, young people before the age of 30 must take the lead in order to release the "grudge" of Jesus. In other words, CARP should be in charge.

"The Yankee Stadium rally marks the crossing and conversion of American providence as Jesus climbs the hill of Golgotha, where his sorrows will not be cleared. Winning this will begin the full-scale work of the Messiah in America. Jesus is asking us to be the key to the final indemnity. If we win, Jesus will bow down to everyone," Rev. Moon said. Nothing could be more gratifying. Besides the fact, he told us that the problem is how to pull in American Christians. Later, Rev. and Mrs. Moon put me in the car and circled Columbia University, saying, "The more important the Yankee Stadium rally is, the harder Satan will attack us. I set the conditions."

Indeed, various persecutions later struck, including the expulsion of Columbia CARP from the university municipality by communist forces working with Jewish and Catholic students, the attacks on Unification Church sisters doing home visits in the Bronx, and the worst kinds of negative articles in the newspapers every day.

The building on West 43rd Street in Manhattan, which was purchased as the headquarters of the Unification Church of America, was formerly used as the Columbia University Alumni Hall. On May 9, 1976, Columbia University alumni from the New York area were invited to a banquet and approximately 200 attended, completely changing our gloomy feelings. Dr. Bergman, our church member and a Columbia alumnus, gave a lecture on the theme "Rev. Moon in America."

On the day of the Yankee Stadium rally June 1, 1976, a stormy rainstorm blew in, and I felt downhearted. The heavy rain reminded me of the tears of sorrow that Jesus shed while dying on the cross 2,000 years ago due to the ignorance of the Jewish people, and I prayed desperately in the rain for the victory of the rally. CARP mobilized more than 10,000 people, and CARP accounted for 10 of the top 12 mobilizers. Rev. and Mrs. Moon presented gold watches to these 12, and I had mobilized 400 people and was awarded second prize.

On June 13, 1976, during lunch at the East Garden, Mrs. Moon whispered something to Rev. Moon and then went upstairs, returning with a white envelope that she gave to him. "You have rendered great service. This is a donation of $10,000 from Germany," he said when he gave it to me. The Korean, American, and Japanese leaders present applauded in unison.

I used $3,000 of that money to make flyers for the upcoming Washington Monument rally. The rest of the money was used to help two Columbia CARP members who were having trouble paying their tuition, and I received the rest and used it for my tuition that fall.

6. Washington Monument Rally (September 18, 1976)

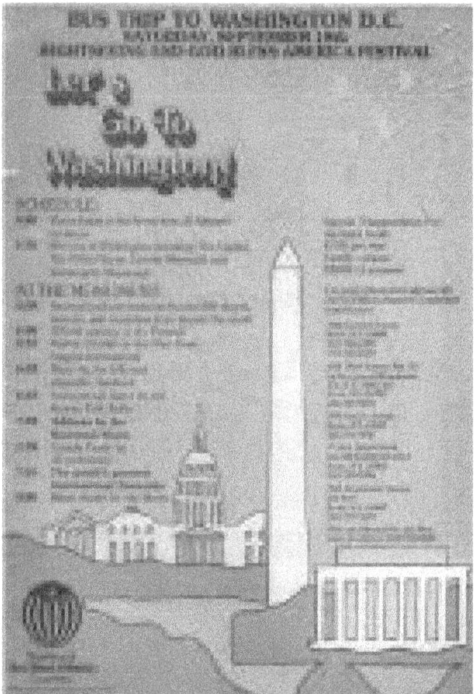

Around 400,000 flyers were distributed

I was in charge of the Bronx area, and 15 other CARP members from other departments filled in to make up the main group. First, we distributed about 400,000 "Let's Go to Washington" flyers before breakfast and then went door-to-door with tickets. The mass distribution of the flyers was so successful that people came to the seven ticket booths to buy the $30 tickets. Every week at night in each community, we showed a film on Rev. Moon in America, using apartment walls as screens, and many people bought tickets afterward. Every Tuesday and Thursday we invited people over for dinner and introduced them to the Washington Monument rally, which was officially called the God Bless America Festival at Washington Monument. On September 18, 1976, the day of the rally, people crowded the seven bus depots from early in the morning, as if it were the eve of the revolution. The entire New York City area sent out 350 buses and about 15,000 people, and in my district of the Bronx, we were able to mobilize 85 buses and about 4,000 people.

Not everyone could come—many buses never arrived to pick up their guests, and other buses broke down on the trip to Washington, D.C. District leaders had to reimburse those who could not make it to the rally.

Around 300,000 people attended the Washington Monument rally

By the time we arrived, the National Mall surrounding the Washington Monument was completely packed. At least 300,000 people came, and the rally was a great success. On the same day, Mao Zedong died.

The Day of the Victory of Heaven was established on October 4, 1976, and Rev. Moon told us that the victory of the Washington Monument rally opened the gates of the home church providence. He said, "If the victory of the 1976 rally had not been made, neither God nor Satan would have approved of home churches, no matter how hard we tried to build them. Before the Washington Monument rally, only individual salvation was allowed, but through the victory of the rally, the way was opened for the whole family to go to heaven through home churches."

I graduated from the school of International Affairs and the Institute of East Asian Studies at the Columbia Graduate School on October 28, 1976. For my graduation thesis, I submitted a paper entitled, "The Possibility of Realizing the Asian Coalition of Nations Concept from the Perspective of International Integration Theory." Mr. Joe Tully became the head of National CARP. From then on, I devoted myself to home church activities under Rev. Won Pil Kim.

7. Receiving the 74 Couples Blessing

After joining the Unification Church, I missed two opportunities to receive the Marriage Blessing. The first was the 777 Couples Blessing in 1970. I missed this Blessing, even though all my conditions were met. Tens of thousands of ancestor spirits behind me cried out in grief and pierced my heart. When I visited Korea in March 1971, Rev. Moon invited me to his room at the church headquarters in Cheongpa-dong and comforted me with many stories. He placed a marble vase between his legs, stroked it, and said, "Don't worry. I can bless you anytime, anywhere. You just happen to have no one who fits as your spouse. In a little while, you'll meet a woman whose nickname is 'White Pumpkin.' The reason for this is that you have a sharp tongue, and if you get into a fight with a normal person, the other person will die. But this woman won't die. She is like a balloon; she goes bang and comes back again. You need someone like that." I was glad to think that I had a future spouse that heaven had already chosen.

The next time I missed the ceremony was in February 1975, at the time of the 1,800 Couples Blessing. Brothers and sisters in the U.S. who were in their late 20s or 30s were beginning to fidget and were buzzing because the 1,800 Couples Blessing was to take place in Korea in early February.

At that time, the person in charge of Japanese members said to me, "Mr. Ikeno, if you go to Korea for the 1,800 Couples Blessing while you have an important mission in the U.S., you may not be able to come back, so Father wants you to stay and take charge of the Yankee Stadium rally, although it may be painful to do so." This was an extremely harsh reply—"Take the providential mission or take the Blessing." Since I came to the U.S. for the restoration of the U.S., I decided to choose the providence for the sake of the U.S. After that, I became so absorbed in the planning for the Yankee Stadium and Washington Monument events that I forgot about the Blessing.

74 Couples Blessing

Suddenly, however, on February 17, 1977, I received a phone call from Mrs. Kanari, who worked closely with Father's family, with a message to come to the main hall at Belvedere by 4:30 PM. When I went there, I was told that the matching for the Blessing would begin at 7:00 PM. During the process of the Blessing, I talked with Rev. and Mrs. Moon about many things, and sometimes they laughed so hard that the water in their cups spilled out. In the end, I was blessed with the 10th person, Mieko Kita. Both of us consulted with each other and reported the results to Rev. and Mrs. Moon. I asked her, "Do you have any nicknames?" to which she replied shyly, "Ever since elementary school, my friends have called me 'White Pumpkin.'" Since I was told by Rev. Moon that my future spouse will be a woman named "White Pumpkin," I agreed to the match without a second thought. Rev. and Mrs. Moon encouraged us to "make a good family."

The Blessing Ceremony for 74 couples was held in the Terrace Room of the New Yorker Hotel on February 21, 1977. This was in some way a unique ceremony. According to the records of the Sunhak Institute of History, it is described as follows.

Rev. Moon said that the 74 Couples Blessing could be given on the basis of the victory of the Washington Monument rally. He explained the significance of the Blessing to the unfortunate members whose earlier marriages were broken or those who were unable to attend the 1975 Blessing Ceremony (1,800 couples) in order to fulfill their providential mission. After our Blessing Ceremony, Rev. and Mrs. Moon took a commemorative photo with each couple for the first time since the 36 Couples Blessing, and a reception was held for the participants. Dr. Bo Hi Pak said, "The venue was overflowing with joy. We have never had a banquet like this before."

Rev. and Mrs. Moon were very concerned that I could not receive the Blessing in 1975 because of the providence. So, he called me directly several times and, when my wife and I started our family life, he told me, "Mr. Ikeno, you had a sign." I wondered what Rev. Moon meant by "a sign," but I guessed he probably meant that my wife was pregnant. I was deeply moved that the Messiah could see through everything spiritually. When our first daughter was born, Mrs. Moon named her.

I recorded the series of events from the Blessing in my diary as follows: "Through this wedding, I will have a child at the age of 33. I am deeply moved when I think of how strongly Jesus wanted this to happen. As I contemplate the conditions that Jesus had to fulfill, here I am going to fulfill them."

CHAPTER 3

The Providence of Home Church and Hoon Dok Hae (Reading-Study) Church

1. Home Church Providence (1977-1983)

Rev. Moon said that home church would never take place without the victory of the Washington Monument rally, and on October 4, 1976, the Day of the Victory of Heaven, Rev. Moon announced that holding a rally in Moscow was his next goal. In his speech at that time, he said, "Without the victory of the 1976 (Washington Monument rally), no matter how much we tried to create a home church, neither God nor Satan could approve of it. Before the Washington Monument victory, only individual salvation was shared, but through the rally victory, the way was opened for the whole family to go to heaven only through home church."

On February 23, 1977, also in the first year of the Heavenly Calendar, he said, "Only after the victory in Washington were the conditions for worldwide indemnity fulfilled, and we can return to our homes. In order to return home, 360 houses in the Cain area have to be saved."

This was the inheritance of the global victorious foundation. He said that from now on, family salvation was now possible. He said that the home church was the only hope. If this fails, he said, there will be no hope whatsoever.

When I understood the words of Rev. Moon after the victory of the Washington Monument, I still thought about the time when I could have gone to Korea as a candidate for the 1,800 Couples Blessing. However, Rev. Moon challenged me with a question and answer. What he meant was, "You have an important providence in the United States. Will you do it? Or, do you want to go to the 1,800 Couples Blessing? If you go, you may not be able to come back."

Anyway, I sacrificed the 1,800 Couples Blessing and chose to work for the providence of the United States. I am very proud of that. So now, there were several paths open to me because I finished graduate school and received my Master of International Affairs. But the most difficult path was the home church providence, since I didn't even know what the heck it meant. I decided to go into that. That was how I started my home church.

I started doing home church with Mr. Sudo in November 1977. At first, it felt like we were searching blindly to find our way. I was asked to work in New Jersey, and surprisingly, there were many Spanish people there. It just so happened that Pastor Casado of the Spanish church joined the Unification Church, and when I asked him how we could develop a Spanish home church, he said the Cubans were very favorable to our movement.

He said these people were very united and the largest Cuban population hub, after those in Florida and Miami, was in Union City, New Jersey.

So, we decided to base ourselves there. And there, gradually, we started focusing on Cubans because they are an anti-communist community and understood us well. We decided to do a home church with mainly Cubans in New Jersey.

Starting in 1979, the annual motto for all five years was the theme of the home church; in 1979, it was "Heavenly Perfection Through Home Church." Gradually, it became an organizing principle that we had to have home churches all over the United States.

These are the members in New Jersey. More than half of them are home church people. There is Carlos here, who is also dedicated and has a wonderful family in Florida with a Japanese sister, Ritsuko Soto. This person is also Columbian. Spanish people are generous, and they eat at home church and sing songs. And these people are leaders of anti-communist groups in Cuba. These people also participated in a big training session and really connected with us.

With New Jersey home church members

At one point, Rev. Moon told us that he was going to train 30,000 Cubans and make them members. There was a large hall called Hudson Hall, which we were planning to buy with the permission of Rev. and Mrs. Moon. It could hold about 400 people in total, and I think that if we used this as our base, it would have been possible for us to restore 30,000 Cubans to our side, as Rev. Moon asked.

However, while the Cubans were very friendly to us, the Italians living in the same city were not. The reason was that the Mafia was very much against us.

To even buy this hall, we would have to get permission from the zoning commission. We were told that the mayor of the city was the boss of the Mafia. And I remember that when we went to City Hall on the day of the zoning decision, the Cubans were running around, and the Italian Mafia men were running around, and the city was in an uproar. From the beginning, everyone was cursing and abusing each other—and, in the end, the Italian side won by a majority vote, and we were not able to buy the place because of the zoning issue. It was very unfortunate.

Home church members with Rev. Won Pil Kim

Next, Rev. Won Pil Kim came from England on September 19, 1979, where he had been in charge of home churches in England. At that time, Dr. Bo Hi Pak was in charge of all home churches in the United States. Then, Rev. Won Pil Kim took over as the head of home churches in the U.S., and there was a great change in the way he conducted home churches. First of all, there was a roster that was created by Rev. Kim, which was written in various ways. He made this roster in England and brought it with him.

There was a World of Hope Festival, a big festival held at the New Yorker Hotel that was Dr. Pak's idea. But Rev. Kim said that this was not rooted in the home church movement and that we should stop this. He also said that we should decentralize, i.e., we should go into 360 homes and give our whole heart and soul to them, doing service activities and so on, and help them by serving them as a servant of servant's position. By doing service activities and so on, we would be able to move from the level of servant to that of parents. In this way, we must serve our home members—that is what Rev. Won Pil Kim believed.

On September 19, 1979, Rev. Kim asked members to move into their respective home church areas. In those days, most of us were single and living in church properties. Still, Rev. Kim told us to move out of the church properties. He said they should take care of their home member's house and do home church activities from there.

Among the members I was in charge of, three of them moved home in that way. They worked on the restoration of families and receiving blessings. I think this was really an important and wonderful change for us. When we decentralized and moved into the community, we did our best, we really loved other people, and when we put ourselves in the position of a father or a mother, the families there would follow us. Those families that entered the community and entered the homes of our home members are still connected, and some of them have been blessed and have become our core members.

The motto of 1980, given at the beginning of the year, was "Home Church is the Base of The Kingdom of Heaven." There was a major personnel change here nationally. I was in charge of New Jersey, but I was asked to become assistant director under Mr. Neil Salonen, the head of the U.S. Unification Church. In my heart, I was not so joyful to leave, but since I received such an order, I gave my area to other brothers, and I worked at the office at West 43rd Street in Manhattan.

Next, Dr. Mose Durst became the head of the American Church, and I became his assistant director, so my main responsibility was to guide home-churched members in all the departments in the New York area.

However, since I could not do home church myself, I decided to make West 107th Street my 360-home church area because my office was located in Manhattan. However, there was a [Karl] Marx Center in the middle of it. I didn't know that, but I found out later.

I was assigned to visit each church as an assistant to Rev. Kim and Mr. Salonen, who were in charge of home churches nationwide. Rev. Kim constantly instructed me on how to be truly mindful. I am grateful to him for his pastoral care, which really touched my heart.

I truly feel that I was raised by him. It is how we can go beyond the servant of servants to the parent level in this home church place of practice. It is really prayer, sincerity, and service. Service is a very unique but important thing for Rev. Kim. Without service, we cannot improve our relationships. When we serve (give) first, we are already filled with the spirit and feel joy. As we truly serve, our relationships gradually move from servant of servants to child, and then to parent position level.

In the process of doing this, various people joined the church. One man named Jeddi King joined our home church in Queens and became a member through the pastoral care and training of Rev. Kim. He became the first Cheonbo

Couple in Florida. My daughter was 4 years old at the time and was cleaning the streets with us.

I was assigned to West 107th Street, where I served 360 households. I always went to my own area early in the morning and cleaned up three streets. I started to get to know some people, and we decided to start a block association there. At that time, we had about 45 members, and we decided to form committees: Member Committee, Information Committee, Public City Committee, Maintenance Safety Committee, and Sunshine Committee. The Sunshine Committee is a beautification campaign. When trees died, we would plant new trees and also plant flowers.

Queens members who attended 2,075 Couples Blessing (July 1, 1982)

The Fundraising Committee was created because, after all, we need money to do something. There were many wealthy people in the area, and some of them donated surprisingly large sums of money. I think we did well.

However, the Marx Center, which I mentioned earlier, was really hostile to us and persecuted us in various ways. The Marx Center had a very sharp view of the world. At that time, the most important place to them was the Korean Peninsula, and the most important issue was how to govern the Korean Peninsula with communism at the center. The director of the Marx Center was a lawyer. He went out of his way to attend the International Communist Conference in Belgrade and would show a video of the May 1980 Gwangju Incident to enlighten people. The Gwangju Incident was an anti-government disturbance that took place in Gwangju City, South Korea. Student demonstrators who opposed the imposition of martial law in South Korea clashed with police and martial law forces, resulting in numerous casualties among civilians.

I was really surprised that the Marx Center was so interested in the Korean Peninsula. Seeing this, I felt that we were really lagging in understanding the current political situation. So, through my experience there, I submitted a 180-page report to Rev. Won Pil Kim on "Communism's Regional Penetration Operations and Our Activities." Rev. Moon appeared to have read it, as he said that the U.S. really had to do something to stop communist infiltration in the region through home church activities.

Next, the issue of building trinities emerged. This is also what Rev. Kim often emphasized at that time. First of all, when a member has 360 homes, he or she must distinguish between those who are "positive, negative, or indifferent," and assign them A, B, or C.

Then, positive home church members must be linked together. When three people are organized as a trinity, they can really devote themselves to it, starting with a servant of servants attitude. Then when they reached the point where they were truly united with us, they could evangelize, and the core group of 12 members would be organized. They would be educated with love and serious education, and through that process, the number of members would expand from 36, to 72, to 120, and so on. We heard this vision many times from Rev. Kim. Due to our lack of ability, we never had the opportunity to break through, but the teaching is still in my mind.

And then there was the challenge of *Topangepa* or community penetration. While many community residents were open and positive, every community had opponents, such as communists or even Christian fundamentalists. The way to "break through" was to look for positive, open-minded VIPs. As friendships formed, these people could use their already established organizations to join with us, and with the combined organizational strength of the VIP organizations there, the negative forces in the community could be dissipated.

2. Providence of the Hoon Dok Hae (Read and Study) Family Church (2005-2009)

In 1981, Unification Church leaders wanted to have a home church model case. Rev. Won Pil Kim asked me to make a model case of the Queens Center, so I moved there.

As part of our home church activity, I became part of the providence of the Hoon Dok Hae home read-study church. I lived 21 years in Queens, and during this time my daughter, who was once a 4-year-old sweeping streets with me with her little broom, turned 25 years old.

We decided to do it together. The important thing to remember is that as we went into an area, we had to consider the unique character of the area. What are they looking for from us? There are various churches as well as religious organizations in the community.

We held a cross-cultural symposium at the Unitarian Church. The theme was the importance of the family. We gathered people from various churches—Catholics and Jews—as well as Muslims and Hindus; there is a large Hindu church there. Many people from these places were interested in participating.

Despite religious differences, when it came to family issues, we all said almost the same thing. In particular, on the issue of sex, they agreed that sexual intercourse was not allowed before having a family. And how can a couple unify their relationship? If the couple cannot be united, the ideal family cannot be built. We were all saying such things.

The next thing was that we picked Martin Luther King, Jr. Day as a day of service. That was a very good opportunity that many churches could co-sponsor with us. About two-thirds of the people were young people. When you put that kind of emphasis on service, you can see that all young people—not just Christian young people but Muslim young people, Jewish young people, Hindu young people—were connected through this service project. Our projects were things like cleaning up the park or going to a nursing home and doing a service project.

Rally together with Queens church members

At this time, interestingly, of the children, one was a Jewish child, one was a Muslim child, and one was a Unification Church child. These were different religious schools, but they served as one. They would come back and give a debriefing, explaining what they thought of it. Jewish, Muslim, Hindu, and Unification Church children came together to paint or go to nursing homes to serve the elderly, or clean up the streets. And at the same time, they would dance a dance of their own creation. You had entertainment. It really showed how important service can be in bringing people together and breaking down sectarian and religious barriers.

This cross-culture symposium was a multifaith gathering, and the person who spoke is a Hindu representative. The next one is a Catholic pastor, and the next one is Kathy, who is a professor at UTS. And the one on the left is a Methodist minister. It is interesting to see that when we discuss the issue of the family, we are united across all denominations.

The difference between the "Hoon Dok Hae Home Church" and the original home church program was that "Reading and Studying" material became the main focus. The core book was about 350 pages long, with a year's worth of material. The content was mostly really short sentences; most are speeches by Rev. Moon but there are also speeches by Rev. Martin Luther King, Jr., and many others. We would use these materials and read them with the home members in a roundabout way. These materials have three or four questions in them, so even if the people at the home were not members, the questions were there, and if everyone read and discussed them, there was a great deal of benefit to be gained.

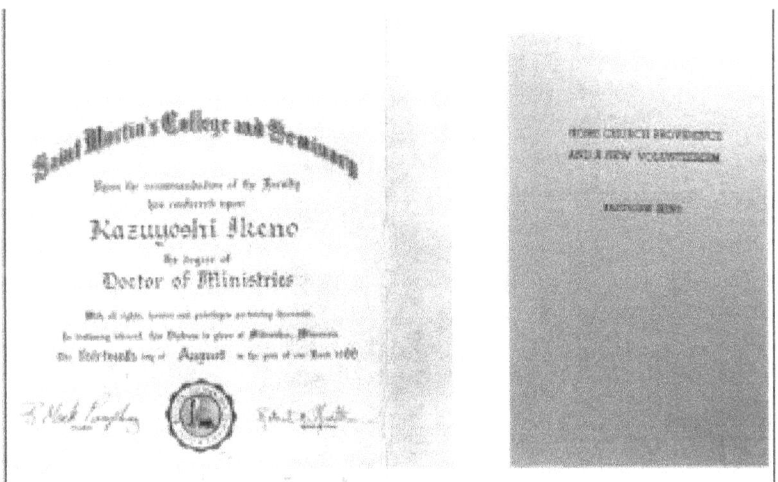

Received Doctor degree by my report of
"Home Church Providence and New Volunteerism."

One time, a young man was killed, probably by a gang. Many pastors and believers gathered for a prayer meeting, and about 500 people marched against the gang. This kind of gathering could happen because people were connected through various service projects. Every year on Martin Luther King's Day, the community would become united through various service activities, entertainment, and symposiums.

We created a variety of issues and involved local people in the process. We used the reading materials to help them understand what we are trying to say, and they became convinced by some parts of what we said. Here in Queens, four or five people have already received the Holy Blessing and become members.

At the end of my six years of home church providence, I decided to compile this valuable information into a book for the benefit of my younger colleagues. I collected every word from Rev. Moon and every story from Rev. Won Pil Kim. The most important factor for Rev. Kim's home church was "service." He told us to "give first," and home church activities would begin with how to give. If one is willing to serve first, the reward for that action is joy and contentment in the Holy Spirit. Therefore, by being willing to give what the people of the community most desire, we feel joy in our hearts, and they feel joy when they respond.

Through this giving and receiving action, the people of the community are filled with the Holy Spirit and revived.

This is called the "new volunteerism." I have again compiled a vast amount of testimonies from members who have continued and won home church. The book, titled "Home Church Providence and the New Volunteerism," was submitted to a local seminary and was so well received that St. Martin's College and Seminary awarded me the title of Doctor of Ministry on August 13, 1989. I am now a Doctor of Ministry. I tried to leave something for the younger generation, and as a result, I received an unexpected blessing.

IOWC Commander (1983-1984)

Today, I would like to present a very fond memory of my work as an IOWC (International One World Crusade) Commander in 1983-1984, traveling around many states in the United States.

First of all, the hasty formation of this IOWC came after the six-year home church providence. Sadly, the home church providence could not bring sufficient results of witnessing and community restoration. I think this was really regrettable for Rev. Moon, and it left him with a big grudge.

Rev. Moon urgently called the Japanese sisters to East Garden on January 17, 1983, and told them that he would mobilize all of them from now on. He told us that all the wives were to go to their respective states to do evangelistic work. Not only Japanese but also American wives were involved in the mobilization. My wife and I had to decide where to put our three children, and we decided to send them to Jacob House in New York.

Having learned from Rev. Won Pil Kim, I really worked hard in the home church activity. When our first daughter was born, I knew that Rev. Moon's wish for home church activity was very serious. Once our daughter reached her 100th day after birth, we took her to be cared for at Jacob House so we could devote ourselves fully to the home church work. When Rev. and Mrs. Moon heard about this, they immediately went to Jacob House to meet with our daughter, and at that time, they knew that we were prepared and told us that we had given birth to a good child.

While I say that the home church providence did not achieve its goal, I truly loved my 360 homes and was determined to evangelize there.

Unfortunately, as I went door to door, apartment by apartment, house by house, visiting the families, I could see the reality of the broken down families in the U.S., and my heart became sad and distressed. I saw that rather than the children being born of their own married parents, one child would be the child of X's husband, while another child was from Y's husband, and so on. The children themselves were raised in a greatly troubled environment.

I recall one sister, a member of mine, who brought 14 spiritual children [new members] through street witnessing. She was very talented, but she also hated or even feared home church work. She said she could not do it because it was too much of a burden to go in there and take care of the families.

There were other people who gave up doing home church activities because they felt they could not help these families restore their moral standards. This was a really difficult journey, and we felt very sad that we were not able to make this home church a success.

This was why Rev. Moon hastily established the IOWC and sent it out to shake up the whole United States. Another reason was that his tax trial in the New York court was gradually going downhill at that time.

A main mission of the IOWC was to remove the negative opinions that the public had about the Unification Church and to create a movement that would increase public understanding and support for Rev. Moon and our movement.

The IOWC was made up of members from Japan, Korea, the U.S., and Europe; we were three teams at first, Korea, Japan, and the United States. I was appointed as Commander on March 15, representing Japan. But after that, as many as 30 IOWC teams were formed, and as these teams moved around the United States, I think this had a really big impact.

One day, about two months after the start of the IOWC, I was at a leaders' meeting and Rev. Moon asked me to stand up. There, he said, in what could be considered a joke, "Have you ever thought you were so short, you should have been born a larger American young man?" Of course, I had never once thought of such a thing, so when I replied in a loud voice, "No, I never thought of that," Rev. Moon praised me, saying, "Wow."

I'm not sure why he praised me. Next, he said, "Because you are short and small, American and European men will think you are stupid, and no one will follow you." I replied, "No, they are big, but they are very obedient to me, a small man," to which he replied, "I understand."

He then encouraged us in this way: "There are two gears in the locomotive, your team and Mr. Reiner Vincenz's team representing Europe, and you should work like one team. You will be one gear and Mr. Vincenz will be the other one, leading the entire team to become a model team and successfully lead this IOWC movement."

This is a picture that someone took of me when I was asked to stand up at the leaders' meeting. There were about 80 members there.

The author answered Rev. Moon's question at the leaders' meeting.

Our IOWC didn't have a home base or mobile home at that time, but we had five or six vans and passenger cars going down the highway. It was a very unusual—I mean great—march, not only by my team but by the 28 other teams all over the country. It was a truly joyful and wonderful experience.

Our IOWC team moved to a different state every three weeks, and I traveled to around 20 states in that year and a half. The places where we worked were Denver, Colorado; Wichita, Kansas; Albuquerque, New Mexico; Lincoln, Nebraska; San Francisco and Los Angeles, California; Las Vegas, Nevada; and Phoenix, Arizona. We also traveled to Seattle, Washington (twice); Portland, Oregon; Missoula, Montana; Minneapolis, Minnesota; Fargo, North Dakota; Sioux Falls, South Dakota; and Des Moines, Iowa. That's like going around half the states in the US.

To improve our track record, I first divided the team into four teams. The most important was the evangelism team. I assigned team members within that team to do the workshops. Secondly, to run this team, we still needed money. Therefore, another team was the fundraising team. The fundraising team would go around to all the states to make money.

Street witnessing IOWC members.

Also important was the liaison team to VIPs. Key people in a state, such as the governor, the lieutenant governor, the mayor, and state and federal lawmakers had many questions for Rev. Moon, so this public relations (PR) team would meet with them. Our messages were "We are now doing this to change America by bringing together young people from all over the world as the IOWC" and "We are promoting a Christ-centered revival of the U.S. culture, which has become decadent." We were able to meet with many political leaders to do that kind of liaison.

Finally, another important team was the one that could do advance work for IOWC activities. This was because the IOWC team would leave for the next state in only 21 days. Therefore, the advance team had to secure a base of operations in the next state. We needed a video center and also a workshop venue because we needed to hold training sessions. In our big churches, there was no problem because they already had training venues. But in about a third of the states we went to, we really didn't know if they had Unification Church members. So in all of those cases, we had to send a team in and set up the training sites.

We also needed lodging. In states where our church was well established, we had accommodations, but in other places, we had to figure out what to do.

I think having our members rotate through these four teams was a good experience. Because the members were constantly moving, doing PR, doing advance work, going to fundraising, and working on the evangelism team, I think our members grew a lot.

Our IOWC days were busy. In each city, we would first give street speeches, and then some of us gave lectures on the street. We would hold an open house, where we invited many people to the church. We would give a brief speech, feed them good food, and then invite them to a two-day retreat.

The total number of participants we brought to the two-day retreat was 612, and the number of people who stayed for the seven-day retreat was 243.

Next was the 21-day training session. This was the most important training session before becoming a full-time missionary. There were 132 people in this group, and 81 people joined as full-time members.

We invited Dr. Durst, the president of the Unification Church of America, as a speaker, and we also invited local pastors to give a speech in order to hold revivals at the end of the three-week campaigns. The total number of participants was 3,633. This final, overall result put our team first among the 28 IOWC teams.

This was how we traveled around the various states. First, the advance team would go and set up a video center there. Then, at night, we called guests to the church, talked to them and then invited them to the two-day training session.

My team was the best team because of the hard work the members put in, not because of what I alone did. But even the ice on the pond starts from a single point, and then it all freezes over at the end. In this way, if I really made up my mind, set up the sincerity conditions, and started to move the spiritual world, the members would be pulled into it, and eventually, the members and leaders would become one, and this IOWC achievement was able to be built there.

My secret of victory was reported to Rev. Moon at the National Leaders' Conference by Rev. Yu in Seattle. When he reported to Rev. Moon that he had seen me leading the way, working from early in the morning until late at night on the front lines, Rev. Yu said felt that this was the secret of victory. Rev. Moon encouraged everyone to do the same. However, these activities alone would not produce results.

One time, a Korean leader overseeing Des Moines, Iowa, asked the members, "What kind of leader do you think Mr. Ikeno is?" When asked, one member replied, "I think he is a man of prayer. I am impressed by his constant and fervent prayer wherever he has free time."

I have found in my experience that the secret of victory is first and foremost prayer. This is the most important thing—it is more important to know how many prayer conditions are established and prepared before the activity than the activity. I am convinced that if we take the lead in frontline activities, the spiritual world will surely cooperate with us, and we will be able to achieve results. Without the cooperation of the spiritual world, no matter what projects or activities you undertake, you will not be able to achieve any results. How do we draw out the cooperation of the spirit world? I believe that is the secret to victory.

Secondly, I think we gained a very big lifetime treasure through the IOWC work. The IOWC met elders who were part of the 36 Couples or 72 Couples Blessings in each state. Whenever we arrived at a city in a state, we were always greeted by these regional directors, and they loved our members very much and provided pastoral care.

Without the hard work of these regional directors, I believe the members working in the United States would not have inherited the tradition of their hearts. Through the regional directors, we were able to know the painful resentment of the living God and the deep parental hearts of Rev. and Mrs. Moon. For that, I can only be truly grateful.

As a commander, I was deeply loved by various elders and received words of encouragement from them, and I truly believe that I was able to grow as a person at this time. Mrs. Gil Ja Sa really loved everyone, the female members loved her so much, and at the same time, she also loved the members more than her own children.

I was really loved by her. At that time, my wife and I had three daughters but longed for a son. She said to me, "Mr. Ikeno, why can't you have a boy? I will teach you the secret and you should tell your wife about it," and I did as she told me. When I reported that our next baby was a boy to her, she said, "I really prayed for you to have a boy."

When married members were sent to IOWC, fundraising teams, or to various states as evangelists, many of them had no place to leave their children. So, the members in Boulder, Colorado, converted this place, which used to be a CARP center, into a nursery. All four of my children were taken care of here.

IOWC members with Ms. Gil Ja Sa in Colorado

On December 23, 1983, a big tragedy occurred. Heung Jin (Rev. Moon's second son) was gravely injured in a car accident and died January 2, 1984. I was instructed to give flowers to Rev. and Mrs. Moon on True God's Day in 1984, but I wondered how they were feeling at such a time, and my wife and I really got serious and went through a prayer situation.

At that time, we had the God's Day celebration at the New Yorker Hotel ballroom. I gave a flower bouquet to Mrs. Moon and my wife gave one to Rev. Moon, who gave us a very big smile. I felt that they truly loved us beyond the pain in their own hearts. I wondered what kind of attitude Rev. and Mrs. Moon must take as parents of their own children as well as parents of all humankind in the world. They truly loved us beyond the pain in their hearts and with constant smiles on their faces.

So, as I mentioned earlier, not only Rev. Moon, but also Korean elders really educated us greatly with their testimonies, especially about their pioneer days' witnessing experiences, and their Ocean Church and other experiences with Rev. and Mrs. Moon. I would like to express my sincere gratitude to the Korean elders because without their sweat, tears, and blood, our activities in America would not have been possible.

Most of these elders have now passed away and are in the spirit world, but when I look at my old photo albums and reminisce about them, they appear to me and say, "Ikeno-kun, we had a lot of fun back then." I am truly grateful for their parental love as they raised us. Also, when I went to Europe as the national messiah, brothers and sisters I worked with at that time would say, "Mr. Ikeno, how much we enjoyed that time."

IOWC members at Albuquerque's training center

In the course of IOWC evangelism and PR, when we moved from one state to the next, we enjoyed barbecues with our brothers and sisters in scenic parks in Colorado. In Yosemite National Park, we enjoyed playing in the water, fishing, and barbecuing in the midst of the magnificent nature. In Seattle, the training center was on a remote island, and we really looked forward to taking guests there by ferry. In Colorado, it snowed and we enjoyed skiing there, or on the way to the Grand Canyon, we would enjoy the beauty of God's great creation. In New Mexico or Arizona, the workshop site was in the desert, and we enjoyed playing volleyball and swimming in the pool during the middle of the day while looking at the huge desert. We all enjoyed these things as we moved from one state to the next.

These brothers and sisters I met in Europe remember these things. They remember well how magnificent Yosemite was at that time, how much fun they had playing on the river, and so on. I think that was really our great treasure in the activities of the IOWC.

We barbecued and played in the river in Yosemite. In San Diego, everyone took a boat ride around San Diego Bay and enjoyed it to the fullest. When we went to Las Vegas, everyone was amazed at how the colorful neon lights were on 24 hours a day. We didn't know this kind of city even existed.

We always had a big meeting at each state at the end of our stay. We had revival meetings with Dr. Durst or pastors we had contact with. We were able to meet with the governor of Montana and the governor of North Dakota because of PR work. When I went to the Montana governor's room, there was a doll of Lord Kiyomasa Kato from Kumamoto, a so-called "tiger killer." When I told him that I was also from Kumamoto, which was a sister city of Montana, he really welcomed me and gave me a wall hanging made of Montana wood with various local products on it.

During our time in New Mexico, President Reagan was visiting, and the opposition was trying to block his visit. There was a surprisingly large number of people at that time—about 75 of us, and with local members, probably a total of 90 people—and we put up banners and placards to support the president. We had more people than the opposition!

Because of that, the mayor was so pleased that he invited us to his residence and gave us honorary citizen's awards and badges. He said, "I was wondering what was going to happen at one point. Because your people got in there, and the Reagan reception was so great that the president was very happy, and he called me. I would like to give you an honorary citizenship award."

While we were in San Francisco, a Korean Air Lines flight was shot down by a Russian missile off the coast of Kamchatka Peninsula in Russia. In response, we joined with CARP to hold a large demonstration in front of the Russian embassy and made a doll of the Russian president at that time and burned it to raise the spirits of the people.

If there was any crisis in those states, we immediately responded to it and supported them. Our territory included Midwestern and Southern states called the Bible Belt. We were persecuted by the negative newspapers on a daily basis. At one point, opponents got together with the police to evict us from a training center I rented.

In Kansas and Nebraska, we had Christian fundamentalists opposing us by making speeches in the streets by the dozen or so, and holding up placards. They would call us "heretics who follow a false Christ," and their group of about 20 of them would protest loudly. They also distributed negative flyers and persecuted us on the streets, saying we were a group of anti-Christians.

Meeting with North Dakota Governor

My viewpoint was that even though we were persecuted, surely one day, these fundamentalists would accept us and Rev. and Mrs. Moon as the Messiah, and surely join together to restore America. They were Christian brothers just like us. I pray that we will be able to restore them.

Revival meetings were held in each state. Gradually, pastors were connected, and they, too, began to work toward Christian revival with us.

The most important thing we did in each state was to meet with the governors there and explain the importance of our movement. Below, you see the governor of North Dakota. He was a very conservative governor, so he knew what we were doing and our activities of Victory Over Communism. When I gave a speech, titled "Vision of the Future," as entertainment, there were so many different people, not only Japanese, but Americans, Europeans, Koreans, and so many other people performed. I think about four or five people joined our church at the university there. I have such good memories.

CHAPTER 5

The Minnesota and Wisconsin Period (1984-1991)

1. Minnesota State Leader

The IOWC was originally scheduled to run for three years, but this changed after Rev. Moon's appeal to the U.S. Supreme Court was rejected on May 14, 1984.

He urgently invited the leaders to East Garden and declared that the IOWC providence was to be dissolved.

"The Unification Church will now enter an extremely difficult path," he said.

However, he encouraged us, saying, "I will choose state leaders from now on, and I hope that state leaders, who are chosen by me, will fulfill their duties and overcome this difficult situation."

Rev. Moon gave several speeches, and then we were all lined up in East Garden, where he hand-picked where we would go, similar what happened in the matching process. For instance, one brother was given the necessary explanation and told to work hard in his area.

Rev. Moon picked me up and said, "You go to Minnesota. There's Fraser over there. You must bring him to his knees."

In 1984, Donald Fraser was the mayor of Minneapolis, but he had a combative history with our Unification Church.

In the 1970s, Mr. Fraser was a U.S. congressman, and he used his House of Representatives international relations subcommittee to investigate Korean-American crimes. He targeted our movement and accused us of wrongdoing. He even made big news one day by claiming that the Unification Church was created by the KCIA (Korean spy agency), not by Rev. Moon.

The Fraser investigation made many headaches for our movement, but Col. Bo Hi Pak defended us. In the end, Mr. Fraser could find nothing wrong with our church and admitted it in his final report.

In 1979, Mr. Fraser gave up his House seat to run for U.S. Senate, but he was narrowly defeated in the Democratic primary. He quickly turned around and ran for mayor of Minneapolis, the largest city in Minnesota, and won that election.

When I was sent to Minnesota in 1984, I was told to make sure Mayor Fraser got restored to God's side. If we could get such a condition by the time Rev. Moon was released from Danbury prison, he would be able to spread his wings wide open.

Meanwhile, all IOWCs were disbanded and the commanders became state leaders.

Rev. Moon was actually imprisoned in Danbury on July 20, 1984, but before that, he appealed to the religious community, saying that his going to Danbury was a form of religious persecution. We started by holding a religious freedom rally in Washington, D.C., on May 30. This was quite a big event, and over 1,000 pastors and others came from all over the country.

I called Mayor Fraser as soon as I arrived in Minnesota as a state leader and asked to meet with him. He didn't say yes initially, so I called him several times and made an appointment on this particular day and went to his city hall.

As soon as he saw me, he cursed Col. Pak with a terrible angry voice, saying, "That Col. Pak is a big liar." He was not so much accusing Rev. Moon, but he was very angry with Col. Pak from the very beginning.

I was worried because I had no idea what was going on. But when he let me out of his office and into his living room, I saw a Japanese suit of armor and a sword. I thought, "What is this?" He told me that his city and Hiroshima have a sister-city relationship. He said he had been to Japan many times, and he really liked Japanese people because they were so kind and gentle.

Rev. Moon in Danbury prison

To my surprise, his previously angry face suddenly softened. This was an ambitious man who unexpectedly lost his chance to be elected to the U.S. Senate. That was a miserable turn of events for him: Only a few years earlier, he had been the powerful chairman of the subcommittee that dealt with national espionage. There had a great deal of news about "Koreagate," the scandal in which the so-called KCIA was trying to manipulate U.S. policy using bribes. As part of this investigation, Mr. Fraser had targeted the Unification Church for their presumed involvement in the internal affairs of the U.S. in cooperation with the KCIA. In other words, Mr. Fraser decided to go after Rev. Moon and the Unification Church because he thought it would make him famous.

Now it was 1984 and I meeting with Mr. Fraser and telling him I would bring him some Japanese rice cakes (mochi). He thought this Japanese person was interesting, and we developed a friendship. So, Satan gradually retreated from him. I met with him six times, and as our last triumph condition, we worked together with Pastor Lewis Jenkins, who was a well-known pastor in the Minneapolis area and also the president of the Black Church Alliance.

We sent Mayor Fraser the request for a permit to hold a religious freedom rally and demonstration march in August 1984. The people who attended would go from a hotel to the big park near City Hall for the demonstration. There would be many placards saying things like "Free Reverend Moon from Prison."

I believe Mayor Fraser had a lot of discussions with the police chief as to what action should be taken about our request to hold this demonstration. But I also gradually softened his attitude toward us and pulled him toward God's side, so he signed the permit, meaning that he was OK with the religious freedom rally. I think that was a very big condition.

We held a religious freedom convention at the hotel, and most of the people there came outside to participate in the demonstration. When Mr. Fraser saw the demonstration from city hall, and saw the placards saying, "Free Reverend Moon from Prison," I think he did not realize he signed the permit for this kind of big demonstration.

A final push for Mr. Fraser was to get his permission for the post-convention demonstration march for religious freedom. We were collecting the signatures of VIPs at the time, and Mayor Fraser finally signed the letter of recommendation of the World Peace Unity Association inspired by Rev. Moon. In this way, I won the victory for Rev. Moon. This was not a perfect response to Rev. Moon's order to bring Mr. Fraser to God, which was the most important part of my mission. But I think that to some extent, he was able to establish such conditions. He signed an important letter of recommendation, so I think he made those conditions to some extent.

In the legal appeal to the U.S. Supreme Court, it says "United States of America v. Sun Myung Moon and Takeru Kamiyama." In other words, the United States, a superpower nation, was attacking Sun Myung Moon, the founder of the Unification Church.

Rev. Moon vigorously appealed the government's so-called tax-evasion case at every level, so it went up from the local courts all the way to the U.S. Supreme Court. That is because this case was really a shameful case of government persecution of a minority religious group.

As Rev. Moon said, the U.S. Supreme Court's rejection of the Unification Church case meant that we had been rejected by this superpower nation. I think about it now and realize that the past seven years were a very difficult journey.

Rev. Moon testified before the Senate Judiciary Committee in June 1984, a month before he entered federal prison in Danbury, Connecticut.

This picture shows U.S. Senator Orrin Hatch, the chairman of the Senate Judiciary Committee. Mr. Hatch held a hearing on religious freedom on June 26, 1984, and invited Rev. Moon to speak in the Senate Judiciary Committee's conference room. Rev. Moon proudly stressed "the need to defend the fundamental principle of America's founding, the freedom of religion."

Since the 1981 beginning of the government's case against Rev. Moon to 1984 when the U.S. Supreme Court rejected his appeal, both white and black church pastors rose up to support him.

Many religious freedom events were held, including a convention in Washington, D.C. Very famous people from all over the country came and gave very passionate speeches in defense of Rev. Moon. Demonstrations and marches were held, including one with Rev. Moon's second-eldest daughter In Jin Moon and Rev. Moon's top assistant Dr. Pak, and so on.

The black man in the middle of this photo is Rev. Joseph Lowery, co-founder of the Southern Christian Leadership Conference and a civil rights icon who had joined Rev. Martin Luther King, Jr., in the 1960s marches for freedom. The black man on the far right is Rev. Leo Champion, pastor of Fellowship Missionary Baptist Church of Milwaukee, Wisconsin. This was the first major religious freedom event.

Freedom of Religion rallies

We held religious freedom events in each state. There were 10 major cities in Minnesota, so we had to have a rally in every city. In some cities, the mayors would participate.

On July 20, 1984, Rev. Moon gave his last speech in the East Garden courtyard where he said, "We must forgive and love America." He then left with Mr. Kamiyama and went to Danbury prison.

At that time, I was so frustrated that I cried. I thought, "What is really going on in America?" Looking at the U.S. at that time, I saw that communism had invaded the nation and its churches in various forms. The neo-Marxist "liberation theology" was popular in many places at that time. People thought that Jesus was a man who wanted to liberate the poor—the so-called proletariat—and so liberation theology gradually penetrated into some black churches.

Rev. Moon's wish was that we must plant the Confederation of Associations for the Unity of the Societies of the Americas (CAUSA) in the churches at the same time we were lifting up religious freedom messages.

The religious freedom rallies were held in different places. In Minnesota, where I was in charge, the mayors of Rochester and a small place called Mankato spoke to the rallies, and a professor spoke in support of their remarks.

The overarching theme at that time was "The United States versus Moon is the United States versus All."

From the smallest city to the largest, religious freedom rallies were held on an ongoing basis. This was a very serious message that any pastor of a church could understand—that if you were a pastor, you would have felt that the church was being suppressed by the government due to tax issues and other problems.

Therefore, the fact that Rev. Moon had to go to jail for tax evasion was not limited to Rev. Moon. There was a sense of crisis within the pastors that they could be the next target tomorrow. That was what appealed to everyone at the religious freedom conferences and rallies: We, the Unification Church, were being impeached now, but their churches would be next.

Put another way, it was clear that the U.S. government was gradually suppressing the religious world. They were infringing on the freedom of religion, which was really the most important aspect of America's founding spirit. Also, this fight was not just about the religious community. We needed to stand up and unite against the government violations of freedom of religion and freedom of speech. This was very much a national issue.

During this difficult time, the blessed families with children were all mobilizing, leaving our children and participating in evangelization work and IOWC activities. We needed a daycare center to care for the children, so we built what was then called Jacob House as a daycare center in Tarrytown, New York. However, Tarrytown City officials told us it was illegal, and we had to close it down and move out.

This was hard on the blessed couples who were on the front lines. In our case, we left our children in the care of members who were not participating in the IOWC.

We had four children at that time. My wife had just given birth to our son, and she was not able to leave right away, so she was resting at a member's house. After that, I worked in a church in Minneapolis, so my family came there later.

CAUSA seminar flyer

Mr. Kamiyama was released from prison in March 1985. Rev. Moon knew how sad the members were to see him in prison and asked Mr. Kamiyama to go and encourage them. So, Mr. Kamiyama began doing statewide tours, giving testimony about Rev. Moon and what happened in Danbury.

Rev. Moon said that the Christian church was in decline because they did not understand communism. This was where CAUSA stepped into the spotlight. We began to hold CAUSA seminars in the many churches that we had contacted. We had the congregations participate in these seminars and explained what communism was all about. It was Rev. Moon's wish that Christians would learn about the atheistic communist ideology and how they themselves could defeat it and protect the essentials of the church, such as freedom of religion and respect for human rights. This had to be done.

After 13 months of hardship, Rev. Moon was released from Danbury on August 20, 1985. That night, a huge God and Freedom Banquet was held in Washington, D.C. Some 1,700 people, including many famous pastors, attended the ceremony and gave speeches to console Rev. Moon and welcome him back. Rev. and Mrs. Moon were very grateful for that.

When Rev. Moon came out of Danbury, he was victorious and became a central figure, especially in the Christian churches. They even made trophies and gave them to him. I attended with about 20 pastors from Minnesota. One man, Pastor White, helped us in many ways.

Rev. Moon spoke to the Christian leaders about how Christianity should be mobilized. He made the great declaration that these prominent pastors from all over the country should now take America and the world in the direction that Jesus and God wanted them to go.

Rev. Moon gave more internal guidance to our members on January 1, 1986. At the 1986 God's Day celebration (one of the holidays of the Unification Church), he gave a very impressive speech in which he explained the history of the Unification Church in detail.

He said, "If you want to restore the free world and restore Christianity, you must pay indemnity. In Korea, there were Christians and some former Unification members who had left and opposed us. Also, there was no sense of unity among the 36 Blessed Couples' families and the True Children who were the Unification Church's central family. How would we pay the price for all of this disunity? That was the price of Rev. Moon's imprisonment." When I heard this speech, I felt a real pain in my heart.

Soon after Rev. Moon came out of prison, he began making personnel changes. My mission in Minnesota ended on September 1, and it was announced that I would be the next State Leader in Wisconsin.

I was asked to go immediately to Wisconsin. But my wife and infant son had just arrived in Minnesota. The center in Wisconsin was small, and it was not possible to get a room for my family. So, I had to send my wife and son to the old CARP Center in Boulder, Colorado, which they had turned into a nursery.

I went to Wisconsin as my new mission.

2. Wisconsin State Leader

The first thing we did in Wisconsin was to hold a seminar at the church of a pastor with whom we had been connected. We appealed not only to the pastor but also to the members of the church about how communism had infiltrated Christianity.

I thought that I had to make a clear about how communism was infiltrating and destroying basic Christian values. At that time, as I mentioned earlier, liberation theology was spreading among various churches in the United States, saying that communism could work together with Christians. But its deceit was so subtle that some pastors could not detect it. Communism is unknowable.

So, "communized" pastors came to have a different view of Jesus that said Jesus Christ came to liberate the poor. The original Christian belief is that Jesus came to liberate us from our sins as fallen descendants of Adam and Eve. But the communists and the pastors they influenced twisted this truth and said Jesus came to save the poor from their plight. "Jesus was the foremost leader of the proletariat." That is how they talked.

In Wisconsin, we decided to establish Unification Church centers in 10 cities and start our activities from there. This was because there were no established churches to support us.

We held CAUSA seminars at churches to appeal to them about how communism had penetrated America and was deforming Christianity. One of the titles of the seminars was "America and the Threat of Communism." Pastors and other church elders gradually came to realize that atheistic communism was a terrible idea.

Before Rev. Moon was released from prison, we distributed 400,000 copies of his *Divine Principle* books and tapes of *Divine Principle* lectures in every state. That was the major mission that was done when he was in Danbury, in addition to the religious freedom rallies that were held during the months when he was in Danbury.

Rev. Moon also decided to send 7,000 pastors to Korea for a pilgrimage to the Holy Land to introduce the path taken by Rev. Moon and to listen to his lecture on the Principle. We sent many pastors to the first ICC Korea (Interdenominational Conference for Clergy), which lasted from April 10 to April 19, 1985. For about two and a half years after that, we searched for pastors from each state every month to send to Korea.

By the way, my four children and my wife were now living at the Boulder nursery in Colorado. They had about 120 or 150 children at that time. The children were divided that into different age groups, from babies to children as old as 10 to 15 years old. My wife was handling one section and taking care of those children. Later, I was able to bring my children and my wife to live with me in Milwaukee.

Rev. Moon spoke at the God and Freedom Banquet (August 20, 1985)

This was a special and welcome time. We received the Holy Blessing in 1977, and our first daughter was born in 1978. But we believed if we didn't put our missions first and develop a home church from that time on, God's providence to restore America would be in trouble. So, we took our child to Jacob House in New York after her 100th day of birth to be cared for.

My wife then worked for CARP and went to various places under Rev. Tiger Park, traveling all over. When I became the IOWC commander, she went to Delaware for missionary work.

So, the first time we started living together with our children was in Milwaukee, Wisconsin. When we could all live together as a family for the first time in eight years, we were very happy.

During my time in Wisconsin, we worked to send pastors to Korea every month, based on the success of the first ICC Korea held from April 10 to 19, 1985. I would often go to Korea, too.

There were events such as lectures and testimonies, and each team had several question-and-answer sessions during the lectures. I was in charge of one of the teams, and the questions from the pastors were really tough; unless you knew the entire 66 books of the Bible by heart, you would not be able to answer many of their questions. But most importantly, I thought we were able to treat them with love and sincerity. In that way, I somehow managed to answer their many difficult questions. I have such memories.

These pastors went to the Korean headquarters church, and they held a revival meeting there. The enthusiasm was so great that our members who attended the meeting were really overwhelmed. We went to the first church of Rev. Moon in Busan which is more of a shack than a church, and to the Rock of Tears behind the church, where Rev. Moon prayed and cried to God for many years.

We established the Morning Calm Association for the pastors who went to ICC Korea and asked them to share their testimonies and help us find other pastors to go to Korea. In total, 7,000 pastors went to Korea and then to pilgrimage to the Holy Land. They listened to the Principle lectures or heard testimonies from our church elders, which was really a spiritual benefit.

With Rev. Lewis Jenkins at CAUSA seminar

And then another big step was taken in the United States—the founding of the ACLC (American Clergy Leadership Conference) from the foundation of the ICC Korea pastors.

The thousands of pastors who went to Korea received really heartwarming hospitality from our members in Korea. When they heard the Principle and learned how hard the path of Rev. Moon was, some pastors were so moved that they became great supporters of our activities in the U.S. from then on.

The 37th and final ICC Korea trip, which I attended, was the biggest gathering, with about 520 pastors attending. Eight of us went from Wisconsin, including Bishop Mann and Pastor Hugh.

In Korea, it was really interesting to see the headquarters church in Cheongpa-dong and the pastors eating Korean food with chopsticks. The leftmost picture was the last gathering of the 37th ICC Korea. At the Rock of Tears, one pastor shared his testimony about how Rev. Moon prayed and wept on this rocky mountain in Busan for the restoration of the world.

The last ICC Korea, 520 ministers attended.

Rev. Moon's first church in Busan, which was made of cardboard and is now in an exhibition room. The pastors went around the exhibition room and could see what kind of life Rev. Moon led 70 years ago. He wrote the manuscript of the *Wolli Wonbon*, the original text of the *Divine Principle*, in a cardboard hut while expressing his devout sincerity. A small desk and lamp were displayed there. The pastors were deeply impressed as they looked at these things.

So, now our providence was going global. For example, the 24th Olympics was held in Seoul on September 16, 1988. This was the first time the Olympics were held in South Korea. At that time, up to 163 countries participated, which means that almost all countries took part in that Summer Olympics.

It is a long story, but I will tell you how much love Rev. Moon showed to the participants, how he prepared suits and delivered McCol (the Korean barley soft drink made by Ilhwa) to the dormitories of each country. He called oversea missionaries from their mission countries and made sure that the missionaries treated the athletes from 163 countries with love and devotion. He asked the missionaries to establish the condition that they would treat the athletes with their hearts and love them with all sincerity. At the same time, the members of the worldwide churches repented of their own mistakes and the mistakes of their national churches while fasting for a week, and united with the missionaries as

Abel and the athletes as Cain. That was how the Foundation Day for the Unified Nation of Heaven and Earth on October 8, 1988 was proclaimed after the Seoul Olympics.

Based on this foundation, Rev. Moon announced a world itinerary worker (IW) system, in which elders traveled to countries to further support the missionaries he had sent to the world. This was the spiritual foundation for the development of our church throughout the world. The 6,500 Couples International Marriage Blessing Ceremony took place on October 30, 1988 at the Ilhwa Ginseng Factory in Yongjin, Gyeonggi Province. Amid such circumstances, President George H.W. Bush was elected as the 41st president of the United States, and the Ceremony of the Settlement of the Eight Stages (August 31, 1989 in Kodiak, Alaska), and the Age of Heavenly Parentism (September 3, 1989) were gradually proclaimed, expanding the spiritual sphere of blessings worldwide. This was the period of 1988 and 1989.

This is why the hardships of the past are gradually giving way to brighter signs. There was a constant flow of pastors who participated in the Korean pilgrimage. When they returned from their monthlong trip, we would greet them with "Welcome ICC Graduates" and new members of the Morning Calm Association. This was how we were constantly taking care of them one by one.

And so, Rev. Moon became active on the world stage from then on. As you know, on April 11, 1990, Rev. and Mrs. Moon held the 11th World Media Conference in Moscow and then met with Soviet President Mikhail Gorbachev. That was the situation that emerged.

11th World Media Conference in Moscow (April 10, 1990)

Rev. Moon urgently asked all prominent people in the U.S. to sign a letter of for the founding of the United Nations for World Peace. This included governors, mayors, congressmen, pastors, professors, famous businessmen, VIPs, and others. Over 4,000 people signed the petition, which laid the foundation for the establishment of the Universal Peace Federation (UPF) in 2005.

This was the condition set by the Seoul Summer Olympics and the Foundation Day for the Unified Nation of Heaven and Earth ("Opening of Heaven Day"). That made way for Rev. Moon's meeting with Mr. Gorbachev. In other words, it led to the global unification of Cain and Abel.

The truth is that Mr. Gorbachev was the kind of person who had tried to kill Rev. Moon many times. But Rev. Moon loved Mr. Gorbachev, the master of global communism, and forgave him with true love, which was more than enough to atone for all his sins. Mr. Gorbachev must have known this, spiritually. And so, he accepted all seven of Rev. Moon's wishes. These included a promise to fulfill the freedom of religion in Russia, and since there is no more need for any statues of Marx, Stalin, or Lenin, they should be removed from the parks.

We invited young people from the Soviet Union to America and let them hear our lectures on the Unification Principles, the essence of Christianity, and showed them American democracy, and then we sent them back. Rev. Moon said, "Send us at least 3,000 students, and we will train more."

Mr. Gorbachev approved of that as well. That was the so-called Soviet students' visit to the United States. Therefore, Mr. Gorbachev's recognition of all seven of these items really created the process of the gradual collapse of communism. At the same time, it provided an opportunity for our Unification Church to expand its roots in the world.

Rev. Moon then instructed brothers and sisters from all over the U.S. to go on a third 40-day overseas mission to 100 countries on October 2, 1990. Seven of us from our state went. They went to Africa, South America, and places like that.

In his instructions, Rev. Moon said, "This 120-day period means 120 years. Before the united kingdom [in Israel] was established, there were three kings, Saul, David and Solomon, and finally the united kingdom was established at the time of Solomon. In this way, the 40 days of the third succession meant 120 days, and 120 years before the unification of the kingdom.

So, that is three generations in the third order. And finally, there will be a unified kingdom. What does that mean? It means that communism will be destroyed, and then the next unified kingdom, the Kingdom of Heaven, will be prepared to be born in the future."

Therefore, we in Wisconsin were connected to the restoration in the midst of such a global perspective. So, when communism was destroyed, the momentum from that was a very meaningful overseas mission, and we created an opportunity by having members from our state go on overseas mission trips. By doing so, communism was destroyed; in other words, East Germany surrendered to West Germany, and they were miraculously unified on October 3, 1990.

So, last but not least, Rev. Moon changed personnel, with Mr. Jin Moon Kim going to New York and Mr. Ki Hoon Kim being assigned as the new Minnesota Regional Director. At the same time, Rev. Moon reaffirmed the basics of the program. For example, he asked each state and city to hold a 21-day conditional prayer service on January 21, 1991. The main content of the prayer was to pray for the settlement of family by breaking through and getting victory to fulfill the providence in Korea.

We created an organization of 1,500 trinity bases throughout the United States. Without it, Rev. Moon said, the U.S. would not be able to build a foundation, and or have a successful World Culture and Sports Festival.

He also said on April 16, 1991, that we must again receive formal education, 21 days, 40 days, and 100 days of training, and that those who have not received all of these must start all over again. He also said that we must go through 3.5 years of fundraising and 3.5 years of witnessing activities and then complete the tribal messiahship. He emphasized that all blessed families must go through this official process.

And finally, in 1991, the "7.1 Day" (or Declaration Day of God's Eternal Blessing) was revealed. At the ceremony to proclaim this, Rev. Moon gave instructions to all members to return to their hometowns throughout the world. This 7.1 Day was a very important providential turning point, as this was where the providence of clan restoration really began.

The explanation given by Rev. Moon at that time was that all people have entered into the sphere of God's direct dominion. This ceremony was to transcend the differences between the democratic world and the communist world, to unify religion and politics, to restore the right of the firstborn, to restore parents, to restore sovereignty, to restore one's true nature, and to restore the sphere of one's mind and heart. Thus, this is a ceremony that will bring about the coming of the original united world. Through this 7.1 Day, we can see this.

I had students from the Soviet Union come to the U.S. on July 1, 1991, but they said they could not train more people that way, so now the U.S had to send staff to the Soviet Union to train more students there. I also participated in the summer seminar starting July 1. Then I was officially recognized by Rev. Moon as the Russian Far East Regional Leader in the winter, and my responsibilities were transferred to Russia.

Since then, we had to send people for world blessings, and at the same time to protect the church from communism. And through our unity with the established Christian churches, we had to bless many members of the church this time. This was a huge turning point for us.

It was then that I moved to my Russia Mission. This long journey gave me a very pleasant, heartwarming, and memorable year with my family. With this, I concluded my seven years as a Minnesota and then Wisconsin State Leader.

CHAPTER 6

Exploration of Russia and China

1. Russian Mission

I have pioneered three countries under the title of Foreign Missionary from 1991 to 2001. I was first involved in two of those countries, Russia and China, as a pioneer from 1991 to 1996.

The reason for this involvement in Russia was that after the Washington Monument rally ended, it was announced on October 4, 1976, that the next rally would be held in Moscow.

I was wondering how Rev. Moon would go to Moscow. However, he had an idea for an event called the World Media Conference, and based on this idea, he invited the heads of state of various foreign countries to attend the historic meeting between Soviet Union President Mikhail Gorbachev and Rev. and Mrs. Moon on April 11, 1990, in the Kremlin.

This was a very important meeting, and, through it, I believe Rev. and Mrs. Moon laid the foundation for the collapse of the Soviet Union's communist regime and its transformation into a new Russia.

In this context, they encouraged our members to go on overseas mission trips for 40 days. We sent missionaries on three separate occasions. Seven brothers from Wisconsin went to Africa and South America. I didn't understand what was happening, but I heard later that this mission led to the collapse of communism. I realized that we needed to follow 100% of the instructions that come from such a person who knew God's Providence.

Rev. and Mrs. Moon's historic meeting with President Gorbachev

Gorbachev agreed on seven items with Rev. Moon, and one of them was to allow us to educate the Soviet students. So, first of all, 2,000 students came to the U.S. from different parts of Russia in October and November, 1990, and they learned the Unification Church's *Divine Principle* here. At the same time, we showed them various places and instilled in them how important democracy and liberalism were.

We achieved the goal of 2,000 students, but many of the students were saying that they would like to come back for more study. However, we had some financial problems, so we decided to go to the Soviet Union and teach the Principle lectures there. I joined as a staff member for about 40 days, starting July 1, 1991.

At that time, students at a Soviet training center in Alante, Latvia, suddenly started making a lot of noise. Many of them left without our permission and returned to Moscow. Then students who had returned to Moscow came back and told other students that Moscow was in serious trouble. They said, "You shouldn't take your training in a carefree manner at a time like this. We need to go to Moscow together." In fact, the situation in Moscow was very difficult.

So, I went to Moscow. Sure enough, a huge number of tanks filled Red Square. Many students who had gone to the U.S. to study and train with us were very angry.

Standing on the tank to stop the coup with Russian students

The guy on top of the tank was named Vladimir. I think he went to 21 days of training, and I happened to meet him at Red Square. He said, "I have to stop this tank, and you have to help me stop it. Let me get on the tank first." As for myself, I was very worried about what would happen if I got on a tank because I was a foreigner.

But many people, especially young ones, stood in front of the tanks and stopped them. I am sure many of the students were among those who went to the United States and were involved in the protest.

Rev. Moon met with President Gorbachev first, then the great Cain of North Korea, Chairman Kim Il Sung, and the Soviet Union finally collapsed as the world leader of the communist state. After Rev. and Mrs. Moon met with Kim Il Sung, we found out later what happened after that meeting. Cain surrendered to Abel, Rev. Moon.

After the summer seminar was over, I attended a winter seminar called the Black Sea Seminar in January 1992. Many of the Belarusian students were going back home. Our leader, Dr. Joon Ho Seuk, asked me, "You go and help them; otherwise, they will be orphans. There is no church to care for them." There were 120 to 200 students who went to the training. Dr. Seuk asked me to take care of those Belarusian students until he could send a care person. He said, "If we could, we like to make a CARP there."

There was a Belarusian National University there, and the daughter of its president was at the seminar on the Black Sea. She was a very interesting girl, and she was on my team. She told me that if I didn't have a place to stay, I should come to her house, so I stayed at the president's house until the next authorized member arrived. I talked with him about many things, and he told me that he would help me to establish the Principle study group (CARP). A month later, my successor came.

The next seminar was at the Black Sea in the Crimea in October 1992. It was a beautiful and scenic place. There were many fun things to do, such as taking a cruise ship there, seeing the site of the Yalta Conference, and visiting Anton Chekhov's home, where he was inspired to write "The Cherry Orchard" and other famous plays.

We came up with the idea to invite teachers from all the republics to come to Crimea and hold public hearings on the Principle. The content was not only Principle lectures but also character education. That was what Dr. Seuk had in mind with his staff.

Many prominent people from the republics came, including a secretary of the Ministry of Education and Culture. I thought that these were excellent people to pioneer Far Eastern Russia in the future.

In November 1992, Dr. Seuk asked me if I would be in charge of Far Eastern Russia. I still had a mission to the U.S., so I could not make a move until I received the proper approval from Rev. Moon. Dr. Seuk immediately consulted with Rev. Moon and got his permission, and soon I was in charge of the eight republics in Far Eastern Russia.

I went to Vladivostok, where I met with the dean of the State Far Eastern University and approached him about several matters. First of all, I asked him if he could extend my visa. This was because the KGB would not be able to interfere with my work as a part-time lecturer or visiting professor as long as the university would provide me with a visa. He readily agreed.

At that time there was no church center. I asked the members who participated in the summer training session to help me with this project, and so it finally began.

These older ladies were the key to bringing stability to Russia. Many of these women were high school teachers. They, in a sense, were the intellectual class, working to build the future of Russia. Therefore, our influence over these teachers was a major factor in moving the Russian providence.

Women supporting education in Russia

My position was the Far East Russia Regional Director, which was a big name, but the only members there were students who studied the Unification Principle in the summer. That was how I started the first cycle of the university's winter seminar on January 25, 1993. I borrowed one lecturer from Moscow.

When I started holding seminars, 126 people came to the first and 152 people to the second. I didn't evangelize anyone, but the secretary of the Ministry of Education gave instructions to each university to send them because there were seminars in Vladivostok. At that time, there was a sanatorium (like a resort or health spa) that had only been used by communist cadres, but since communism collapsed, it was left alone. It could be rented at a really low price, $2 per person per day, and inside was a luxurious building with a marble swimming pool and other amenities. We welcomed the students with open arms.

It was important that I kept personally meeting the secretaries of Ministries of Education in each republic to thank them for their service and ask them for their continued support. The purpose of these tours was to ensure that communication between each secretary of education and us was kept up to date. That was the most important purpose of my visits. Look at the number of people in this picture. Isn't it amazing? There are almost 150 students; that's a huge number.

Russian participants Black Sea Winter Seminar

So now, in the spring, there was a very luxurious Russian youth camp (*okeah* in Russian) for elementary, middle, and high school students built by the Communist Party. Okeah means "by the sea." Teachers and staff were a bit concerned about sending just the high school students, so they came along with them.

I wrote in my diary something like this: "It has never happened before that young men and women from eight republics in the Far East gathered together and competed with each other's strengths. God must have been moved to see this. The young people are really on fire when they hear our Principle lectures. I feel that God would be pleased if He could see these young people."

Spring seminar of high school students in okeah (Russian youth camp)

Students and faculty came there during these three breaks: summer, winter, and spring. There was the triangle of Russia, China, and North Korea. In April 1993, at the end of the spring break period, under Dr. Seuk's guidance, the whole staff prayed on the new Holy Ground for the victory of the post-Soviet Commonwealth of Independent States (CIS), the unification of North and South Korea, and Mrs. Moon's visit to Moscow. At that time, Mrs. Moon had an invitation to go to Moscow.

We continued to conduct seminars for university students, and a lot of university presidents from various republics came. University presidents who sent their students came to find out what their students were doing. They, too, saw that the students were really lively and left with a very good impression. So, they started sending more students.

This was a really good opportunity for us. For example, we were trying to get those who attended the seminar on the Principle studies back on track, so we continued with the Sunday services. At that time, on Easter Sunday in Russia, we had a really large number of students and teachers participating—between 150 and 170 people.

Gradually, through these experiences, I came to understand that faculty members were very important in Russia. So, I started to organize Principle seminars for faculty and staff, constantly at the same time as the students.

Touring snowy Komsomolsk

I would go around to different regions. Wherever I went, the first people I would meet would be the republics' secretaries of education. I would explain to them about the current status of the seminars and ask them to send more people in the future. We had around 200 students from various republics coming to the training seminar every week. We did not evangelize them.

The training hall had a very large auditorium, so it could easily accommodate about 500 people. The facilities at the sanatorium were the best. Students enjoyed staying in such a place and eating delicious food that they had never eaten before, so more and more students and teachers were really looking forward to going to the seminar.

I went on the Kamchatka and then the Sakhalin tour, and met with the secretary of education there and kept in constant communication with him. Many students and teachers came to the Sunday service. Follow-up was very important. We always invited the students to our meetings, sang, danced, shared testimonies, cooked meals, and ate with them. We repeated this process many times.

If we had tried to invite 200 people by plane, the airfare would have been ridiculous. So, to reverse the situation, a workshop team visited each republic and held a training session there. We saved 75% of the cost of the seminar. The finance director at that time was pleased. He said, "You've come up with a good idea. This would save a lot of money." And since the training was held locally, it was rooted in their community and was a win-win situation.

During this period, I had to travel a lot. The traffic in Russia was really terrible. Once, on my way back from Moscow, there was an announcement that the plane was running out of fuel and everyone had to buckle up their seat belts. Our plane made an emergency landing somewhere, but then we had to wait, shivering, in the cold airplane for about eight hours until the army gasoline truck came. You couldn't go to other republics by driving, only by plane. But airplanes were not that reliable. We went out and witnessed in such a difficult situation in Russia.

In November 1993, I visited Komsomolsk, a town created by Stalin. It had tasteless buildings and apartments, but there was a very active missionary named Kenzo Endo in Komsomolsk, and he did a good job of evangelizing teachers there. In Kamchatka there was a mountain bigger than Mount Fuji and nicknamed Kamchatka Fuji. There is a hot springs there, and I took a bath in it with Mr. Kenichi Ito who came as a Russian missionary from Burkina Faso, Africa. I thought that if they could develop the area a little, they could build a great hot springs hotel, but they didn't know how to market it for tourism. They filled the pool with hot water from the hot springs and swam in their bathing suits. I thought it was not used well for economic development.

The spring seminar ended and the summer one began in full scale. At this time, we were not continuing the five-day training as before. Since 2,500 people have already undergone training in the Far East alone, we educated them by conducting three-day, seven-day, and 21-day retreats. At the same time, at the regional headquarters in Vladivostok, we were constantly renting a sanatorium, so there were not so many instructors for the 21-day training. So, we sent students for the 21-day or the 40-day training to the regional headquarters. Of course, the 40-day training had to be organized in the district headquarters.

Around this time, I had a harrowing experience where I was attacked and beaten. Vladivostok is a mecca for the local mafia. I tried to be very careful in my travels and regularly gave money to a Russian driver who had a car to cover his services and the cost of gasoline. One day, however, his car broke down. Days later, I had to give an evening speech at the completion ceremony for the seven-day course, where I gave participants certificates of completion. I then had to walk back to the center.

My intuition had become sharper in Russia, and I noticed that someone was following me. I became concerned because I was carrying a lot of money. There were four of these training sites, and I had to give them money for rent, so I had been converting dollars into rubles that evening. Now I was carrying a shoulder bag filled with $6,000 or $8,000; I don't remember exactly, but anyway, my bag was filled with money. I thought this was dangerous, so I started to hold my bag with both hands and started running a little faster.

However, five or six mafia members knew exactly my way back to the center. They were lurking in the shade of a tree, and suddenly they attacked me. They wanted to get the money in my shoulder bag. I knew that if they took the shoulder bag, it would be the end for me, so I was really desperate to protect it. A big, tall guy kicked me in the head. My glasses were blown off, blood was spurting out, and it was a terrible scene. I was wearing a brand-new suit my father-in-law had bought me, and now it was covered in blood and torn off like the legs of an octopus.

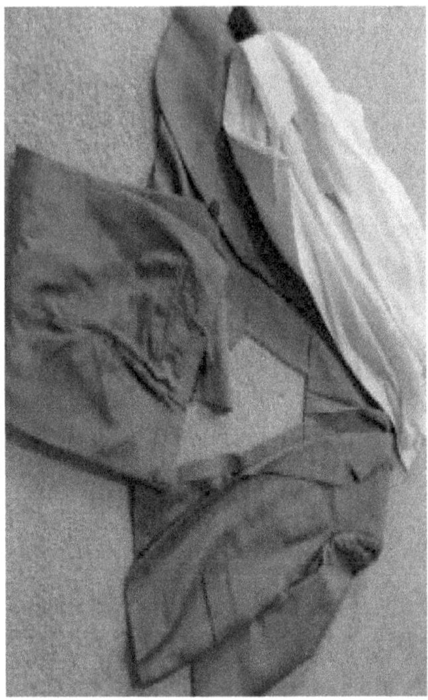

Suit and shirt torn by six mafia men

However, I was able to remain very calm in the midst of all that. I think God protected me. I really felt the kind of merciful feelings as Jesus had towards his tormentors, wondering what on earth they were doing. I thought calmly, "This is public money. If this public money is taken, hundreds of lives will be lost. This mafia group is trying to take it away. It is unforgivable." I guess robbery was their habitual life. My shoulder bag had not been snatched yet, but I still prayed, "If they would take away the money, God will reimburse me 100 times for it." Satan heard my prayer and said that he had to approve this.

The thieves still had their eyes on the shoulder bag. There was a bit of a slope all the way down to the beach. They kicked and hit me on the head again. I was about to faint, and my body rolled down that slope. There was a young couple at the end of a slope, and the female screamed.

The mafia men thought it must be time to end the attack and ran to escape; they stole my wallet with about $300 in it. But they only took the money and threw away everything else in my wallet. That was helpful. I had my credit cards in there, too.

I had this kind of experience three times, but my mission in Russia was a bloody one. However, during the mission to Belgium, a small miracle occurred. When I was in the most difficult time in my finances, 30,000 yen was turned into 3 million yen. The current exchange teller was probably a newbie and didn't know how many francs one yen was, so he miscalculated and multiplied it by 100 times and gave it to me.

Let me get back to my original topic. Character education and curriculum seminars were gradually gaining support from schools, generally from high schools. We selected about five people from among the high school teachers who had participated in the curriculum seminar and sent them to Moscow, where they took a training course and became full-fledged instructors. These people came from many different republics, and indeed, many different regions found this curriculum valuable. We did this three times at Ussuriysk, which was an agricultural university on the outskirts of Vladivostok. Most of the republics participated, and everyone was grateful for the opportunities they received.

About 4,000 textbooks were delivered from Vladivostok. We gave about three copies to each participant. They were so successful that they were given to school principals and directors of the Ministry of Education. This spread to other schools, and we received a steady stream of phone calls from people asking us to sell them textbooks. We also sent more and more books by plane to the various republics.

I must say again, the older women were the key to Russia. These were the people who ran everything. I think that the fact that we realized this and opened a curriculum and seminars there was a great success.

We had a really busy summer. We were constantly doing three-day, seven-day, 21-day, and 40-day seminars at the three training centers, so the staff had a busy time with lectures. Finally, we took a three-day break and went to the new Holy Ground. We prayed fervently for the success of the world tour of Rev. and Mrs. Moon, the unification of North and South Korea, and the establishment of a firm foundation for Russia. The Holy Ground is in a scenic place, and on the way there, there are rivers, lakes, seas, and mountains. I realized that when we made a Holy Ground and prayed there, it was clear that God was listening to our prayers.

Dr. Seuk came up with the idea of a Chinese providence at the national leadership meeting of the CIS on October 29, 1993. We would consult with the heads of universities in Harbin and Changchun in northeastern China, recruit students, bring them by train to Vladivostok, and hold an international leadership seminar. He encouraged me to take charge and carry out this project.

I was busy in Russia, but here I was given the responsibility of China's providence. I was concerned about whether I would be able to do both projects. However, I was attracted to China—in the old days, my grandfather was a member of the Kanton Army (Japanese army in Manchuria). He worked there, so I always heard about China and Manchuria from him. When I was asked to work in Manchuria, I thought it was because of my ancestors, so I gladly accepted the China mission.

2. China mission

Starting on December 20, 1993, we spent 10 days visiting all the universities in Northeastern China (Manchuria in the old days), starting from Harbin, Shenyang, and Changchun, to ask them what they thought of our project.

First, we arrived in Harbin, where we were met by Mr. Wu, who had already become a member of our group. Then we went to Harbin Institute of Technology. The vice president of the university here showed his interest and promised to give our projects more consideration.

Rev. Moon once thought of creating a large industrial zone between Harbin and Khabarovsk. That is quite understandable. The reason is the sheer scale of the Harbin Institute of Technology. This university is known as the MIT of China, and all of China's current satellites and rockets are made at this university. That is why the state is assisting in a semi-private, semi-governmental way. Khabarovsk also has a good university, the Khabarovsk Polytechnic University. These two universities have been in contact with each other for a long time.

Next was Heilongjiang Provincial University. When I met with the president of Heilongjiang University, I showed him a large and magnificent book on our activities in Russia. The president looked at it, pointed to a picture, and said, "This is the ICUS meeting I attended in 1987."(ICUS is the International Conference on the Unity of the Sciences.)

"I was the first person from China to participate in ICUS, and you can see me here," he said. The president understood our purpose very well, and he gave us a good reply saying that he would consider this positively.

We went to Changchun and met Mr. Wang the head of the Public Affairs Section of the Ministry of Education at Jilin University. I brought Natalia with me because she was the director of the Public Affairs Department of the Ministry of Education in Primorsky Krai, a city of Vladivostok. They have known each other for a long time.

The president of Heilongjiang University who attended the first ICUS

The conversation went well. Natalia spoke a little bit of Chinese. So, rather than me telling him, she told him what we were doing, educating a great number of students, saying he should definitely send them there. She did a good job. He was very pleased and took us to a very fancy restaurant and treated us to a great meal.

There were leading universities, and all of them were very welcoming. I arrived in Vladivostok in time to spend December 31, 1993 and God's Day 1994, so it was a hectic 10 days. I am glad that I was able to fulfill my mission and report everything back to Dr. Seuk.

I had to work for Russia and China. No matter how many bodies I had, it was never enough. But I was still young and energetic, around 45 to 50 years old at the time. I remember how many training sessions I had in a week. I was also traveling to China, doing things that would be impossible to do nowadays. That was how passionate I was when I was young. I believe God and my ancestors supported me.

Rev. and Mrs. Moon invited Gorbachev and his wife to Hannam-dong Korea, and they had a real chat like old friends. The Soviet Union had ended, and he only had the title of former president of the Soviet Union, but as his friends,

Rev. and Mrs. Moon said, "Well done, Mr. Gorbachev." I don't know their actual conversation, but Rev. Moon would say, "Because you fulfill my requests, many young people's lives are now being saved." He invited Mr. and Mrs. Gorbachev to Hannam-dong with that in mind.

Unification Church's 40th Anniversary Founding Convention.
May 1, 1994) Seoul Olympic Gymnastics Stadium

On May 1, 1994, I was in Hannam-dong, Korea, for the 40th anniversary of the founding of the Unification Church and the International Leadership Conference (ILC), where the new Family Pledge was announced. At that time, I wanted to meet the president of Far Eastern University, where I would work as a visiting professor in the future. I received some information that the president of Far Eastern University was currently in Niigata, Japan, attending a conference of the Japan Sea International Academic Research Association. So, I rushed from Korea to Japan to meet him.

As soon as the 40th anniversary celebration and my visit to Japan were over, I went back to northeastern China. During this time, Dr. Seuk, Jack Corley, Ittetsu Aoki, and other key CIS missionary leaders visited the universities I had approached, and we checked whether our plan could be implemented. The three of them and I, together with a Taiwanese woman named Wong-Lin acting as interpreter, were to visit all the universities, including places I had visited before. The universities already knew we were coming, and they were very welcoming. So, we started to work out the details of our visit with them.

Meanwhile, in Russia the issue of the Marriage Blessing Ceremony was brought up. The first stage of the 3.6 million Couples Blessing was coming soon, and we were told to prepare a ceremony in each region. We thought that we were going to send candidates to Korea, but then we were told to hold a ceremony in each region. One more challenge was how to introduce the Blessing Ceremony to the local youth in Russia.

During this time we met the great Russian writer Aleksandr Solzhenitsyn. He had been in Zurich, Switzerland, for 20 years, and then changed his base to Vermont in the U.S. In May 1994, Solzhenitsyn decided to return to Russia to give a speech. Because he was going to Moscow via Vladivostok, I could see him again. He gave a speech at Far Eastern University. I didn't understand Russian, but a student I knew interpreted it for me. I felt that he loved Russia so much and was a true Russian. We went to his hotel for our third meeting the next day. I gave him lots of ginseng tea as a gift. He didn't know what ginseng tea was, but I explained it to him. He seemed to understand the benefit of ginseng.

And the next visit was to the Far Eastern Institute of Technology, which was producing more and more excellent scientists. We asked the president of the university to participate in the Seoul Sports Culture Festival. He attended there.

I received more big news. There would be the World Student Conference in Beijing in June, and I was asked to send 10 representative students from Far Eastern Russia. This World Student Conference was planned by Rev. Moon, and the first one was to be held in Moscow, and the second one in Beijing. The conference was designed to address the issue of North-South Korea unification, and there was a condition that North Korean students had to be included. If we had both North and South Korean students, these Cain and Abel students, when they become one, a miracle could happen.

What was this miracle? I did not understand it at the time. I thought it would be a wasted opportunity to send only students, so I asked the president of the Far Eastern Institute of Technology, whom I mentioned earlier, to be a speaker, and he agreed to come.

Dr. Seuk and his group were visiting more and more universities. They sought to see if a leadership seminar would be possible. This was how we would go around to each university, and ask, "Would you like to come to this kind of event?" They all said yes. However, if they were teachers in charge of students, they might think that Vladivostok was a dangerous place, a mafia town. They were concerned about what would happen to young students.

They said, "Let me think about this for a while." The heads of each university's public affairs department began to voice their support for the purpose of the International Leadership Seminar, but they were concerned about sending students to Vladivostok. Dr. Seuk also wondered how to respond to their concerns, as he knew I was beaten and robbed there. So, we suddenly decided to bring people not only from Russia but also from various other countries to China to hold an international leadership seminar there. That was the decision we made.

In Manchuria, there happened to be a small, very famous place in Yanbian called Yongpyeong, where Mr. Kyong Ho Kim joined the Unification Church in Russia. He was witnessing to his clan in China and teaching the Unification Principle more and more. Eventually, he asked us to send someone to give a formal lecture on the Principle. Mrs. Liu (Principle lecturer) was sent there for about two weeks, and we were impressed that she was giving lectures to Mr. Kim's tribe.

We went to her place to congratulate and encourage her. As soon as we got there, we saw that three white cars and a big truck were parked in front of her house. To our surprise, we were immediately detained. We wondered what was going on, and later we learned that Mrs. Kim's aunt's fiancée had called the Chinese police to complain about her. She said she was teaching some religious theory to his clan. That was why the police came in.

We were interrogated at the local police office. "Why did you come here? What are you teaching Mr. Kim's clans? What is the name of the main leader?" When we answered them honestly, the local police officials said that this didn't make sense, so they contacted the police department at the headquarters in Beijing.

The response from Beijing was very interesting, saying "Rev. Sun Myung Moon's group is a very unusual one, they invest in China despite the Tiananmen Square incident, while most of the others pull out of their business from China. In that aspect, we owe a debt of gratitude to Rev. Moon's group."

The Beijing officials said that they could not be friends with Rev. Moon's group, but if it became their enemy, this would bring a terrible consequence. They asked the local police to release us immediately and send us right back to where we came from.

We knew that the World Student Conference was to be held on June 21, 1994, in the People's Auditorium in Beijing. If the detention had been prolonged, I would not have been able to attend the World Student Conference or host the 12 Russian students and the president of Far Eastern Institute of

Technology. Fortunately, the restraints were lifted after about two days, so I was able to attend the conference, which was really a blessing.

Holding the World Student Conference in the Great Hall of the People in Beijing was very significant. Only a very powerful person could rent the main auditorium, the center of the government, for such a conference. I can't tell you why, but it was because we had a connection with Deng Xiaoping's group. China is controlled and driven by five families. One of them is the Deng family. It was with the help of Deng's son that we were able to hold Mrs. Moon's Women's Federation for World Peace conference at the Great Hall of the People.

That was how we had the World Student Conference, where one of the students I invited was supposed to give a speech, and the university president was supposed to give a speech as well. But the Chinese officials wanted me to submit a manuscript before I gave my speech. When I submitted the manuscript, a third of it was erased in black ink.

At that time, I felt that freedom of speech was a wonderful thing. Today, under the leadership of President Xi Jinping, freedom of speech is even more strictly controlled than it was then. When you think about that, you can understand much we appreciate freedom.

One of the points that Rev. Moon made in planning this project was that if North Korean and South Korean students could unite, a miracle would happen. At the end of this event, the two groups of North and South Korean students got together shoulder to shoulder at the farewell banquet and sang "Urie So Wonun Tongil (Our wish is unification)." It was a wonderful Abel and Cain unity.

South and North Korean students join to sing "Our Wish is for Unification"

This is how the World Student Conference was held at the Great Hall of the People. Look at this group of North Korean students. They all wore the same red ties with new suits and Kim Il Sung badges on the right side, and when the leader of the group said something, they would do it like a lightning strike. It was as if the North Korean students were part of the military. About five of them were students from Kim Il Sung University, and the rest were from organizations sent by the government.

The Korean students' talks were refreshing. They were students from the various elite collages and some of them were also CARP members. The president of the Far Eastern Institute of Technology gave a speech and said some very good things.

In the aftermath of such an emotional experience, I said goodbye to the Russian students and temporarily returned to Changchun. On July 9, 1994, Mr. Kyung Ho Kim came to my hotel and knocked on the door in a hurry. "I heard terrible news. Kim Il Sung is dead," he said. I was also surprised. Soon I realized that this was what Rev. Moon meant when he said that a miracle would happen. Later, Rev. Thomas Hwang told me, "Col. Park just went to the North Korean Embassy in Beijing to offer his condolences, and he received an invitation to attend the funeral. So, he will be going to the funeral."

Newspaper information on Kim Il Sung's death (July 8, 1994) and funeral

I was supposed to go to Beijing to prepare for the next International Leadership Conference, so I traveled to Beijing on July 17. When I was watching TV in my hotel there, I saw many North Korean citizens—it seemed like millions of them—crying like crazy next to this car carrying Kim Il Sung's body. I was not sure if they were really crying or if they were doing it because they had to, but it was a bizarre, odd atmosphere. They were hitting the road with their fists, and even though their fists were bleeding, they kept on banging and crying.

I thought about how we could make the International Leadership Conference, which was to be held in Beijing, successful. The International Friendship and Exchange Federation, a group of NGOs with which we had a long relationship, was one such group. They, too, suggested not sending participants to Vladivostok. They warned us that no university would send students to Vladivostok if we said we would do it there.

So, we met with the head of the Public Affairs Division of the Ministry of Education in Harbin and asked him to allow us to use Harbin Normal University as the venue for the seminar. They gave us permission and allowed us to use their university. I met with the president of the university afterward, and he said that he would fully support the project and that we could use the university.

At that time, Dr. Seuk suggested going to Mount Paekto in North Korea and creating a Holy Ground there. Since that place was a symbol of the unification of North and South Korea, we would pray for the unification of North and South.

Meanwhile, I returned to Vladivostok and soon became worried about what had already happened there. As expected, a terrible persecution had arisen against the Unification Church in Vladivostok, and the auditorium of the museum, which had been used for Sunday services, was no longer available. I was kicked out of the Far Eastern University, and the KGB revoked the visa I had received. I was being blocked in every way.

I provided information to Moscow, and a man named Peter, who was in charge of legal affairs, came to Vladivostok and did various things. I asked him, "How is the religious persecution in the other republics?" And he said, "Not as much as in Far Eastern Russia; we have been able to register [the church] in other places." "After all," he said, "it seems that only Vladivostok and Khabarovsk were severely persecuted."

In some respects, I was relieved to hear that. I was very worried because soon I had to go back to Harbin to join the International Leadership Conference, and if the persecution was a little more severe, I would not be able to go there. But that was not the case, so I went immediately, and the ILC seminar was held at Harbin Normal University.

This university is very famous, and they let us use all of their facilities. And the Chinese who participated in the program were amazing. They spoke fluent English, and some of them spoke fluent Russian and were very smart. Some of them even spoke Japanese. I was really overwhelmed by the level of Chinese students they sent. The Unification Church has a rich international flavor, and the Chinese side was wondering how we had gathered such an international group with American, Russian, and Japanese students. Even though they were students, they were all missionaries. When we gathered all the missionaries, it became a substantial international conference with a total of 100 people. The president was very pleased, and the officials from the Ministry of Education who were sent from Beijing were very pleased. The breakout sessions were very good, with prominent Russian and Chinese professors speaking on the main theme, which was very good, and everyone was very impressed.

On October 29, 1994, the last day of the event, a cultural evening was held, and the Chinese side performed a Chinese opera. We danced and sang Russian folk songs, and the Japanese also sang and danced, and at the end, everyone danced in a circle. It seems that the officials of Beijing reported to their superiors that our organization was holding a very good seminar. The students were more than happy to express their opinions, and they asked and answered questions. And the entertainment was really interesting, and the seminar was a great success.

What ended up happening was that we were permitted to conduct this seminar from January 22-27, 1995, at Beijing Normal School, the most excellent teacher training school in China. This was a really big accomplishment.

3. First Blessing Ceremony in Far East Russia

On January 17, 1995, the Hanshin-Awaji Earthquake hit Japan and killed more than 5,000 people. Several months , in May, a similar large earthquake hit Russia's Sakhalin Island, killing several hundred people.

In the case of the Hanshin-Awaji earthquake, the area was restored within two years, and a highway was built that was even better than before. Sakhalin, on the other hand, was completely ruined and never rebuilt. I thought there was a considerable difference between Japan and Russia in terms of technology and compassion for the people.

Earlier, in the last weeks of 1994, Mr. Zin Moon Kim, as well as the president of Sun Moon University and his delegation, suddenly came to Vladivostok to give a seminar for our members in Far East Russia. Then, separately, Mr. Chang Sheng An came.

They seemed to feel some spiritual urgency to come here. Mr. An went to Khabarovsk for the Blessing Training Seminar, and then to Yakutsk, the furthest away, for another Blessing Training Seminar, and I wondered what was going on there. I did not invite them, nor did I give them any money. But they came of their own will and held seminars and Blessing seminars for the members and even donated money. I was really grateful that the spiritual world was cooperating with them.

I had to move from Vladivostok to Khabarovsk in a hurry because the KGB was coming after me more and more. One time, in the middle of the night, about six police officers with machine guns banged on my door and said, "You have to leave today." Apparently, when I returned from China, I was already on the blacklist. The police said they would give me a visa for only three more days, and then I had to leave for somewhere. They issued a deportation order by the KGB in a threatening way.

I held the last Sunday service and told many students and teachers, without explaining the situation, that the next Blessing Ceremony would be held in Khabarovsk and that they should come, too.

The president of the Technical University in Khabarovsk told me that he would be participating in a sporting event in Korea. I had to move to Khabarovsk from then on and get another visa. So, I signed a contract as a visiting professor at the Khabarovsk University of Economics and Law, and I got a visa from there.

I did not know how or where it came from, but they considered me a very famous scholar, and I was asked to give a speech at the 25th anniversary celebration there. Of course, they asked me to do it in English. I gave a speech in front of about 1,500 students there.

Since that time, we held Blessing Revival Seminars in Vladivostok, Khabarovsk, and other republics, and there were about 3,000 people who received the training. From among them, we explained to them what the Holy Blessing was, what lineage conversion was, and so on, and then recruited them to participate in the seminar. That was the new trend.

We held many meetings of all the missionaries in the Far East. From time to time, Dr. Seuk and other executives would come and give us all kinds of information about what was going on in Moscow. It was a wonderful give-and-take exchange, and we received a lot of stimulation. We asked that centering on missionary Shuji Igarashi, not only missionaries but also brothers and sisters become instructors in their respective republics. It would be very strong if there were about five lecturers in each republic. Therefore, we held several seminars for the training of lecturers.

I started doing more and more Blessing workshops in various republics. Dr. James Baughman, who was president of the Unification Church of America until he was replaced by Dr. Tyler Hendricks, helped us. Dr. Baughman was now the executive director of the International Education Foundation, which was founded by Dr. Seuk. Dr. Baughman came to our Far East region, and we decided to hold a Blessing seminar at the Khabarovsk retreat, which 42 people attended.

Gradually, the lectures got going, and Dr. Baughman spoke to 42 candidates at the training center over a period of five days. He was very smart and could convey the significance of the Holy Blessing very well, so his lectures really revived many people.

The first Blessing Ceremony in Far East Russia

Dr. Seuk asked me to officiate the Blessing Ceremony in each region. I couldn't do it without my wife, so I decided to call my wife and two daughters to Khabarovsk.

We solemnly performed the Holy Wine Ceremony for the first time with the 43 couples matched by True Parents.

Next, after receiving the holy wine, we held the Blessing Ceremony that same day around noon. My two daughters took the bowl of holy water to the 43 couples.

It was a truly moving Blessing Ceremony. The main venue for the ceremony was Khabarovsk, but we also held Blessing Ceremonies for three couples and seven couples in Magadan and Yakutsk, due to the far distance. Fifty-three couples participated in this Blessing Ceremony in the end. The dinner that night was really exciting. The entertainment was really good, as well as the testimonies of the couples, and we had a wonderful day.

In September 1995, at the CIS Leaders' Meeting, I was instructed to assume responsibility for Northeast China, which was a great responsibility. It took me a while to make up my mind because I was told to take on the Russian Far East as well.

When I went to Khabarovsk, the University of Economics and Law was a sister school of Niigata Sangyo University in Japan. When I happened to visit the school office, Dr. Kaneko, the president of Niigata Sangyo University, was visiting there. He invited me to participate in an international conference in October. It was a symposium of about 18 countries that were coming. He said, "You are from the United States, you are Japanese, and you are in Russia, so this will be a perfect symposium for you. Please come and join us."

I said I was not sure if I would actually be able to find the time, as I had a lot of work to do. I didn't say yes, but I kept getting calls from him, and finally, I accepted the invitation. I sent in my manuscript and attended the symposium on October 25. I made a presentation on the theme of "Securing a Sea of Peace and Prosperity: A Proposal for a Northeast Asia Regional Forum and a Northeast Asia Free Economic Zone".

Let me talk about China, where I was in charge of providential activities at Dr. Seuk's request. There was missionary Han, who was appointed by Mr. Hwang, and who had been living in Harbin for a surprisingly long time, which I did not know. However, Mr. Hwang knew him, and he and Han came to Harbin because we were going to gather there. Mr. Hwang was sent to Beijing quite some time ago as a missionary. However, due to various difficulties in Beijing, he temporarily moved to Hong Kong and then returned to Beijing.

Overall, Mr. Hwang was in charge of the five or six missionaries in China, taking care of all of them. He encouraged them to obtain a doctor's degree in their schools. In the case of Dr. Seuk, the character education curriculum became very popular, with each province inviting him to come to their province, so over the long term, the character education curriculum was expanded, and Dr. Seuk came to have jurisdiction over all of China.

I, on the other hand, was more focused on the main cities of Northeast China, such as Changchun, Shenyang, and Harbin. I mainly developed relationships with Chinese universities. However, Dr. Seuk told me that Shanghai would be important in the future. He said that if we could get a hold in Shanghai and Beijing, it would be the same as if we held China. He wanted me to visit Shanghai to find out what was going on. On November 26, 1995, I traveled to China's east coast to visit the huge seaport city of Shanghai.

Weeks later, I received a letter informing me that I was a candidate for National Messiah and I should prepare to go to Korea to attend the 40-day training session in Cheong Pyeong. At that time, I wondered what on earth this National Messiah was.

I eventually received an invitation letter to attend the 40-day retreat from August 1 to September 9, 1996.

I was to go from Shanghai to Korea. I notified my wife that we should go to Cheong Pyeong as a couple, and we agreed to meet in Gimpo International Airport sometime soon.

Shanghai has really changed its appearance in a modern way, and even from that time on, I realized that there was great momentum in China.

I thought I was going to stay in China and had already received a visa from the Chinese Embassy in Tokyo on July 5. However, I had to get a Korean visa as well, since the 40-day training workshop was longer than the no-visa limit of 30 days. I got a Korean visa in a hurry and went from Fukuoka to Seoul, meeting my wife who had arrived from the U.S. in Gimpo for the 40-day training.

This marked another new beginning for me and our family. The providence of the pioneering work in Russia and China was truly a miraculous movement in some respects, made possible by the cooperation of the spirit world and the Japanese missionaries. Because I was persecuted by the KGB and the mafia, the Russian state-run TV interviewed me for about three hours. But then they twisted the whole thing and aired a great criticism of the Unification Church and Rev. and Mrs. Moon. The TV program was so negative that two of the candidates for the Holy Blessing dropped out after seeing it. There was severe persecution both inside and outside the church, but I believe that God protected us.

Shanghai (top) and the Great Wall of China

I was not shaken at all by the persecution. The more persecution came, the more excited I became, and I came with the mindset that if I could overcome it, victory would not be a problem. If my foundation had become this strong, I could easily overcome the persecution even if it came. Thus, when I was in my 40s, running around Manchuria and Far East Russia and being persecuted, that was a most glorious time in my life, and I think now that I was happy.

CHAPTER 7

National Messiah Providence in Belgium

Up to now, I have had the shared responsibility of pioneering Russia and China, and I was excited about this mission. I was in charge of China and Russia, especially Far Eastern Russia and Northeastern China, the two regions of old Manchuria. I thought it would be one of the best memories of my life to go from Russia into China and from China into Russia, and run around in that magnificent wilderness when I was in my 40s.

I had planned to spend more time in China and got a long-term visa to China. But at the stage where I was about to go to China, another providential development took place.

It became known as the "National Messiah Providence." Japanese members who had been more than 30 years in the church were candidates for a National Messiah posting and were asked to participate in a 40-day training session. Since that direction came from Rev. and Mrs. Moon, I could not refuse. So, my wife and I agreed to participate in the 40-day National Messiah training session in Cheong Pyeong beginning in August 1996.

About 180 Japanese candidates for the National Messiah mission gathered in a hut-like place in Cheong Pyeong. At times, there was drumming, clapping hands, and reading the scriptures in a circle. Occasionally, Mrs. Hyo Nam Kim came and spoke to us.

Mr. Chung Hwan Kwak would come and explain to us the providential significance of the National Messiah. As I listened to these things, I gradually came to understand this new providence.

Then, before the end of the 40 days, there was a lottery to decide who was going to which country. I was concerned about which country would be my next mission. Even when I came to the training session, my heart was still pulled back by China and Russia. But with renewed determination, I drew the lottery with the mindset that I would love the country drawn in the lots more than anyone else. It was Belgium.

During the lunch break, the European member I worked with asked me which country I drew. I told him Belgium, and he said, "That's a tough place." When I asked him why it was so difficult, he replied that Belgium is a country where Catholicism is the national religion and the Unification Church is regarded as a heretic. First of all, he said, "you can't get a visa" for religious purposes. This meant I had to think about how I could work there for a long period of time.

Then he added that the Unification Church in Belgium was very difficult because of internal divisions. I recalled that when I was a IOWC commander, a national leader from Europe came in as a commander. At that time, Rev. Moon was very angry with one of the women in the room. "If you behave like that, the spiritual world of that country will slander you," he said. I remember thinking to myself, "There is no need to say such a thing to a female leader," but she was the national leader of Belgium.

After the 40-day retreat in Cheong Pyeong ended on September 10, the Korean National Messiah had already been assigned. I went to the home of Rev. Chan Kyun Kim, one of the 36 Blessed Couples, to greet him at his home in Seoul. He explained more about why Belgium was a very difficult situation. The woman who was formerly the national leader of Belgium had a conflict with the former continental president, and she took the best people and formed her own group. Now only a few members remained in the Belgian church, and some of those had problems, too. So, the challenge was to bring these divided church groups back together.

I went to Belgium in October. There were already several Japanese missionaries working there, and they welcomed me at the airport. As soon as I arrived, I was told that Mrs. Moon was going to have the founding event of the Family Federation for World Peace and Unification (FFWPU) in Vienna, so I flew straight there. Then she came again to Paris for the founding convention of the FFWPU.

Welcomed by Belgian members at Brussels Airport

Most importantly, we ourselves had to hold the founding convention in Belgium. We had made hotel reservations, banners, and various other preparations, but then the hotel where we planned to have the convention received huge objections from the Catholics and asked us to cancel the event. It was outrageous to cancel two days in advance, and I was pretty pissed off and tried to negotiate a way for us to stay on schedule. But in the end, they canceled.

So, we had to find a new hotel and make a reservation under the name of the Women's Federation for World Peace. Somehow we were able to hold the founding convention of the Family Federation for World Peace and Unification in Brussels. We spent a lot of time advertising, but the location changed, and we asked for help from our members in Luxembourg. We were very disappointed that only about 46 people attended.

After the event was over on November 23, 1996, we decided to hold the "True Family Values" seminar every Saturday and Sunday. This was very well received, and our members said they could invite many people to the seminar, and it was surprisingly successful.

Next, I had to create CARP, so I opened a CARP center at the Free University in Brussels, where I started two activities simultaneously: the church and CARP. But just as I was gearing up my evangelistic activities, my three-month visa was about to expire.

I knew that I would never be able to get a religious visa, so I asked the president of Sekai Nippo (World Daily) to let me stay here as a correspondent and send them new articles, while, at the same time, do evangelistic work since I came here as a missionary. Especially now, I had to work toward the "preliminary blessing" goal, which was a huge goal. So, I asked him to help me get a correspondent's visa.

The founding convention of the Family Federation
for World Peace and Unification in Brussels

The head of the Foreign Correspondent's Office of Sekai Nippo prepared the necessary document, and I went to the Belgium Embassy in Japan to get a correspondent visa. But they flatly refused, saying, "No, we cannot grant a visa for Sekai Nippo. You are a sectarian newspaper and not a member of the Japan Newspaper Publishers Association, so how can we give you a correspondent's visa?" I was very disappointed and wondered if this would make it more difficult to get a correspondent's visa, so I went back to Belgium again, this time with a three-month tourist visa.

On January 1, 1997, I met with the members again, and we planned to spend God's Day with them at the home of the national leader, Yvo Bruffaerts. Rev. Chan Kyun Kim's wife was there, too. We had a prayer meeting outside that day, and I encouraged everyone in a strong tone of voice with the theme, "God's Providence and Me." My message was that brothers and sisters had to think of their lives centering on providence rather than doing something else.

In the meantime, Blessing Ceremonies were held in Europe from time to time, including one in Vienna, Austria, on January 12, 1997. Mr. and Mrs. Modessa from Belgium were to receive the Holy Blessing, so I attended the ceremony.

Mrs. Moon spoke at the founding convention of the Family Federation for World Peace and Unification in Vienna

It was a very nice atmosphere at the ceremony, and Rev. and Mrs. Kwak performed the main service. Soon after that, the European Leaders' Conference was held in Austria, and we discussed the 3.6 million Couples Blessing. Each country had its own goal for preliminary blessings, and Europe's goal was 1.2 million. ("Preliminary blessings" meant people received candies sanctified with holy wine as a condition to receive the Holy Blessing one day.) We had a target of 150,000 couples at that time.

We constantly used the "True Family Values" slides and gave weekly seminars, sometimes on weekends and sometimes over two days. Surprisingly, our members started bringing guests, and it became very exciting.

The slides from our "True Family Values" workshop were so popular that people from other countries wanted to borrow them, so we shared them. I heard that they used them to hold workshops at their own centers. In the meantime, my three-month visa expired, and I returned to the United States.

Anyway, I looked for different ways to get a long-term stay if possible. I went to a local city hall to negotiate a visa but was rejected. I was concerned about how I could stay in Belgium for a longer period of time, as we would not be able to achieve any results with me going back and forth. I decided to rent an office as a U.S. correspondent for Sekai Nippo and then apply for a correspondent's visa at the Belgian Consulate in Chicago.

Meanwhile, until I could obtain a long-term visa, I returned to the U.S. I had to do something to help out in Wisconsin, so I called on pastors I had been connected to before and held blessings at the Milwaukee Cultural Center, and so on. Preliminary blessings had begun in the U.S., so I gradually blessed various people and also blessed pastors together with the holy wine.

While I was in the U.S., I received some very good news. It was about the leader couple of the split in Belgium, an outstanding member named Philippe and his wife, a Japanese woman named Yoko. We received information that they had returned to our side. This couple was the so-called assistant leader of the split group, the right-hand man in charge of all the finances. It really gave me hope that the church group that had left could be brought back together.

In the meantime, another person from Zaire (Democratic Republic of Congo), whose father worked at the Zairean Embassy in Switzerland, came back to us. She was a black woman with a very good credentials, and she was smart and capable. Meanwhile, the former national leader and her husband divorced. So, that group fell apart. There were four or five excellent members in their group and we wanted them to come work with us again, but their hearts were so broken that they rejected our proposal out of hand.

In that context, I was very happy to be able to participate in the East Garden ceremony on True Day of All Things as a Belgian representative. While I was waiting for the report from the Belgian Consulate in Chicago, I blessed Mr. and

Mrs. Way, a university professor, and Pastor and Mrs. McFee at the home and Mrs. Ferry, a friend of ours.

The preliminary blessing of the 3.6 million Couples Blessing worldwide was accomplished on April 15, 1997. We blessed 283 couples in Wisconsin. At that time, the Pure Love Alliance (PLA) was touring and holding purity rallies all over the United States. My three daughters participated in the project, and my wife and I went to pick them up when they arrived in Madison, the capital of Wisconsin. When 3.6 million couples had received the preliminary blessing, Rev. and Mrs. Moon said it was completed, and they proclaimed the Universal Sabbath Sphere.

In the midst of all this, I received a notice that the Belgian Consulate in Chicago wanted to interview me for a correspondent's visa. On October 6, 1997, I was able to obtain the long-awaited correspondent visa, and I was really happy from the bottom of my heart. I immediately flew to Belgium. I received a temporary press card from the media office of the Belgian Ministry of Foreign Affairs. All the members in Belgium were really happy, and when we had Sunday services, all joined in because I was back again.

At that time, Belgium had set a national goal of finding 500 couples for the Blessing Ceremony, but we were short by 96 couples. We all went to the Grand Place and successfully found those couples. I remember that we all had a victory party to celebrate.

In the meantime, I had to return to the U.S. again because the second stage of the 3.6 million Couples Blessing Ceremony was to be held at the Robert F. Kennedy Memorial Stadium near Washington, D.C. My eldest daughter was going to participate in this Blessing Ceremony, so I headed to the U.S. with national leaders from Belgium and some Japanese missionaries. The event was held in a very large, outdoor sports arena, and it was a really impressive and splendid Blessing Ceremony.

I also reported to the head office of Sekai Nippo that I had received a correspondent's visa and asked what they expected of me. I discussed these matters with President Kinoshita, Director Kabe, and Director Yamamoto of the Foreign Correspondent Division. When I returned to Belgium, I had a clear understanding of how to harmonize my activities as a correspondent and as a missionary.

Belgium European Union Headquarters with Rev. Chang Kyun Kim

On January 5, 1998, I successfully received a correspondent's visa from the media office of Belgian Foreign Affair Department. They were expecting a lot from me. Brussels is not just the capital of Belgium; it is the capital of the European Union (EU). The headquarters of NATO is also located there, so Belgium is the political and military center of Europe.

Since there were no correspondents there, Sekai Nippo had very high expectations of me and wanted me to send them at least one article every week. That was a lot of work. At the same time, I had to do the preliminary blessing of 150,000 couples and then 500,000 couples. I further had to hold a weekly seminar on "True Family Values" and visit members' homes. So, I was very busy being the Japanese National Messiah of Belgium.

In the meantime, there was a leadership meeting in Budapest, Hungary, in Europe, and we were given a goal of giving preliminary blessings to 150,000 couples.

It took a lot of money to buy this candy. Belgian church members made tithes and donations, but this money was mostly used for rent, utilities, and food for the Sunday service. The money to buy candy had to come from the missionaries in Japan and me.

We decided to start a 40-day campaign, with the encouragement of the continental president Rev. Sa. The members in Luxembourg said it would be easier to do in Belgium, so they joined us to do the blessing activities in various places in Belgium.

But buying candy was a very big financial burden in itself. At the same time, I had been to Japan and the U.S. so many times—every three months—that I was becoming very financially strapped, and my missionary work was becoming a hindrance. At that time, the only cash balance I had left was the 30,000 yen I had brought from Japan. But I had to buy candy, so I decided to withdraw it all.

I went to my bank and told the teller to withdraw the full amount, but I wanted the full amount converted into Belgian francs. I realized later that the bank employee transferred 100 times the amount of my money! He probably made a mistake in converting the yen to Belgian francs and increased the number of zeros by about three more.

When I saw the amount of francs I received, I had a hunch. I remembered that when I was in Vladivostok, I had converted the money to rubles to pay the seminar fee in Russia, and the mafia followed me. They tried to steal that money, and five or six of them attacked and beat me. I told them that the money was for the people who participated in the three training sessions and that it was for their eternal life. Anyway, I did my best to make sure that I would never give them this money even if I died. They got away with $300 in my wallet.

At the time of that beating, I really thought they were wretched and pitiful but I prayed for forgiveness. But I also asked God to reimburse me a hundredfold for what they had taken. The promised amount of money came back to me when I needed it the most. This allowed us to buy 150,000 or 500,000 candies for the preliminary blessing. God knows the situation well, doesn't He?

I got a long-term visa, I got money from Satan, and I started working toward a preliminary blessing of 150,000 couples for the first time and toward a blessing of 500,000. We worked really hard, and the Japanese missionaries and I worked as one, and gradually the Belgian members started to follow.

On April 2, 1998, I was in London for the Second Asia-Europe Conference, a meeting of Asian and European political leaders. I was able to meet and interview world leaders such as British Prime Minister Tony Blair, South Korean President Dae Jung Kim, and Japanese Prime Minister Ryutaro Hashimoto. This allowed me to broaden my perspective.

At the same time, I was able to exchange feelings with my brothers and sisters who worked with me in the U.S. and Russia. In that sense, coming to Europe really broadened my horizons, and I am grateful to God for that.

From time to time, we held leadership meetings at our training center in Austria. Austria is a beautiful place, with mountains and rivers. We have two training centers in such a place, with one located right next to a river. So, the meetings were held every three months in a truly wonderful environment.

Antwerp is home to major paintings by Peter Paul Rubens, including "The Elevation of the Cross" and "The Descent From the Cross." There is also the famous tragedy story called, "A Dog of Flanders," which is about a Belgian orphan boy and his dog. We went around such famous paintings and the place where the story was told while doing the blessing activities, and although it was very hard work, we were able to have fun and enjoy the blessing activities together.

At the same time, I sent one report a week to the Sekai Nippo headquarters in Tokyo. That alone was a lot of work. First of all, I had to go to the briefing at the EU headquarters, and then I had to go to the briefing at the NATO headquarters to file the article, but at the same time, I had to do blessing activities, and I had to do workshop meetings every week.

I was able to really unite my emotions with the members, and I have many happy memories. For instance, there was a Christian festival at Antwerp that drew many people to see special scenes of angels and Jesus riding on a donkey. We thought this was a good place to give people holy candy. Another time, there was a big fireworks display along the beach and a great number of people gathered. We went to the town and gave a preliminary blessing to many people. We went to most of the Belgian cities by car.

All-European Blessing Ceremony held in the Slovak Republic

When there were festivals, like the Doudou Festival in Mons, a couple of our members, Simon and René, who were elders, lived there, and we stayed in their house. A great number of people—about 120,000 tourists— came to the festival. We had eight teams, and over two days, we brought all the candy we could find, prepared with holy wine, and then gave them to 46,842 people. That was the biggest number we've ever had.

Because of this 46,000, on June 10, the national goal of 150,000 was achieved, which was 111.98% of the goal, and made Belgium third-ranked out of 35 countries in continental Europe. Before that, Belgium was ranked 34th or 35th out of 35 countries, or at best 32nd, but suddenly we were third. All of my brothers and sisters were very happy to see this.

In the meantime, this time on June 13, 1998, there was a big Blessing Ceremony in the United States. We decided to do that in Belgium as well, in Bratislava, the capital of the Slovak Republic. From Belgium, a black Zairean woman named Lily, who had been on the other side of the split, came back. She had done really good work—always helped with the blessing activities and was really dedicated to church activities—and she was going to receive the Holy Blessing this time. We went to Slovakia with her.

This Blessing Ceremony was unique. For the first time, Rev. and Mrs. Moon blessed 34 Couples in the spirit world. They also gave Blessed spouses to four great saints as well as four evildoers, Hitler, Stalin, Mao Zedong, and Kim Il Sung.

That was how the sister of Rev. Chan Kyun Kim, our Belgian National Messiah from Korea, received a spirit world Blessing with the philosopher Socrates.

Our sister Lily got a really fine husband, and with this, the divided Belgium became one again.

Then the European Leadership Conference was held, where the testimony meeting and a new preliminary blessing goal was given to each country. At the awards ceremony, Belgium was honored with the third place in achievement.

I immediately went home and told the members to prepare the holy candy so that we could work toward the new goal. My wife knew how busy I was. She was a high school teacher at the time, and high schools were closed for two months during summer vacation. She came to Brussels to help with the blessing activities, and her arrival was a very significant and wonderful human resource. From that time on, together with my wife, Japanese missionaries, and Belgian members, we set out for the next preliminary blessing of 500,000 couples.

Blessing activities at the 550th anniversary of Rubens City

We went to many cities: Antwerp, Ghent, and the city of Brussels. Whenever there was a festival in those places, we would follow the information and go to that city. One time, there was a famous festival in a village with only about 600 inhabitants, but 70,000 people from all over the world came to the festival. We went out again to those places and gave everyone a preliminary blessing by giving them holy candy.

After that, we continued to work with members in all kinds of festivals. There was a leadership conference of all European brothers in a place called Slovenia. Japanese missionaries also went. We had an award ceremony and a departure ceremony for the next 3.6 million preliminary blessings.

Slovenia is a beautiful and scenic place that faces the Adriatic Sea. We relaxed there for about three days, swimming, playing soccer, and splitting watermelons. At the same time, there was a testimonial meeting, then an awards ceremony, and finally a rally for the new 3.6 million preliminary blessing. At the same time, we had to prepare single members for the Blessing Ceremony, as well, and we gave them the preliminary blessing. Such a meeting was held at this scenic place.

In the meantime, as our activities grew, the Belgian Ministry of the Interior and secret police officers visited our church and asked us if we were planning a big demonstration. They had heard about the Pure Love Alliance (PLA) rallies in the United States and suspected that the Belgium Unification Church might do something like that. But they left us, realizing that with only about 12 families as members, we were not likely to do such a thing.

Next, we continued to go to bigger and bigger festivals, driving to a festival in two cars and blessing up to 20,000 people. The Belgian members became excited to participate in blessing activities together. There were fireworks displays along the coast in various places in the summer, and we rushed there with all the holy candy we could find.

In the meantime, my biggest headache stemmed from a government investigation into my activities as a news correspondent for Sekai Nippo. Mr. Emmanuel Conou, the lawyer I hired at the time, told me that the Ministry of Foreign Affairs' Press Bureau had been asked to look into my case. They were to check on the legality of Sekai Nippo and, if possible, kick me out of the country. Mr. Anthony Gidden, who was Mr. Conou's assistant, told me how to deal with the government inquiry. We went over it piece by piece.

The authorities were eager to see the Sekai Nippo's holdings made public. The ministry's press bureau suspected that the Sekai Nippo was mostly owned by Rev. and Mrs. Moon and their executives, and that it was published for a private audience, such as only Unification Church members. If the government could brand Sekai Nippo as a sectarian newspaper, they could take action against me. But we could easily prove that Sekai Nippo was a general interest newspaper published to serve the public. It is available on the internet, so all people can see it if they want to.

As part of my defense, I immediately contacted the headquarters of Sekai Nippo in Tokyo and asked them to send materials on Sekai Nippo's financials and proof that it is publicly published and sold on the internet and in print. They understood and quickly sent me a considerable amount of material. I handed this over to Mr. Gidden, who spent three days researching it all. When he was done, he told me that he thought we would win.

On September 22, 1998, an important hearing was held. Eight representatives from the Ministry of Foreign Affairs, the Ministry of the Interior, and the International Press Center participated in a tense question-and-answer session, which lasted about three hours. Their intention was to say that Sekai Nippo was a newspaper of the Unification Church, which was a heretical organization in the eyes of Catholics. They said that such a thing would not be tolerated in Belgium. In fact, they said, there was no correspondent in Belgium for the Akahata News, which was owned by the Japanese Communist Party, or the Soka Gakkai's Seikyo Shimbun (Japanese Buddhist newspaper).

In that sense, if they saw us as heretics, it was certainly a natural view for them to see the Sekai Nippo as a sectarian newspaper. But Mr. Gidden said that based on the three documents he has collected so far, the Sekai Nippo was by no means an organ of a single religion. He really made an eloquent defense. The hearing ended with another hearing set for October 27, at which time the decision would be made.

For the second hearing, I wrote a statement and distributed it in advance to all the participants, and then I was given time to read it out loud.

The decision was finally made at the hearing when the chairman said, "Sekai Nippo is not the organ of a sectarian religious organization." It was determined to be a public media, and I, as a correspondent, should be granted a permanent correspondent's visa. This became a symbolic victory for us against Belgium's huge Catholic organization.

At that time, both in Europe and in the U.S., a book written by Nansook Hong (Rev. Moon's former daughter-in-law who published a negative book about Rev. Moon) brought about a crisis of faith within the Belgian church. In Austria, many members left the church. I desperately testified of my absolute faith in Rev. and Mrs. Moon, with whom I had come into contact, and I was very happy that not a single person dropped out of the church in Belgium.

Still, in this situation, we agreed to make a change in the Belgian national leader. Aiden Cunningham of Ireland, whose wife is Belgian, was elected as the new national leader.

It was during this time that the hearings on my news correspondent qualifications were held. We could see that the Catholic Church was quietly working against us. They didn't like it when we said that the Catholic Church's weakness in sexual harassment is because it still forbids priests and nuns to marry. There are a lot of ex-priests in Belgium who were excommunicated from the Catholic Church because they got married.

I contacted a man named Paul Bourgeois, who was excommunicated from Catholicism and was the general secretary of the Federation of Married Priests in Europe. He said it was unacceptable that sexual harassment had come too far in the Catholic Church and the solution is to permit their clergy to get married. We agreed that we had to create such a movement, since some of our members came from the Catholic Church.

Cardinal Danneels

This headquarters was in Rome, and they held a general meeting twice a year. Archbishop Stallings, Archbishop Milingo, and others had left the Catholic Church but received the Holy Blessing from our church. I asked them if they could join this group and participate in the Rome conference for married priests.

At the same time, we pursued the married-priest issue in another way. A Catholic clergyman named Cardinal Godfried Danneels had jurisdiction over France, Belgium, the Netherlands, and about five other countries; his residence was in Antwerp, Belgium. We went there to meet him and found that he had a very positive attitude toward the married priests.

This made him liberal in the eyes of mainstream Catholics. However, from our point of view, he was the right person to make a breakthrough and solve the problems in Catholicism. So, we met with him several times, gave him a letter from the spirit world, and asked him to please seek election as pope. I spent a long time with the Belgian members, offering amazing prayers for him to be pope.

In the end, Pope Francis was elected. We were disappointed, as we thought Cardinal Danneels would have made more bold reforms if he had been the one elected.

On November 10, 1998, all the Japanese national messiahs were called to attend a 40-day retreat in Fuerte Olimpo in Paraguay. It seems that just at the right moment there is always such a change of providence, and a different mission comes. I went to the Brazilian Embassy to apply for a visa.

On November 15, the Belgian members gave me a big farewell party. I comforted them, saying that a national messiah, as Rev. and Mrs. Moon said, is permanent and no one can change it. This means that once the national messiah is decided, that person is the national messiah of that country permanently. I told them that I would always be willing to come back and help.

By the way, in July 2016, the Belgian national leader Mr. Philippe Jacques passed away suddenly. At that time, my parents' house was recovering from the Kumamoto earthquake (April 16, 2016), and after visiting my mother in Kumamoto, I flew to Belgium to participate in Philippe's Seonghwa Ceremony (funeral). I said to the members, "I told you so. I told you that the national messiah has to take care of this country permanently. I told them not to leave you alone and go to the next providence. I told them not to worry. I will come back again."

Belgian members gathered to send me off to South America

Most of the members came to see me off at the airport. I loved them like my own children, and my heart was filled with painful reluctance to leave them. On November 21, 1998, I arrived in the village of Fuerte Olimpo. On November 28, Rev. and Mrs. Moon arrived at the retreat and spoke at length about the Pantanal providence.

I listened to Rev. and Mrs. Moon's talk, thinking that my new mission was here.

CHAPTER 8

The Pantanal and Leda Providence

1. Significance of the Jardim Declarations

I would like to explain about the Pantanal and Leda providence. The origin of God's Providence in the Pantanal can be traced back to 1965 when Rev. and Mrs. Moon toured the world. When they flew over South America's highest mountain, Aconcagua in the Andes Mountains of Argentina, Rev. Moon was very moved when he looked out of the airplane window and saw this vast, marshy plain below him. This was the Pantanal, which extends across four countries: Argentina, Paraguay, Brazil, and Bolivia. Its wetland area is as big as the main island of Japan.

However, Rev. Moon received a revelation that there was no one to take charge of it. So, in the 1990s, he decided that he had to do it himself and went to the land of South America to cultivate it. He planned a big project in the Pantanal and called it Jardim. Later, he directed that a village with water and electrical services be built nearby, which was called the Leda project.

Rev. Moon entered Paraguay when he was more than 75 years old. Everyone said it was an impossible job, but Rev. Moon made a promise to God and jumped in. When he saw the Pantanal, he came to love it very much. He saw the Pantanal in its natural state, with its amazing variety of fish, animals birds, insects, plants, and flowers. All are still largely untouched by human hands. He felt that this was the very nature, like a garden of Eden, that God had given to Adam and Eve.

In such a situation, he used logs to build a large hut on the fishing grounds with a sleeping area on the second floor. At night, mosquitoes were very active, so he built a fire pit on the first floor and burned different kinds of wood to get rid of the mosquitoes.

World's largest marshland, the Pantanal

When I joined this Pantanal providence, I wondered why in the world Rev. Moon would go to such a place in South America where there is no civilization and what he would do there. The Fifth Jardim Declaration was announced when I arrived. If there was the Fifth Declaration, there must have been four other Jardim Declarations before that. I immediately began to study.

The First Declaration was issued surprisingly early, on April 3, 1995. It was based on the three concepts of absolute faith, absolute love, and absolute obedience, which were the three concepts on which God created the heavens and the earth. If this is the case, then we human beings, the so-called center of creation, must take charge of all creations with these three concepts in mind.

The Second Jardim Declaration was that we must create ideal couples, siblings, children, and families that are absolute, unique, unchanging, and eternal.

The Third Jardim Declaration stated that God was the first creator, Adam and Eve were the second creators, and the descendants of Adam and Eve were the third creators and the ones who could realize God's ideals.

The Fourth Jardim Declaration is a very difficult philosophical phrase called "Liberate God by Fulfilling Our Destined Parent-Child Relationship." I think its contents have a very deep meaning.

The Fifth Jardim Declaration is the proclamation of the family Sa Sa Jeol (4-4 Day). The same Sa Sa Jeol appears again later in the Seventh Jardim Declaration.

The Sixth Jardim Declaration is about the Liberation Ceremony for Spirits.

The Seventh Jardim Declaration, which was held in Punta del Este on January 1, 1999, was proclaimed on God's Day as the Cosmic Expansion of the True Blessing and Complete Liberation from Satan's Lineage. Rev. Moon said that while the Fifth Jardim was for family, he added Cosmic Sa Sa Jeol to the seventh one. In other words, the Sa Sa Jeol means the four-position foundation and the four great realms of the heart. The Messiah came and took back 4-4 from Satan and restored the 4-4 that had been destroyed by Satan. That is why the Seventh Declaration is named the "Cosmic 4-4 Day." The Seventh Jardim Declaration was the motto for that year and proclaimed at the same time as God's Day 1999.

And, finally, the Eighth Jardim Declaration is that all humankind must return to Heavenly Parent. That is why Rev. Moon created the Cosmic Federation of True Parents.

The Jardim Declarations are the standard that Rev. Moon strictly adhered to, completely adjusting the effects of the spiritual world and principle and building up the sections step by step. This is a symbolic declaration to be proclaimed and realized in the physical world. This was connected to the coronation ceremony of God's Kingship on January 13, 2001, when Rev. Moon made the Eighth Jardim Declaration, taking into consideration the state of the spiritual world.

This led to the Jerusalem Declaration of May 18, 2003, made in Israel, and the founding of the Universal Peace Federation (UPF) in 2005. Mrs. Moon's speaking tour of 58 countries successfully ended up in Beijing. Because of her victorious speaking tour, Foundation Day was finally proclaimed on January 13, 2013 (February 22, 2013, on lunar calendar).

By dividing the spiritual world under different declarations, one by one, and attaching one declaration to another, the Pantanal providence was proclaimed in the earthly world. I think this is the most important thing about the Pantanal providence.

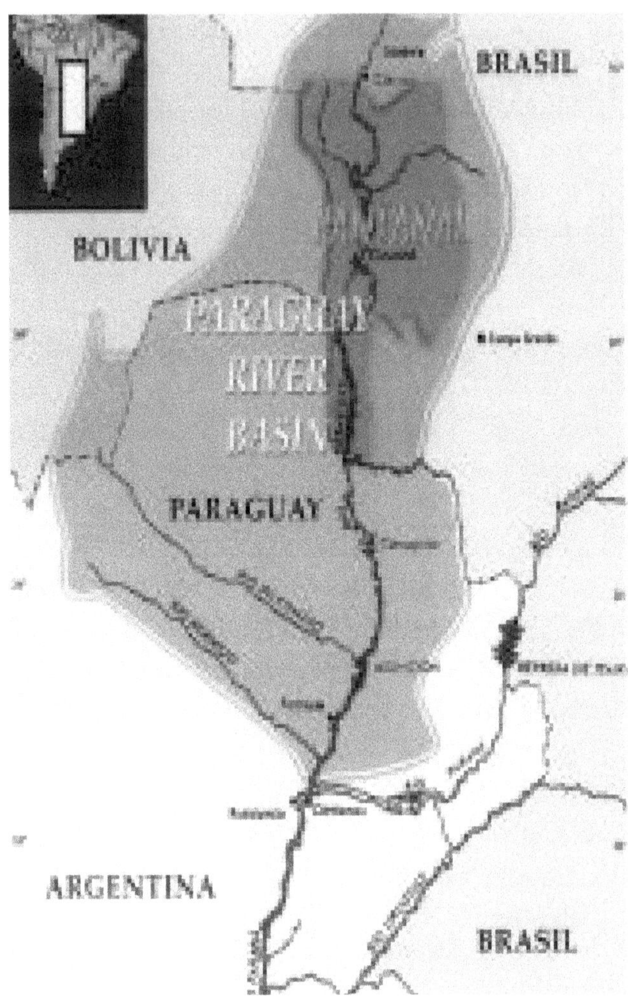

In our base in the Pantanal, Rev. Moon liked to fish all the time while he made his sincere devotions. The upstairs where he stayed had the sleeping quarters, and the kitchen was below. Mrs. Moon became good at fishing and caught big pacu fish. Their grandchildren sometimes came to Jardim and played at the foot of the river in Jardim.

The Pantanal has many tributaries. One day, Rev. Moon chose one of the tributaries and went straight to it. Paul, the boat captain was a local man who knew the area well. But Rev. Moon went there in the middle of the night and ordered him to drive the boat at maximum speed.

I went fishing once with this captain, and he told me about that trip with Rev. Moon. He said that his teeth were shaking, even though it was summer, because it was that scary. He knew that if a tree or something had fallen in the river, he would surely have had a big accident going at this speed in the dark. Still, Rev. Moon told him to go as fast as he could.

We learned later that Mrs. Kim, who was in charge of this house during our tour of the holy ground in Salobra, Paraguay, told Captain Paul that Rev. Moon had gone to the spirit world and went to the bottom of hell to liberate the heads of the demons, and that was why what he did seemed so reckless. Rev. Moon set such really serious sincerity conditions.

In this way, the Pantanal was not just a place for sightseeing, fishing, or scenic beauty as we think of it. Rev. Moon chose the Pantanal as his fighting ground with the spirit world.

The São Paulo Declaration was proclaimed on March 31, 1995, followed gradually by the eight Jardim Declarations. This is truly a principle within principles, as Rev. Moon conveyed in each of his declarations. He had been doing his utmost to correct such internal traditions. He paved the way for the realization of world salvation, which is the historical longing of all humankind through the blessings of the spirit world and the earthly world.

On November 7, 1998, I received a call to go to Jardim, and I left Brussels immediately for Jardim. But Jardim was not my destination; it was Olimpo in Paraguay on November 21. As soon as I arrived, I heard that President Kuboki of the Japan Unification Church had passed away, so we sent him off in the form of a testimonial meeting, mourning him together.

This Olimpo retreat had a surprisingly slow schedule. The reading sessions were held in the morning and afternoon, and each brother's testimony session was held in the evening. Rev. Moon had purchased an abandoned building in Olimpo, and we Japanese national messiahs were asked to fix it up as a training site. It was a lot of work, and there were many things that needed to be done. We didn't even have a water pump, so how in the world were we going to provide water for the trainees when they arrived? We couldn't even paint without water.

We tried to dig a well, but only salt water came in. So, we learned that the people of Olimpo collected rainwater and drank it. It is the same as in Israel.

In such a situation, Rev. Moon visited us several times, and we had a very pleasant time singing songs and giving testimonies. At the end of the meetings, Rev. Moon asked us to gather together and take pictures.

Despite sweating, hard work, and service, these 40 days of training and sharing testimonies were very enjoyable. At that time, we were informed that God's Day would be held in Uruguay, and all Japanese national messiahs were requested to participate. We went by bus from Jardim to a place in Uruguay called Punta del Este. On the way, we saw Ignace Falls. We did some fishing in the Atlantic Ocean after God's Day. We caught a different kind of fish there.

Mother prayed at the Japanese national messiah's
40-day workshop (Americana Hotel)

Mrs. Moon had been traveling around the world, making speeches in eight cities in Korea, 16 cities in Japan, and 12 cities in the U.S., as part of the "Global Expansion of True Families." But on the occasion of God's Day, she suddenly returned to Uruguay. So, of course, we were able to celebrate God's Day with Rev. and Mrs. Moon.

This Day of God, you see, is a duplication of the Fifth Declaration of Jardim. As I mentioned earlier, the 4-4 Day is something that Adam and Eve, the false parents, destroyed. It is the four-position foundation, or the four great realms of heart. True Parents won the victory and returned it to Heaven on September 8, 1998. On January 8, 1999, it became Cosmic 4-4 Day. Rev. and Mrs. Moon were very confident. They said that there would be a great change in the universe.

In Japan, True Mother gave lectures in 16 cities, and it was clear that she was gradually encircling Satan, rooting everything out in a very gradual manner, and the New Year's motto for God's Day, January 1, 1999, was "Blessing the Heavens and Eradicating the Satanic Lineage," which was correctly said in the Jardim Seventh Declaration. That is why it became the motto for that God's Day.

At this time, Rev. Moon asked Ms. Erikawa why she could not conduct 360 million Couples Blessings in Japan. He said that it should be done in Japan. Ms. Erikawa said that she wanted to do it, but that realistically it would be difficult. Rev. Moon was a little angry, but he decided to do it in Korea, and on February 7, 1999, the first wedding ceremony of 360 million couples was held in Seoul.

Next, Mrs. Moon came to the United States, and on March 19, 1999, in Washington, D.C., she spoke at Congress. Finally, on May 28, the last of these 34 countries, the last of the eight cities, she spoke in Beijing. She had a successful conclusion of the speaking tour.

Because of her conditions, Lucifer (Satan) was completely humbled on March 21, 1999. Mrs. Moon had done this great work, and Lucifer gave letters of apology to God, Rev. and Mrs. Moon, and mankind. The place where this great historical event took place was the room of Rev. and Mrs. Moon in the Americana Hotel in Brazil.

I was fortunate enough to visit Rev. and Mrs. Moon's house several times. It was shabby, what can I say, better than a shack, but it was all made of wood. It was like a cottage attached to the side of the main Americana Hotel building, and it was Rev. Moon's room.

Annex of Hotel Americana where Lucifer (Satan)
naturally surrendered to Rev. and Mrs. Moon.

Mrs. Hak Ja Han Moon traveled to eight cities and 34 countries like this. That was quite an accomplishment. She didn't even seem to get tired. When Mrs. Moon came to Uruguay, she was really beautiful and very energetic. She sang many songs when Rev. Moon asked her to sing. God knew more than anyone else that this world speaking tour was important to bring Satan to his knees. Therefore, God supported her spiritually, and she brought victory.

Mrs. Moon returned to East Garden in New York on May 30, 1999, and so Rev. Moon named the day as the True Parents' Earth Star Victory Proclamation Day.

March 21, 1999, had been the day of the complete surrender of Lucifer (Satan) to True Parents. On May 14, 1999, the Day of Proclamation of the Liberation of the Cosmos was announced, and then on May 30, 1999, True Parents made the Day of the Declaration of True Parents' Global Victory (East and West Global Victory).

On June 14, 1999, at the same time as the 37th True Day of All Things and True Parents' Cosmic Blessing Declaration at the Seoul Olympic Stadium, Rev. Moon presented a large plaque and a certificate of commendation to Mrs. Moon. I can only imagine how happy he must have been. With this, the foundation for victory was firmly established, and I believe that Rev. and Mrs. Moon were truly happy.

2. Jardim World Peace and Ideal Family Registration Workshop

This time we finished our 40 days in the Pantanal as national messiahs, and we celebrated God's Day in Punta del Este, Uruguay. After that, I went back to Belgium to gather my possessions. But this time, I was told that there would be a 40-day retreat for registration in the Ideal Family for World Peace. This was an important event, and it was up to our couple to decide whether or not to enroll our family. I was happy to receive the notice, and I went there.

Soon after, I flew from Belgium back to Wisconsin, where my family was based. I bought tickets to Sao Paulo, Brazil, and arrived in Jardim on June 16, 1999. There was an evening orientation, and my wife and I were assigned to the ninth group and elected as its general group leader. The next day, the 40-day training session began.

Of course, there was a morning service, three prayer bowings, the Family Pledge, a prayer meeting, and a lecture by Rev. Yun. His talks had very deep content. After breakfast, there was a morning reading session, and then three hours of free time in the afternoon. Then another reading session from 4:30 to 6:00 in the afternoon. The reading sessions were all held at the same time. The reading material was decided, and each person stood up and read it. After this, it was dinner time.

There was two hours of free time in the evening, from 9pm to 11pm. During this free time, everyone was wondering what they should do. Since I was the leader of the general group, everyone came to me asking, "What should we do?" I told them to follow their conscience, study if they wanted to, do preparatory work, or if they had any questions, they could ask the senior members of the group, who were all here. However, during the last 30 minutes, they must write a reflection essay. I advised them to keep that to themselves, leave the rest to their initiative, and work freely.

With my wife at Ignace Falls

Being responsible while living life was the rule for these 40 days. There was a pilgrimage to the holy ground for about five days. In the Pantanal, Rev. Moon created many holy grounds; this one is the only place in the world that has three names.

First of all, its names are: Original Holy Ground, Root Holy Ground, and Victory Holy Ground. If you speak out these many times, you cannot help but be impressed with these names. Rev. Moon came here to fight, love, and liberate the heads of all demons. He was able to bring Satan to the natural surrender, and then he loved them. I thought that this is the deep meaning of the Original Holy Ground, Root Holy Ground, and Victory Holy Ground.

Our couple was fortunate enough to sit in the very front of the room for a long time to listen to Rev. Moon's speech, so we received many scoldings, praise, and consolations. I took notes on all of them, receiving profound benefits. I read them over from time to time to correct my life of faith.

Trainees came from all over the world. In the case of entertainment, there were people not only from Japan and Korea, but also from Europe, the U.S., and of course South America. The entertainment was colorful. I was impressed by how different dances and music were in different countries, whether they were singing or dancing.

As for the children, Rev. Moon said you could not leave the little ones at home. Rev. Moon's true wish was that everyone should bring their families, if possible, despite financial problems. So, some parents brought their small children with them. They learned songs and performed them in front of Rev. and Mrs. Moon, and they did their best and sang loudly.

This was a pilgrimage to a holy ground, and the training center we had built in Olimpo was also a holy ground. We also visited a place called Beljid, which has a beautiful waterfall. Of course, we also visited the Americana, the historic hotel where Satan succumbed and where Rev. Moon lived.

Rev. and Mrs. Moon prayed at God's Day in Punta del Este, Uruguay, 1999.

The workshop was not just a 40-day special training session but a more in-depth training session for registration. So, at the end, the couple or the family had the opportunity to have their picture taken with Rev. and Mrs. Moon.

You might think this is a normal picture, but it is not. When we were standing next to each other, Rev. Moon was praying. He said, "This couple and I become parent and child. I will try to make that causation now, so God, ancestors, acknowledge this kinship that we have become blood relatives." I have this commemorative photo in a large frame in my study room. Whenever I look at it, the relationship between parent and child comes to mind. I have taken a lot of pictures so far. There are also photos of me with Rev. and Mrs. Moon. However, this photo is the one that moves me the most deeply.

Family registration picture with Rev. and Mrs. Moon at Jardim

As I mentioned earlier, Mrs. Kim, who was in charge of this house during my tour of the Salobra holy ground, told me that Rev. Moon drove a boat through the hanging trees and dangerous rivers at high speed until midnight, and plunged into the spiritual world. He went to the bottom of hell where the heads of demons hung out and released hundreds of millions of demons and evil spirits. Because of this, Lucifer (Satan) naturally surrendered to God.

At the same time, on June 13, 1998, at Madison Square Garden, four great saints and also the worst criminals of Kim Il Sung, Mao Zedong, Hitler, and Stalin, each received God's blessing. Rev. Moon said that the spirit of the Pantanal is to eat the whole fish, including their bitter guts. That is the spirit of the Pantanal. With that spirit, he blessed four saints with holy women, and also found wives for the heads of demons. He told us that he blessed Hitler, and he (Hitler) began to bow down, too.

We took our registry photos, and when we came back from our last pilgrimage to the holy ground, it was already about 40 days. On the way back, my wife said that she had not been to Ignace Falls and she wanted to go, so we went there with Mr. and Mrs. Lee, the regional director of Minnesota at that time.

We met some couples who are in a sisterhood relationship with us. Rev. and Mrs. Moon are in a photo with us, and the two sisterhood families were behind them. This man is Valdir, with whom I worked for about three years in Far East Russia. His wife is Korean. I missed this man, and I am amazed that God made this kind of person into my sisterhood couple. I asked Rev. Moon, "Valdir, whom I used to work with, became my sisterhood couple. Is this God's plan?" He told me that it was.

3. Japan National Messiah, Pantanal Special 40-Day Retreat

When the Jardim workshop was over, I received another summons. This time, all the Japanese national messiahs were instructed to stay behind and come to Olimpo for a special 40-day training session in the Pantanal. Olimpo is a small town facing the Paraguay River and is part of the Pantanal.

How many times have I attended the 40-day retreat already? First of all, I attended the first 40-day training session in Olimpo on November 13, 1998. Then the second one was the registration training session in Jardim. The third special 40-day training session of Japanese national messiahs was in Olimpo.

Fortunately, I was in Jardim when the third training was announced, so there were only four of us—Mr. Oyamada, Kunitoki, Aoki, and myself—who were trainees at that time. I went to the room to greet Rev. and Mrs. Moon. All participants had been notified and knew that there was going to be an opening ceremony, but there were only 13 people gathered in Rev. Moon's room.

He said, "I don't know if I should do it or not, postpone it or not, but August 1 is the most important day of the month. So, although there were only 13 national messiahs, the special training session for Japanese people should start from August 1 to September 9." This would be the ninth day of the ninth month and year of 1999, 09:09 AM and 9 seconds would be eight of the number nine.

Rev. Moon had to finish, and then he had to proclaim another big ceremony. That was why he said we had to start it on August 1.

At that time, Rev. Moon had already had various ideas and kept talking about them to us. What was also very unique was that he prayed first. Then he said to Mrs. Moon, "Pray for God's support for these Japanese national messiahs." Although Mrs. Moon prayed in Korean, I think she prayed earnestly for two things.

Japanese national messiahs with Rev. and Mrs. Moon at Olimpo training center

First, we must work much more before the year 2000. Second, for the providence of the Pantanal to triumph, Rev. Moon called the Japanese national messiahs. She was praying that the Japanese national messiahs would unite and win the victory, not only in the 40 days but also in the subsequent period of the Leda pioneering. I found out the content of prayer later in Japanese.

Leda is located two hours upstream, by boat, from Olimpo. So, we moved to Olimpo again in a hurry, and from there we would spend another 40 days. Mr. Kajiguri was very adventurous, and since the Leda project was given to the Japanese national messiahs, he wanted to go and explore it. Mr. Oyamada said that since we did not have enough people yet, Mr. Kajiguri and three others could go there, investigate, and report back to us later. But there was no word from them. We didn't even have cell phones. Mr. Oyamada asked me to go and find out what kind of situation they were in.

Rev. Moon speaking to Japanese national messiahs at Olimpo training center

I went there alone and hired a motorboat captain. A few more Japanese members joined us soon.

That place was already a tough place. There were about four huts, but they were not the kind of housing that people could live in. When we tried to find a place to sleep in one of the huts, we found snakes of all colors coiled around it. And at night, poisonous insects stung us, and all of us were very swollen and hurt a lot.

I wondered what would happen if I stayed the night, and sure enough, it was extremely noisy outside. The cows were screaming. And at the same time, some kind of beast was screaming, "Gaaaah, gaaaah, gaaaah," as it killed the cows and ate them. It went on for about four hours, and I couldn't sleep.

When I woke up in the morning, the area was covered in blood and gore. And all that was left was the head of a cow that had been eaten by a jaguar. I went back to Olimpo and reported to Mr. Oyamada. Because there was a great need for supplies of food and water, I went to buy them and send them urgently. We also dispatched an additional four new members to reinforce the team.

Since it was so hot, we would go to the Paraguay River to cool off and wash ourselves. There was no drinking water at that time, so we boiled water from the Paraguay River and drank it.

This training session ended on September 9, 1999, at 9:09:09 AM. Rev. Moon said this was what he wanted. By restoring the lost nine numbers, Rev.

and Mrs. Moon said that a new era had arrived in which all things related to Satan could be liquidated and Heaven on Earth could be built. They named it, "The Day of the Parents of Heaven and Earth Opening the Realm of the Unity and Liberation of Heaven and Earth." After that, at 10:10 AM, Rev. Moon proclaimed something called "Sam Shib Joel" or "3-10 Day."

The entire universe is made up of numbers. Therefore, Rev. Moon was trying to establish the Kingdom of Heaven in the real world by using the numbers in a truly wonderful way, making each number like a bamboo joint and proclaiming it to bring Satan to his knees. So, what is significant about the 3-10 Day? He needed to go beyond the buffer zone of nine numbers, which Satan could not cross, to make 10 numbers, and perform the completion ceremony in the name of Yahweh to proclaim God's direct sovereignty. And so, he proclaimed the 3-10 Day.

On September 14, 1999, there was another important change in the closing of the prayer. Now we were allowed to pray in our name.

Since the National Messiah Training Seminar held in Olimpo, Rev. and Mrs. Moon often visited us in Olimpo and talked about the significance of the Pantanal Project and why they chose Japanese national messiahs to serve there. Why did he choose Paraguay? Everyone in South America is poor, and South America has suffered the most persecution of all. They have been persecuted by Christianity. During the Cold War, Soviet KGB spies built a power plant in Paraguay and used it as a base for the Soviet KGB.

At the same time, the U.S. was also using Paraguay to put about 200 CIA special agents in a power plant they built elsewhere with a headquarters. In that way, South America was really abused by the so-called superpowers. Also, Paraguay is different from other South American countries in that it is the only one that still has diplomatic relations with Taiwan, despite the fact that all the other countries are beholden to China.

Paraguay is a really interesting country. There was once a famous movie called "Mission," wasn't there? The Guarani tribe were there. The Catholic Jesuits were really sacrificially converting them to Christianity and creating an ideal world. But Spain didn't like the Guarani tribe and destroyed them all.

However, now we invited members of the Guarani tribe to attend a 40-day separation (sexual abstinence) workshop to prepare for the Blessing Ceremony. I think this is the third time now; later, because of the COVID-19 pandemic, the workshops stopped. In any case, the couples would go home after 40 days of training and conduct the three-day ritual. In this way, about 250 people have already passed the 43-day consecration and become Blessed Couples. Now, some people, led by Mr. Minoru Nakata, are going there for missionary work. I think this will bring great good news.

In 1999, we spent 40 days reading, testifying, and serving. At lunch, Rev. Moon called us all together and said that today we would have a fishing contest. He also urged us again to make up our minds to develop this Leda project.

The speeches that Rev. Moon spoke at the 40-day special training sessions are truly amazing words. It is not only a guideline or a compass for the future development of the Leda project, but also a guide to the spiritual world. Also, wherever Rev. Moon goes, he is ultimately concerned with the unification of North and South Korea. It is not easy to understand how the Pantanal providence can unify North and South Korea, is it? But Rev. Moon shared the secret with us.

The collection of Rev. Moon's speeches during the 40-day workshops is about 60 pages long and is the bible for the Leda pioneers. Everyone reads it constantly. Even when they go to Leda, Japanese national messiahs read this book over and over again, whether they are in Japan or in the United States. I have read it so much that the cover of my book is now gray instead of white. It is such a valuable bible for the pioneering of Leda.

4. Pantanal International Conference

Fortunately, the second International Pantanal Conference was in Washington, D.C. As organizers, I and Mr. Oyamada were allowed to attend it. The director general of the United Nations Environment Programme, who was at the conference, was going to give a talk.

Do you know what a crested ibis is? The director of the United Nations Environment Programme was told that the last surviving crested ibis was on its deathbed, so he immediately bought a ticket and went from John F. Kennedy International Airport to Narita, Japan, then from Narita to Noto, and from there to Sado Island. What was he going to do? It's one species, you know. But this species is now disappearing and he said, "This is a very serious matter."

That's why he went there at the time of the death of the last crested ibis. I was moved. I think everyone was moved. I reflected on the need to take care of all things in the world with that kind of love. I thought this is exactly what the Third Jardim Declaration is all about.

I then came back to the U.S. and participated in God's Day on January 1, 2000. Fortunately, I was able to invite all my family members to participate with me.

This was the second international conference of the Pantanal. Everyone loves nature, loves the Pantanal, and loves these species in the wetlands. They were trying to keep them alive. Some of the participants were millionaires, right? They were willing to give as much as they could for the preservation of the Pantanal. One of them told me, "If you are doing the Pantanal, I will help you." He said he was always willing to help.

I went back to Leda with great joy at this news. But, as I thought, the mainstream opinion was that we should do things on our own. That was why I did not receive his support.

This is Sekai Nippo. At that time, Mr. Yuji Yokoyama came and wrote an article. Since then, he has written several articles on the significance of the Pantanal.

I made the 60-page book of Rev. Moon's speeches. Under the direction of Mr. Oyamada, I recorded the entire process, including True Mother's prayer, on 26 tapes, which were edited by Mr. Toishi, Mr. Owaki, Mr. Iwaoiji. With the help of Mr. Ezwa and Mr. Katsuno, the book of Rev. Moon was completed.

This has truly been a wonderful resource for posterity. The workshop period was from August 1 to September 26, 1999. Even though the order was given, members could not all gather at the same time. Sometimes there were 10 people, sometimes three, sometimes six, and so on. The day when all the members gathered was August 14, 1999. The 13 members who joined the training from the beginning finished 40 days on September 9, 1999. Some members came late, so the end of the workshop ended September 26.

The 400 million Couples Blessing was possible, from the point of view of Rev. Moon, because the spiritual world was organized. Fortunately, my second daughter also received the Blessing in Korea at that time. I also joined the ceremony there on short notice. At that time, there was a world leaders' conference at the central training center, so I attended it. It was a very unique leadership conference. The Jardim Eighth Declaration was issued at that time.

Rev. Moon also founded two organizations. One is called the "Cosmic Federation of True Parents" and the other is called the "Family Party for Universal Peace and Unity." These are what this last Jardim declaration is all about. We must be present to the Cosmic Parents. Therefore, we are the United Federation of True Parents of the Universe. After these eight declarations were made, the "Enthronement Ceremony for God's Kingship" was held for the first time on January 13, 2001.

5. Pioneering Leda

On January 13, 2001, the "Enthronement Ceremony for God's Kingship" was held in Cheongpyeong, South Korea. After participating in that ceremony, I went immediately to Jardim and then on to Leda. Rev. Moon asked that as many of the Japanese national messiahs as possible come and participate in the workshop one more time because it was the final goal.

When I went there, Mr. Kamiyama, a leader of the project, said, "Mr. Ikeno, we will be receiving many tourists from now on. We need to know where the best spots are and what kind of fish can be caught, so that we can guide these tourists.

Since you like fishing, I want you to do it this time." That made me very happy. I was really surprised that I could devote myself to fishing like this.

Caught a pacu in the Paraguay River

It was not that I didn't like this labor, but I have a very slender body. I couldn't work as hard as the locals. But what I was doing now was fishing in the Paraguay River, which is about 100 kilometers long. We dug holes for a fish tank to put in different kinds of bait.

A local guy named Aron knew the best places to fish. While getting bait from somewhere and buying them, I went to the spots he guided me to and caught a variety of fish.

By the way, Rev. Moon asked especially for the Korean national messiahs to catch four kinds of fish in the Paraguay River, 40 fish each, for a total of 160 fish. These 160 fish were such an important mathematical condition that it would determine the fate of the Korean national messiah's assigned country.

Boga, like the crucian carp, were very easy to catch. The hardest to catch was a golden-colored fish called dorado. The pintado was a big catfish. And then there was the pacu, which has the most delicious flesh. These were the four types of fish I just mentioned. The dorado, the most difficult fish, jumps three times, twisting its head up to about three meters, even after being hooked. So, the hook was usually broken there, or the fish would spit out the hook anyway. So, even though I caught 40 other kinds of fish, the dorado was the most difficult. I could catch 26 dorado but no more.

The fish fed us all. Pacu was deliciously grilled with salt. Pintado was really tasty when it was cooked in sweet soy sauce, and the oil was released when it was boiled for a long time, and it was tender. Boga was often caught but it was not a popular fish, and I didn't want visitors to catch it. It was not very tasty and had too many small bones.

Every morning at Leda, we got up at 4am and had a reading session at 5am. During the reading session, we read many times from the 40-day Pantanal Training Course book of Rev. Moon. He said, "This Paraguay is a land of resentment. If you become the best workers, even surpassing the local people through sweat and tears, you will be able to get rid of the resentment of this land. This is to create an open area for God. There is nothing more wonderful than this. Therefore, you must become the best workers under the sun." At Olimpo, Rev. Moon gave us a pep talk many times.

There were only four humble shacks when we started to pioneer, right? However, Leda now has modern buildings to be able to have an international conference and a pool. Even wealthy people who attended the Pantanal International Conference came here. Our members who pioneered Leda said they didn't know how this area was transformed, but it was wonderful. An ideal world was being created here.

After the 40-day workshop was over, we went to see a game of our soccer team in Jardim, CENE Jardim (Centro Esportivo Nova EsperanÁa, or the New Hope Sports Center). Rev. Moon wanted to make it bigger and bigger, and he wanted to combine it with a big soccer team in Sao Paulo. At one point, this team became so good that they became the best in the region.

Watched CENE Jardim's game

Rev. Moon thought he could draw North Korea out through soccer, and this CENE Jardim team traveled to North Korea to play a friendly match. Later, they trained the North Korean women's soccer team by having them stay at a dormitory in Sao Paulo. When North Korea heard about Brazilian soccer, they were surprised that Rev. Moon had the world's strongest soccer team, and that he was doing such a great job. He also invited a youth soccer team for training and games.

CENE Jardim was getting stronger and stronger. Then Rev. Moon moved a certain number of players to Sao Paulo and bought a soccer team in Sao Paulo, while keeping CENE Jardim there. That is amazing, isn't it?

Now, to change the subject, this Enthronement Ceremony for God's Kingship was not made suddenly, was it? There were seven Jardim declarations, and Satan gave in, and then God was enthroned. At the same time as the Enthronement Ceremony, the headquarters of the UPF South America was opened. As I mentioned earlier, this is where two presidents (current and former) of Uruguay and 400 prominent people gathered. This is an amazing building just by looking at it. It has a fountain. There is no other building like it anywhere.

Rev. Moon bought two places here in Paraguay. The first place was Leda, which was being developed by the Japanese national messiahs. However, he bought a place about three times larger than Leda, which is called Casado. He said, "We must keep alive Japan and Korea with a focus on North and South America. If the Catholics and the Protestants conflict, this is a big deal. When the Protestants of North America and the Catholics of South America become one, the Korean Peninsula will be unified." He talked about this very important thing. I think that is the reason why Rev. Moon named the Leda pioneering project "South and North America Sustainable Development for World Peace."

And then there's the other one, the Casado. There are all kinds of animals in this Casado. Jaguars, for example, and other big cats come to eat villagers' cows, sheep, pigs, and so on. So, when I went to Leda last time, I saw cattle being killed by a jaguar. The width of the river here is twice as wide as in Leda.

What is going on with the Casado is complicated now. Just when we thought that Hyun Jin Moon had taken control of the place, a mafia-like group took it away from him. And then they put it on trial. Well, you can't rely on Paraguayan courts. Even though we had already paid for the Leda property, someone who used to be the owner came to court with some documents and they won. They then took the property and sold it to the Brazilian mafia at a high price. So, unfortunately, now it is a chaotic situation for ownership.

Next, the Third International Pantanal Conference was held in Ascension, Paraguay. Four or five famous scholars came from the United States, and two from Japan—a professor from Utsunomiya University who worked at the Botanical Research Institute for Tropical Climates, and a woman from Sophia University who was also a researcher of tropical plants.

*Received the Overseas Missionary Achievement Award from True Parents
at the 50th Anniversary Ceremony of the Unification Church*

So, what was very good this time was that these participants decided to do a fact-finding tour. They were the first ones to come to our Leda. A biology professor from the most famous university in Chile came. The former ambassador of the United States to Paraguay is now on the board of an important diplomatic institute. Five of these important visitors came to Leda.

One thing people talked about was how Leda Director Minoru Nakata made the Paraguay River water taste delicious. When these people drank the water, they said it tasted so good, maybe it's even better than Evian in France. I thought, "Well, then, let them make a toast with this—toast to God and to the pioneers of Leda—and be victorious."

On May 1, 2004, at the 50th anniversary celebration of the Unification Church, I was fortunate to receive the Overseas Missionary Achievement Award. This was a wonderful and precious honor. At that time, Mr. Sano gave a report on Leda using a PowerPoint presentation at the United Nations Economic and Social Council. I never thought that the Leda project would be presented at the UN.

GPA (Global Peace Academy, our church's youth training) members also visited from the U.S. and stayed for two or three weeks. They helped with various things, like building an elementary school and a park in a local Indian village. They were taking taro, a potato-like plant, out of the swamps and processing them into food.

The issue of climate warming, or the so-called "weather problem," is of great concern. If we, American Christians, Protestants, and South American Catholics, can work together, we can protect the South American Amazon and the Pantanal. Such religious cooperation would be good, both from a humanitarian point of view and from a climate change policy standpoint.

Last but not least, from the perspective of the unification of the Korean Peninsula: If Protestants in North America and Catholics in South America are united, we will be able to see progress in the unification of North and South Korea.

CHAPTER 9

Pastoral Liaison and Clergy Blessing

First, I would like to talk about "Pastoral Liaison and Clergy Blessing Activities."

This pastor liaison began when Rev. Moon was imprisoned in Danbury in 1984 and asked that 400,000 videotapes be sent to all American churches.

From Rev Moon's arrival in the U.S., the most important thing for him was "how to restore Christianity." Therefore, I think that this pastoral liaison was also the main purpose of Rev. Moon's 50-state speaking tour in the U.S.

In 2002, for one week from March 7, Rev. Moon called the Korean national messiahs in Kona, Hawaii, and held a workshop there. After that, all the Korean national messiahs were excited (or frightened) to see what the next order would be. To their surprise, they were all ordered to go to the United States. What did Rev. Moon wish for? He asked them to bless 144,000 ministers. This must have been a great surprise to the Korean leaders.

In such a situation, Rev. Moon said, "You are not to do this alone." He asked them to call on the Japanese missionaries under their command, who were mostly women.

In Queens, New York, three national messiahs had gathered. One of their mission countries was the Caribbean island of Grenada. This country had many missionaries in South America; in fact, each country in South America had about 120 missionaries. The Korean national messiah from Grenada asked for a large number of missionaries to come to Queens. In addition, there were missionaries called from Belgium and Liechtenstein. On average, 45 missionaries slept and woke up together in the Queens church center, and we blessed 144,000 people.

Rev. Moon, at the age of 80 years old, made up his mind to give one state lecture a day in 50 states. We, too, determined to evangelize Christianity once again with spirit and truth, and began to work so his 50-state tour would be successful.

Rev. Moon spoke in Milwaukee as part of his 50-state speaking tour

I came back to the U.S. from Leda at this time and helped with this tour in Wisconsin, where I have my own home. Rev. Moon came to Wisconsin, and as I visited pastors, I connected with them one more time. They were all very eager to see Rev. Moon, and they brought all their church members. Other states were also experiencing this response. So, when Rev. Moon gave his speech, everyone clapped. Especially the Pentecostals, who felt the Holy Spirit descended on them, were jumping up and down while listening to Rev. Moon's talk. I think this was a wonderful foundation.

Rev. Moon's 50-state tour took place over exactly 50 days from February 25 to April 17, 2001. The transcript of his lecture was published in an excellent 468-page book with photos, "We Will Stand in Oneness!" As the culmination of the 50-state tour, a Blessing Ceremony was held on May 25 at the New York Hilton Hotel for 60 clergy couples. Among them were Rev. T. L. Barrett, Archbishop Milingo and Archbishop Stallings. The marriage of the two Catholic bishops caused quite a stir, as The New York Times ran a story with a picture of

Archbishop Milingo and his wife. Four pastors from Wisconsin, who have been with us for a long time, were also blessed.

Archbishop Milingo's Blessing reported in the New York Times, May 25, 2001

In such a situation, we were asked to work with a total of 144,000 ministers. At that time, there were about 130 Japanese working on the Leda project, and half of them were told to return to the U.S., and the other half were told to continue the Leda project. I was told to come back to the U.S. and go and work with my Korean national messiah, which, strangely enough, was in Queens, New York.

I went to Queens and worked with 45 to 60 women missionaries. We were trying to figure out how we were going to do it since most of the missionaries could not speak English.

But these women were well trained. They understood what was important. They said it was important to move the spirit world because if the spirit world could not be mobilized, 144,000 blessings would be impossible. So, we started the program by getting up early at 5:00 AM, doing a short reading, and then doing 40 bowing conditions. After that, we would have another prayer meeting. The Korean national messiahs were mostly elderly, but they worked together with the young missionaries to fulfill these conditions. The Queens church's goal was to do 3,200 blessings. It took until the end of September, but during that period, the Japanese missionary sisters were constantly fulfilling the conditions.

The Korean national messiahs also did it, and I did the same. In such a situation, we can visibly understand the workings of the spirit world. To give you an example, one time a missionary in Grenada was resting because she was ill. In a dream, a young couple came to her bed and said, "You are working hard. Thank you very much. We will lay hands on you and pray for you, and you will surely get well." She testified that a warm spirit covered her, and she felt better and better. She was able to work the next day.

I believe that the young couple she saw in her dream was my late daughter, Seong Ae, and her husband, who is also in the spirit world. They received the spirit world Blessing on February 16, 2002, at the Seoul Olympic Stadium during the 400 million Couples Blessing.

Yong Jung Ho (my daughter's husband) had told his mother (Mrs. Seon Ji Jeon of the 72 Couples Blessing) in a dream that they had to go to America to assist in the providence of True Parents. He said that his wife's father (meaning me) was participating in that providence, and they were going to cooperate and assist with our activities.

My daughter Seong Ae was born prematurely when we lived in Queens, New York. My wife was visiting her neighbors with her children on Halloween in her home church area when her amniotic fluid bag broke. Seong Ae was born prematurely and died within a few days. Mrs. Seon Ji Jeon was a well-known evangelist at Ewha Woman's University, where she led many members to the church. She was seven months pregnant when she went out to evangelize, but after giving birth to Yong Jung Ho, both mother and child suffered from infections due to poor sanitary conditions. He died at the young age of a few months. Because of the similarities between Seong Ae's and Yong Jung Ho's circumstances, our families are bound by a deep emotional relationship. I was able to know that the spirit world was also moving in response to the providence.

Blessing ceremony with Pastor Boyd and 800 members

Of the three Korean national messiahs in the Queens church, two of them were called Kim, and Rev. Chan Hyun Kim was the National Messiah of Belgium. The one on the right is Rev. Won Jong Kim, the National Messiah of Grenada. And Rev. Pyeong Geun Shin was responsible for Liechtenstein. There were about 20 women who were missionaries in Grenada.

We each formed a team, and at first, we went around on a really serious prayerful foundation, trying to go around the entire Queens borough, which had 8,000 churches. The missionaries didn't speak English. But what moved them was that Rev. Moon called them because he loved American Christianity and to restore America. They said, "If we inherit the sphere of Rev. and Mrs. Moon's heart, this is a goal that we can surely achieve." I was convinced that blessing 144,000 pastors was something we could surely do.

We chose New Greater Bethel Ministries, which was a Queens megachurch of about 8,500 members with three branches. Dr. Boyd was a head pastor. Our missionaries were able to bless 800 people in this church. Japanese sisters would hold the Blessing Ceremony. Because 2,000 people came, even though the sisters went to New York City to buy trays of holy wine, they still didn't have enough. So, they decided to split it up into two because they have three Sunday services. So, we asked the pastors to hold their Holy Communion Service once during the morning Sunday service. Then, the next time we did it, we had everyone drink the holy wine during the noon service, and the ceremony was complete.

At that time, there were five items in the Blessing vows. The secretary of the church read them one by one. Then she asked everyone to say "Yes" in a loud voice in advance and everyone said yes. Then she said the second item and said this Blessing vow again. It was very spiritually exciting, and at the end of it all, I asked them to drink the holy wine, facing each other as if they were married couples. If they were single, they drank it as it was. And if one of their spouses was not with them right now, I instructed them to leave half and go home and have their spouses drink half.

Japanese missionaries rejoicing with Pastor Boyd after the Blessing

This church was unique, and they started their early morning service at 5:00 AM on Tuesday mornings. The line to get in was extremely long, so it was very difficult for everyone to get there. We heard rumors about this church, and we decided to ask Rev. and Mrs. Moon to bless this church, and we offered a special prayer to this church. The spiritual world was moved in that way, and these

Japanese sisters were really devoted to heaven. They brought not only beautiful paper cranes but also various other things.

Even though they could not speak English, the pastor felt something from them. What was it? I think it was love. Love is invisible, and love is more powerful than anything else. The Holy Spirit can move clergy more than words, and when they feel it, they listen to us unconditionally and work with us.

In these activities, I can say that mobilizing the spiritual world—and especially the Holy Spirit, the embodiment of True Mother—is important. Then I believe that this pastoral liaison is a victory. When we challenge these people in various theological debates, they tend to close their minds and are reluctant to even talk to us. But what moves the clergy is prayer, humility, and the desire to be filled with the Holy Spirit. Churches can become the place that God wants us to be and revive Christianity in the United States.

When I saw the miracle of 144,000 Couples Blessing, I wondered why Rev. Moon called Korean national messiahs who did not understand English. Or, why he called Japanese missionaries who did not understand English and had never even opened a Bible. That is where we can see the great achievement and triumph of this amazing secret technique. The missionaries' sincerity, not because they knew the Bible, but because they knew the wishes of Rev. and Mrs. Moon and wanted to fulfill them, was important. Because they got up early in the morning to pray and did the 40 bowing conditions. Some people even got up earlier in the morning to do a cold shower condition. It is a clear fact that the accumulation of such conditions moved the spirit world, the Holy Spirit, and even the pastor of a large megachurch of 8,500 people.

Therefore, many Japanese members understand that the spirit world will move if they pray with confidence and devotion in the morning.

Dr. Boyd, the pastor of this megachurch, has already passed away, and his son has succeeded him. Initially, the son told his father that he did not want to be a pastor. But when it was time to bring his father's hearse and bury him in the grave, the son felt his father come out in spirit and ask him, "Which path are you going to take? … Which way are you going? Do you long for the things of Caesar or do you follow the things of God?" Then the son's eyes opened, and he answered, "Father, I will go your way." And so, once and for all, he withdrew from the business world and began his journey as the pastor's successor.

This person, strangely enough, really admired Bishop Noel Jones. He bought a video of Bishop Noel Jones for all his speeches, imitated his gestures, and tried to rebuild this church in a similar way.

Around this time, he went to Madison Square Garden, then Nassau County, New York, and then the Prudential Center in Newark, New Jersey, to hear True Mother speak at "Peace Starts With Me" rallies. At Nassau County, he filled four buses with church members, and then we went to Nassau County in high spirits. Our connection with his church is still strong, and when I heard his sermon, I thought, "Oh, he has really grown up." And we're getting more members again, in the same way that Bishop Noel Jones did with his speeches.

Pastors are spiritual people, and if we pray and set conditions, they will be sensitive to it. I would like to share that with you all. I don't want you to feel weak because you didn't go to seminary and don't know the Bible, but out of these 1,200 or so missionaries who came to the U.S. to help, maybe only 5% of them understood English. Of the 80 people who came to Queens, only two could speak English and the rest could not at all. However, those who could not speak English achieved more results.

The blessing of 144,000 ministers in the U.S. began on March 15, 2002, and it took about six to ten months to achieve the goal, although the goal differed from region to region. Japanese missionaries have also been in charge of this providence, taking over from one another, and by 2003, it was decided that there could be no true Christian revival unless we address Jesus' unresolved grudge. From this time on, the stage was expanded to Israel, as in the "Middle East Peace Initiative."

My second daughter Akiko spoke in front of 30,000
about the unity of three religion through service of youth

On December 22, 2003, the "Jerusalem Peace Rally" was held, and a ceremony was held in Victory Park in Jerusalem, where representatives of the Jewish, Muslim, and Christian faiths offered crowns to Jesus in a ceremony to release him from his grudge. Approximately 3,000 Unification Church members from all over the world were mobilized for this rally, which eventually became a 30,000-people congregation. Pastors, rabbis, and Muslim clergy who had been connected in the U.S. attended the conference. In order to make the rally a success, I paired up with a local member for about 40 days and went door-to-door in Jerusalem to invite people to the rally.

*Members of the three major religions gather in front of the Dome of the Rock,
the sacred site of the three major religions.*

However, some areas were exclusively Jewish while others were populated by Palestinians, and if you asked them to come to the "Peace Rally," they would tell you that, for them, "peace" will come only when the other side completely disappears from the world. The local member explained at length how many of his relatives had been killed by the other side while showing us a thick album. The magnitude of the feud between Jews and Palestinians was immeasurable.

To remove their hatred, we explained that the three religions originally came from Abraham, and Jesus is the fruit of these religions. If the leaders of the three religions come together to put the crown on Jesus, the resentment of Jesus would be removed and wars in the Middle East would be resolved. This rally would have been very meaningful.

My second daughter, Akiko, spoke proudly before an audience of 30,000 people at this time. That's because the youth of the three major religions, centering on the service of the youth, had achieved unity.

CHAPTER 10

Las Vegas Providence

I would like to talk about my time in Las Vegas. Rev. Moon stayed in Las Vegas for about four years before he ascended to the spiritual world, and he performed various important providential acts here.

I attended the GPF (Global Peace Festival) Washington Rally (August 9, 2008) while working at hoon dok hae (read and study together) home church in Queens, New York. We worked to mobilize my connected home church people, pastors, political figures, and even members of Congress. We brought success to the GPF event. A few days after the conference, I was to attend a breakfast meeting of pastors, but just before I entered a church in Queens, I felt a pain as if I had been hit on the right side of my head with an iron bat, and I blacked out.

A brother noticed that something was wrong with me and called for help. A doctor from New York Family Church named Dr. Adachi happened to be there and immediately told them to administer three aspirin pills to me to counter the stroke. I was taken straight to the emergency room.

When I recovered enough, I returned to my home in Milwaukee for further testing. When I went in for an MRI, there were about three doctors there who were specialists, and they decided to operate on me. I was in rehab for about four or five months.

In the midst of all this, my wife attended the "Original Divine Principle Workshop" training session of Rev. Kyok Jeong Eu. My wife received spiritual benefits at the workshop. She met Dr. Cho there and told him about my condition. Dr. Cho explained that if I would come to Las Vegas, he would heal me completely. Dr. Cho was so convincing that my wife and I decided to go to Las Vegas to start treatment immediately.

At the same time, I believe that Rev. Moon had been thinking of the Las Vegas providence as a last trump card for a long time. Of course, during that transitional period, he was thinking of making the Pantanal the site of the so-called "Kingdom of Heaven," but as soon as the communist government came to power in Brazil, they began to impose a huge tax on our property and educational centers, and this almost destroyed the goal we wanted to achieve. Because of this and other factors, it was difficult for Rev. Moon's providence to progress smoothly.

Moreover, a few weeks earlier, on July 19, 2008, Rev. Moon and Mrs. Moon were involved in a catastrophic helicopter accident behind Cheongshim International Medical Center in Korea. Several of their grandchildren were on board. Miraculously, no one died, but several people were injured and shortly after everyone was evacuated from the helicopter, it exploded. It was such a catastrophe that I wondered how anyone could survive something so severely damaged. Satan caused this, and Rev. Moon said that he was sent to hell. He said that the Kingdom of Heaven will come to the earthly realm only when all evil spirits are liberated, including those in Las Vegas, the city of sin where lewdness and greed hang out, and in Hollywood, which is a sub-city of Las Vegas.

On August 27, 2008, 40 days after the helicopter accident, Rev. Moon said it had the same meaning of liberation and release as the 40 days after Jesus went to the cross and ascended to heaven. And that is how the Las Vegas providence began. According to one theory, Rev. Moon's Las Vegas providence was as much of a hardship as his years in Hungnam prison (North Korean labor camp), where Satan caused suffering to such an extent the point that Rev. Moon almost lost his life.

From that time on, Rev. Moon thought that this final battle would have to be fought in such a place where gambling and whoremongers hang out. I do not know if I actually knew the city of Las Vegas at that time, but I was thinking that the final battle would be fought in a place of great sexual sin and greed and that Satan would be completely overthrown there.

Rev. Moon developed many activities in Las Vegas with the idea of bringing Satan down to his knees in the city where Satan hangs out. One of them was a "dream team" as some people called it, composed of about 12 outstanding American brothers, such as Michael Jenkins; Mark Anderson, who is now a retired state lawmaker and judge; Patrick Hickey; Mike Smith; and so on. However, they were given very difficult tasks as there was a great deal of spiritual pressure to follow this providence. One or two people dropped out, and eventually this dream team, the PR team, dissipated and eventually disappeared.

Wreckage of the July 19, 2008 helicopter accident

Rev. Moon instead began looking for 21 righteous people. What kind of people? For example, there was Mimi, who was the vice president of the Ariana Hotel at that time. Others included Ms. Reiko, a descendant of the Tokugawa family; Fred Nassiri, the former owner of IPEC (International Peace Education Center); Mr. Lee, who was in charge of the construction of IPEC, and so on. They were all excellent, capable people who were also independent-minded, had big capacities, and had a lot of money.

Rev. Moon said if we could find 21 righteous people in Las Vegas, the city would be turned upside down, and Rev. Park and others worked hard to find 21 righteous people. Unfortunately, this search for righteous people did not go well. Rev. Moon also decided to leave the East Garden in New York and purchase a new house in Las Vegas. On December 7, 2009, he purchased a house in Las Vegas, which is now called the Cheon Hwa Gung. Before that, in 2008, he purchased the first Shin Hwa Gung, which is now occupied by the Kwon Jin Moon's (Rev. Moon's son) couple.

On May 5, 2009, Rev. and Mrs. Moon held the Settlement of the Abel UN and the Golden Wedding and Memorial Celebration of Ascension and Unity. In other words, this coronation ceremony was held in conjunction with a ceremony to commemorate those who had already passed away and who had made great spiritual achievements. Rev. Moon prayed at different places and times, held special prayers, and made certain proclamations.

On June 19, 2010, at 2:20 AM, Rev. and Mrs. Moon prayed a special prayer and made a fresh start before heaven. They were going to declare to hold this proclamation conference all over the world from now on. Rev. Moon held the reading sessions irregularly. Sometimes he told us to gather at 3:00 AM, sometimes he told us to come at 2:30 AM, and so on. It was not a regular meeting that started at 5:00 AM and ended at 8:00 AM. Sometimes he talked about the Word of God for 14 hours.

Rev. and Mrs. Moon fishing at Lake Mead

Las Vegas members fishing

Rev. Moon caught a golden carp at Lake Mead

Then again, Rev. Moon was constantly fishing. What is that? He said evil spirits from all over the world gathered at Lake Mead. He also said the spirits of people who have died in water-related accidents also came here. They constantly went out to Lake Mead to fish.

This one on the right is a golden carp. When this photo was taken on June 7, 2011, it immediately had to be rejoiced by everyone, so the whole world was instructed to read the designated book there at 5:00 AM Las Vegas time, all together.

There were also conditions for catching fish. For this 24-hour period, both the boat captain and Rev. Moon himself set conditions for fishing. Lake Mead has quite a lot of striped bass, and at the very bottom you can catch catfish, really big catfish. At the same time, you can catch a lot of carp; the lake practically crawls with them. Rev. Moon's condition was that striped bass meant white people, catfish meant black people, and carp meant yellow people. He put harsh conditions on the boat captain and himself, saying that unless he caught four striped bass, four catfish, and four carp each day, for a total of 12 fish, he should continue to fish.

As you may know, Las Vegas gets unbelievably hot in the summer. At times, the temperature rises to about 45 degrees (115 degrees Fahrenheit). It is no mean feat to spend a whole day on a boat without getting any sleep and making conditions. Japanese boat captains who completed this mission include Mr. Kensaku Takahashi and Mr. James Nada. Therefore, when Rev. Moon was in Las Vegas, he devoted himself to fishing, and he set up another condition, a condition of releasing evil spirits.

Another providential development in Las Vegas was to distribute 120,000 copies of Rev. Moon's autobiography in Las Vegas. This was a huge task, so volunteers from all over the country were called to Las Vegas. Mrs. Kyoko Yamaguchi, the oldest member in Las Vegas, advertised the autobiography on billboards. We bought billboards and tried to promote it there for two or three months. We decided to buy three other locations until we distributed 120,000 copies. We were able to do so with donations from various sources. We reached the distribution of 120,000 books on July 4, 2011, Independence Day in the U.S. I remember that we had a big barbecue in the Cheon Hwa Gung to celebrate Independence Day and the victorious distribution of 120,000 copies of his autobiography.

Rev. Moon had high expectations for the Ariana Hotel. There was a person named Mimi who was the vice president of the board of directors of the hotel, and she made various arrangements for us. At the True Parents' 51st wedding ceremony, many brothers, sisters, and leaders gathered at the hotel, and the speeches lasted about 12 hours. He explained to us that the Coming Age of Heaven had started once before, but that it would essentially start today. The Coming Age of Heaven was on April 18, 2011. The book that Rev. Moon would have to read was called, "The Proclamation of the Establishment of the Word of True Parents of Heaven, Earth, and Humankind," the last spoken word that Rev. Moon loved the most. He would proclaim it throughout the world for a long time to come. The first event was held at the Ariana Hotel. At that time, the national messiahs of Korea, Japan, and the U.S. came, as well as state leaders from all over the U.S., and we held a grand event at the Ariana Hotel.

Rev. Moon always had the restoration of the Christian churches in mind everywhere he went. When he was in Las Vegas, he listened to the report of 120 pastors who had visited Korea, selected 12 of them, and asked them to come to Las Vegas immediately. At that time, 12 leaders from Korea were also there, and he asked us to put 24 of them on a boat and go fishing. That was one of the major conditions.

The reading sessions held by Rev. Moon were not like those held at East Garden or Cheon Jeong Gung in Korea, where the reading starts at 5:00 AM and lasts for four or five hours. He started at 5:00 AM and continued until 7:00 PM, or 14 hours of passionate talks while pouring out his sweat.

One time, brothers and sisters from Saitama, Japan, were in Las Vegas, and he talked for 14 hours straight. They wanted to go to the bathroom but could not easily do so. Some of them endured these 14 hours while squirming. They came in large numbers once every two months from Japan, met Rev. and Mrs. Moon at Cheon Hwa Gung, and then visited places like the Grand Canyon, etc. They were given a lot of love and returned home fully satisfied.

I think the most moving of these was still Rev. Moon's reading of the scriptures or speaking of the Word of God at the Cheon Hwa Gung. I especially treasured his commentary on the final speech, "The Proclamation of the Word of the True Parents of Heaven, Earth, and Humankind," in which he explained the Word of God word by word. I attended several times and took notes of the commentary that was given. Even now, I still find the content of Rev. Moon's talks to be profound and valuable.

Another thing that Rev. and Mrs. Moon needed to do in Las Vegas was to promote Happy Health in Las Vegas. Many people, especially hotel owners, are sick, and Rev. and Mrs. Moon wanted to prove that Happy Health could treat them and solve their various problems.

Dr. Cho was called from Korea. His whole family are church members, and his lineage comes from Mrs. Moon's Cho family lineage. It is a really meritorious family.

Dr. Cho studied under a famous 90-year-old doctor in Korea in the field of acupuncture and Chinese medicine. From there, he learned oriental medicine like acupuncture and moxibustion. Rev. Moon asked him to investigate how to apply Happy Health to Oriental medicine, and that was why Rev. Moon invited him to Las Vegas.

Wongu Oriental Medicine University

Rev. Moon said, "In the future, we are going to establish a graduate school of oriental medicine here. You have to be such a pioneer." Earlier, when I had had my stroke, my wife met Dr. Cho and he told her she should call me immediately, saying "I will treat your husband's illness myself and heal him completely." I came to Las Vegas and received treatment from Dr. Cho every morning and evening. Because of this, I found that the aftereffects of my stroke were gradually being healed.

Mrs. Moon told me that I could do more while I was receiving treatment to regain my health. She said the Japanese missionaries visiting Las Vegas needed more training. I was chosen among Japanese leaders to give them education and teach tradition.

I've been with them for about two and a half years, I guess, and there are people who have grown into highly competent missionaries now. One missionary went on an overseas mission to Moldova, which is located next to Ukraine. Another went on a mission to South America. It moves my heart that these Japanese missionaries grew up so well, despite facing various difficult places, and that they courageously chose to go and succeed on overseas missions.

Rev. Kyok Jong Eu lectured on the Principle at the South Point Hotel, which has about 3,000 rooms. Rev. Moon wanted to purchase such a hotel and invite leaders from around the world to hear lectures on the Theory of Original Substance of the Divine Principle; he wanted to see people transformed from the bottom up. This was the most important ideal of Rev. Moon's vision. Unfortunately, some of the leaders said that it was not economically feasible to do this. In the end, while Rev. Moon was unable to buy a large hotel, he built the IPEC (International Peace Education Center), which can accommodate around 800 people.

In the process of doing so, Rev. Moon also issued several important instructions. On July 12, 2011, he said that because God's providence was now completed, all blessed families around the world should read the scriptures and inherit the victory sphere on that day. This was the second time on July 12, wasn't it? In this way, we can see Rev. Moon's desperate desire to have blessed families inherit the spiritual foundation that he achieved while looking at the whole world.

While I was in treatment at Happy Health, I helped educate the Japanese missionaries and the guests they brought with them. I occasionally conducted service activities such as two-day retreats for those they had evangelized, Sunshine Cleanups, sports tournaments, etc. I helped them with a sincere heart.

Rev. Moon said that although Las Vegas is located inland, it is an important base of oceanic providence and is even the base of the Pacific Rim civilization. He further said that this triangle of Hawaii, Alaska, and Las Vegas is the central base of the Pacific Ocean providence. Thus, a shipyard had to be built here, and the Won Mo (mother ship), a very light but fast ship, was built in Korea and brought to Las Vegas. The launching ceremony was held at the Las Vegas Peace Palace, a name that was later changed to IPEC when IPEC was established.

Important people in the business world, such as the hotel owners and the right-hand man of the governor, the mayor, and so on, were invited to the launching ceremony. They knew Rev. Moon would do something unusual—he was going to build a shipyard in Las Vegas. They said this was interesting and they wanted to go there, so they joined us. When they saw the Won Mo, they were truly surprised. They were amazed to see such a smooth hull running at such a high speed, and they thought it had amazing technology.

When we explained what kind of shipbuilding we planned to do, they said that it was not impossible to build a shipyard in Las Vegas. We came to the point where we, as a company with a financial base in Las Vegas, decided to invest in Las Vegas. That is why Rev. Moon established the Won Mo Pyeong-ae Peace Foundation.

Next, regarding the pastors of Christian churches, we were told we had to get 3,000 people to attend the Original Divine Principle training sessions. We were given a deadline, but our foundation was not as big as we needed. Rev. Moon compromised and said, "Well, at least, hold a big conference in Las Vegas." The name of the event was the "Registration in God's Homeland." The main pastors who participated in the event were given the names of the main Korean clans. These pastors were all in harmony and received Korean names because they had helped lift Rev. and Mrs. Moon to the top in the United States.

IPEC opening ceremony

Rev. Moon has been constantly promoting the restoration of Christianity, the unification of the North and South Korea, and the restoration of the United States. These things were always in his mind wherever he went.

On December 17, 2011, North Korea Chairman Kim Jong Il passed away. Mr. and Mrs. Hyung Jin Moon (Rev. Moon's son) went to Kim Jong Il's funeral. Rev. Moon gave various instructions to Mr. and Mrs. Hyung Jin Moon before their leaving for the funeral.

In Las Vegas, Rev. Moon's two major projects were to create IPEC and educate many thousands of people there. The other was to develop oriental medicine, with Dr. Cho as the core. At first, Dr. Cho held training sessions and gave treatments in his own small house, but eventually, the Nevada State Council of Oriental Medicine recognized him and established an excellent graduate school here, called Wongu University of Oriental Medicine.

The IPEC building was once owned by one of the 21 righteous men in Las Vegas. He was so inspired by Rev. Moon that he wanted to help him as much as possible. As a result, he sold our church two valuable buildings at a very low price.

I was able to spend the last four years of Rev. Moon's life around him. I think I attended 70% of the reading sessions at the Cheon Hwa Gung. I have 38 notebooks of notes alone. These are precious speeches from Rev. Moon's hoon dok hae reading sessions

In 2012, Rev. Moon returned to Korea. He gave his final public speech, on the Abel Women UN Inauguration, at the Cheongshim Peace World Center on July 16, 2012. Fortunately, I was able to participate in this event.

Rev. Moon's last public speech on July 16, 2012

After the ceremony, Rev. Moon came to the reading session to celebrate the formation of Abel Women's UN, and it turned into a long celebration. It just so happened that on July 1, 2012, Rev. Moon's best friend from his Waseda University days, Dr. Duk Moon Aum, passed away. Perhaps because of this, Rev. Moon spoke fondly about his Waseda days and his many different memories from that time. For instance, Rev. Moon recalled being a student at Waseda University. One day, he saw a friend walk by with a dark face and he began to cry, thinking, "Why couldn't I save this person?"

Rev. Moon also recalled meeting Dr. Aum, and then how he was tortured at the Totsuka police station in Japan. His deep memories of his Waseda days moved me since I am also a graduate of Waseda University. I was interested to learn new things about Rev. Moon's Waseda days, and this became an invaluable lesson reading session.

After this speech, though, Rev. Moon's health took a turn for the worse. I heard that he went to Geomundo Island in Korea after the fishing tournament in Cheongpyeong. He had been fishing there and fell ill during a rainstorm, so he came back to Seoul. Mrs. Moon said that since her husband's condition was getting worse, it would be good for him to be admitted to the Catholic University's St. Mary's Hospital in Seoul. Despite everyone's efforts and prayers, his blood oxygen level fell to severely low levels, and his condition worsened again, so he was transferred to Cheongshim International Medical Center.

Rev. Moon's condition continued to deteriorate, and as you all know, on September 3, 2012, at 1:54 AM, he was consecrated in the presence of Mrs. Moon and their children at Cheongshim International Medical Center.

Rev. Moon's Seonghwa Ceremony

I believe that Rev. Moon never stopped thinking about how to establish the Kingdom of Heaven on Earth and live there, even for a second. When I went to Korea in 1971, the first speech given by Rev. Moon was about the "establishment of God's homeland." I wondered how God's country would be created. However, the God's country that Rev. Moon was talking about was a community of the heart. As it turns out, this means a community of blessed families whose original sin has been removed, and they were connected to God's lineage and freely operate in that realm. That is what expanded the Kingdom of Heaven.

In 1971, Rev. Moon did not use the term "Cheon Il Guk," but he said that it was the Kingdom of God. He has been saying the same thing for 50 years now: "I am going to establish the Kingdom of Heaven, the Kingdom of God. That is why I came here."

Even though Rev. Moon had been preparing for Foundation Day in 2013, he had to entrust the entire mission to True Mother (Mrs. Moon). How disappointed he must have felt. Furthermore, I wonder how much it must have pained Rev. Moon to see his children pushing their own authority to the fore and being at odds with Mrs. Moon or being at odds with their brothers and sisters. I can't help but cry when I explore Rev. Moon's feelings. How can we release Rev. and Mrs. Moon from their bitterness and at the same time, how can we establish God's Kingdom, which he has been talking about his whole life, in this land? This is an important task for all our blessed families and CheonBo families. This is the most important task that we must accomplish during the lifetime of Mrs. Moon. On September 15, 2012, when I participated in the Cheongshim Peace World Center's Cosmic Seonghwa Ceremony (Rev. Moon's funeral) in Korea, I vowed to create an ideal country, the Kingdom of Heaven, here in this land.

In the meantime, on October 26, 2012, Mrs. Moon returned to Las Vegas, where the 20th anniversary of the Women's Federation for World Peace (WFWP) was held. Sun Jin Moon read the Founders' address on behalf of Mrs. Moon, but Mrs. Moon also suddenly came out and spoke at the event. She was wearing sunglasses because of health-related pain in her eyes, but her speech touched my heart.

On October 28, Mrs. Moon began a journey across the U.S. in a wonderful Mercedes Benz bus that she had purchased. She traveled the United States, together with members, in the spirit of the late Rev. Moon, taking into consideration the 40 years of hardships in the United States.

She finally reached New York City, and on November 4, about 3,000 people gathered at the Manhattan Center to hear her speak.

Mrs. Moon had difficult words for our blessed families. She said that our work for the U.S. providence had failed. It was truly heartbreaking for us to hear that. She said if we did not fulfill our responsibility this time, the United States, the world, and our descendants would bear a greater burden of indemnity. We thought we had done our best, but the revival of Christianity, in particular, had not progressed as fast as we had hoped. I felt truly sorry to Rev. and Mrs. Moon to hear this.

But this time, Dr. Yong (former continental director of South East Asia) came to the U.S., and I believe that we are now in such a time of the Great Spiritual Awakening Movement, where we have to mobilize the spiritual world, restore the Christian church, restore the United States, and restore the world.

It reminded me of Rev. Moon's Las Vegas providence. It was a gambling spirit, spending money on it constantly, losing and losing, but eventually winning. Have you ever seen Rev. Moon gambling? In that unusually tense situation, mainly at the gambling hall of the Ariana Hotel, from morning to night, Rev. Moon didn't actually gamble, but he stood there and gave instructions to Dr. Yang or Dr. Kim. Even if he lost, he would spend twice the amount of money and eventually win. This means that one should not look at Rev. Moon as if he is gambling. In this Las Vegas gambling hall, where Satan controls all things through the mafia, the Messiah would win over all the gambling champions and won a lot of their money. The Messiah won that fortune from Satan. That is the purpose and challenge of Rev. Moon's one big thing called gambling.

Another thing is that we don't have money, so we don't understand the seriousness of gambling, but there are people who lose, say $20 million, which is an order of magnitude larger than the amount of money they lost. How do you think that person feels when he or she goes home? They would be out of the game for about six months because they lost $20 million.

Then Rev. Moon came up with an idea that he said should be shared with casino owners by Mimi. He thought, "What if we set up something like this, where the various owners donate one-tenth of their gambling money from the 30 or so gambling parlors. Then that money would be used for education in Africa and other emerging countries, even if they lose $20 million. If we set up such an institution, even if gamblers lose $20 million, they would not mind losing. One-tenth of the loss would go to education in underdeveloped areas. The Sahara Desert is expanding and consuming arable land because of desertification. What if we planted trees there and made the area greener so that more people could live there again?"

The idea was that even if people lost $20 million to gambling, if it was to be used for the greening campaign in the Sahara Desert, they could think they had done a good deed, wouldn't they, these wealthy people? That is why Rev. Moon initially came to us and told us to form a dream team and meet with major hotel owners to persuade them about this idea.

Again, the idea was not to just gamble to make your pocket bigger, but to use a tenth of it for the children in those underdeveloped countries, or for people who are struggling with desertification, or for people who are suffering from various viruses. If we make and distribute vaccines to these places, they will stand up for that. That's what we are contributing with this one-tenth donation. The Las Vegas hotel owners are doing a great thing. Everyone does not mind losing in gambling.

Rev. Moon also wanted Lake Mead to be a place where families could come and enjoy themselves.

We respected Rev. Moon's desire to change "Sin City" 180 degrees through education, and we prayed that IPEC will become a mecca for education. With these words, we conclude our providence in Las Vegas.

CHAPTER 11

The First Seven-Year Course of the Heavenly Cosmic Canaan Restoration (2013-2020)

1. Foundation Day Proclamation

Mrs. Hak Ja Han Moon named the period from 2013 to 2020 as the First Seven-Year Course of the Heavenly Cosmic Canaan Restoration.

After the death of Rev. Moon on September 3, 2012, we entered a difficult time emotionally. However, Rev. Moon had repeatedly said that we would hold the Foundation Day celebration on January 13, 2013. Finally, on January 13, 2013 (February 22), the Foundation Day was celebrated by True Mother (Mrs. Hak Ja Han Moon) in Korea.

The Foundation Day had two primary elements: One was the ceremony for the enthronement of Heaven, Earth, and Humankind, True Parents, and Cheon Il Guk (Kingdom of Heaven on Earth). The other was the Marriage Blessing for Registration in Cheon Il Guk. Therefore, Mrs. Moon herself wore a purple gown to perform this ceremony at the accession ceremony of Cheon Il Guk. Next was the Blessing Ceremony. At this time, she was dressed in pure white and wore a small, woman's crown on her head.

Mrs. Moon at Foundation Day 2013

What is this Foundation Day, and what is its significance? To put it simply in the words of Rev. and Mrs. Moon, on January 13, 2013, Cheon Il Guk Foundation Day was proclaimed. They said that Foundation Day marks the beginning of the substantial Cheon Il Guk and is a day of joy in the history of humanity. True Parents said that it was the day when a new history would begin and that it was a day that must come despite the fallen history of mankind. In other words, we always hear about the "God Kingdom of Heaven," but this Foundation Day is the foundation for the start of the creation of the real Kingdom of God. That is why it is called Foundation Day.

During Foundation Day, there were several events. The Cham Bumo Gyeong (True Parents' speech) book was published. Later, the first meeting of the Committee for the Reestablishment of Heaven and Earth was held on May 12. Mrs. Moon also retraced True Parents' steps and went to the top of 12 mountains in the Alps to lay conditions for the success of the 13 regions. She succeeded despite setting a demanding schedule for herself and others.

True Mother was in mourning for three years at that time, so the flow of the providence slowed somewhat. The most notable event of these years happened in 2014. Dr. Balcomb, who was newly appointed to the president of the Family Federation for World Peace and Unification-USA, started the God's Hope for America tour, in which he and other blessed families visited the 50 U.S. holy grounds that Rev. and Mrs. Moon had established. I think Dr. Balcomb took more than two months to do this 50-state memorial tour. The tour group, which traveled in a caravan, would visit holy grounds every day. The members of each state would get together at the holy grounds, and Dr. Balcomb and others would remember Rev. and Mrs. Moon.

In 2014, on December 21, in Las Vegas, Mrs. Moon and pastors gathered together. That was the first time she declared herself the "Only Begotten Daughter." I think this is very significant. In such a situation, Hyung Jin Moon went his own way, and on March 4, Sun Jin Moon was inaugurated as the World President of the Family Federation for World Peace and Unification (FFWPU), replacing Hyung Jin Moon. On May 28, 2015, we had the opening ceremony of IPEC (International Peace Education Center). It took three years for its construction.

The grand opening of IPEC inspired many nostalgic feelings, as old missionaries from Japan and young missionaries came to the event. Mrs. Moon also gave us her words, and the children sang with great energy.

2. Madison Square Garden "Peace Starts With Me" Revival Rally (July 15, 2017)

Finally, in 2017, True Mother (Mrs. Moon) started to move more boldly and instructed us to hold the first "Peace Starts With Me" rally at Madison Square Garden in New York City on July 15, 2017.

This was a daunting task for us, but everyone was determined to do it with the attitude of "Let's make it a success."

With Lifeline Church members at Madison Square Garden

On June 24, 2017, we had a meeting of the American Clergy Leadership Conference (ACLC). The main concern of the heads of the churches in that area was how to shake these sleeping brothers and sisters once again and push them forward to Madison Square Garden. Fortunately, these three Japanese missionary sisters were assigned to Queens where I was. Dr. Ki Hoon Kim thought these Japanese missionaries probably could not speak English, so he decided to leave them to me.

This was a big mobilization. However, as I had experienced during the blessing of the 144,000 clergy, the Japanese missionaries innately knew how to win the hearts of pastors even if they could not speak English. So when I was told, "He will send three missionaries to me," I felt that I had already won.

Immediately after Sunday service on July 6, 2017, I got my rental car together and started going around to churches from morning to night. If the pastor wasn't at the church, I would go to his house. We planned our schedule with this in mind, and we set an aggressive schedule for the Madison Square Garden activities. On Sundays, four teams would visit 12 churches. These included: Bishop Blackwood's New Jerusalem church; Pentecostal Lifeline, a church that we have known for about 40 years; and Pastor Raphael's church. We faithfully visited the churches we had in contact with over the years.

Japanese missionaries could not stay at Queens Family Church because it was already full, so they stayed at the New Yorker Hotel in Manhattan. Because of this extra travel time, they often returned home after midnight. We had a hard schedule, with our members driving their own cars to take them to New Yorker Hotel. In addition to that, they went from church to church. I think these three Japanese missionaries were a real catalyst for the victory of Madison Square Garden.

About 10 days passed and Dr. Kim said to me, "The missionaries are doing an incredibly hard schedule. I heard that they haven't done a single wash. Mr. Ikeno, please think about this for a minute. I don't mind the hard schedule, but they are women, too, so please take care of them."

Dr. Kim gave me money and I invited the missionaries on a cruise on the Hudson River. It was the Fourth of July holiday, and we had a nice dinner and watched the big fireworks. They were really happy, and after watching the fireworks display for about an hour and a half at night with wonderful meals, they were able to regain their energy and work hard for the Madison Square Garden rally.

Independence Day fireworks on the Hudson River

For this first rally at Madison Square Garden, we did not concentrate only on Christian churches but visited other religions, such as Buddhism, Tenrikyo, Mormonism, Judaism, and Hinduism, with which we have been in contact. This area of Queens is said to be a melting pot of religions, and if you take a short walk, you can find temples of different denominations around the Queens Family Church. At first, I went around with Japanese missionaries to the denominations as much as I could. But gradually we narrowed our focus to Christian churches. One place is called Pentecostal Lifeline. After the Sunday service was over, we set up tables, put on music, and showed a video on a monitor while church members came out of the exit. Many had heard about the July 15 Madison Square Garden rally, but some of them missed getting the bus tickets. To completely mobilize all of the church members to the event, we set up tables, got everyone to sign in, and gave them the vouchers.

Gradually, specific numbers of tickets or buses began to be discussed at leadership meetings. We started to fill in the pastors of the churches we had been visiting with specific numbers of people who would be coming. At this leaders' meeting in New York City, led by co-chairs Dr. Balcomb and Archbishop Stallings, we were estimating that Queens would have roughly 12 buses.

The Christian members were quite interested in who the gospel singers were going to be. Almost everyone knew the name of Bishop Hezekiah Walker, and I think the 2,000-voice choir captured the hearts of the participants. And then the powerful singer Yolanda Adams, I think, had an impact beyond what they expected. I think that gospel singers were the key to this Christian rally.

About 600 young people who attended the Generation Peace Academy (GPA) and the young people who graduated from the workshop joined the group, and everyone danced and sang "Everyone Praise" under the direction of Pastor Curtis Farrow. That was a truly appropriate song. The choir, the young people, and all the people were standing up, singing, and dancing. Mrs. Hak Ja Han Moon talked about the role of Christianity, which she called "Peace Starts With Me," and how world peace begins with the unification of one's mind and body. She emphasized that although it is true that external things such as the prohibition of war will lead to peace, such a world will be realized through the unification of our individual minds and bodies, and through harmony within our families.

I worked with members of the Lifeline Pentecostal Church. They were all delightful people, and many of them were of Caribbean descent, like Jamaican. There was already a big choir on the bus. We made a lot of sandwiches, and one, two, three, everyone ate well, sang well, and there were a lot of very happy people. The co-chairs, Dr. Balcomb and Archbishop Stallings, were harmonizing moderators.

The victory celebration after the July 15 rally was held at East Garden and Belvedere. Many young people came, and Mrs. Moon spoke to the members. We attended the victory celebration at Belvedere. Then, because my wife brought a guest from Wisconsin, we took her to various places in New York City, such as the memorial for 9/11 Ground Zero, and other places.

Months later, in November 2017, a rally was held in Seoul for the peaceful reunification of North and South Korea. Bishop Noel Jones participated in this rally. It was cold outside, but what moved him was the spiritual aspect of the event. Especially when Mrs. Moon hit the gong three times, he said it was a prompting "from God to me." He said, "This is the group that can truly unify North and South Korea peacefully and create world peace." He received such a shock, just as Paul was choked by God, and since then he has become deeply involved with us.

After this, Mrs. Moon's world tour started in Senegal. On January 18, 2018, the Africa Summit was held there. She also visited the island of Gorée, where she prayed for the liberation of 200 billion spirits. Mrs. Moon emphasized the importance of Christianity and the need to create an interfaith association, so the International Association for Peace and Development (IAPD) was officially launched at the 22nd True Family Values Banquet in Chicago. Bishop Wood from Wisconsin, who had worked with us for a long time to overcome persecution, joined us and received the Distinguished Service Award.

Madison Square Garden "Peace Starts With Me" rally

3. "Peace Starts With Me" Nassau County Coliseum Revival Rally (November 12, 2018)

In the meantime, the decision was made to hold another rally on November 12 at the Nassau County Coliseum. I immediately accepted the invitation and went up to New York. An advantage this time was that not only were there Japanese missionaries to help with outreach but also Pastor Tanya Edwards' brother, Joel Barnaby, who is a Pentecostal pastor and has a fine, old church in Pennsylvania. This pastor's grandfather was the founder of the oldest church in Jamaica, so if you say that it was my grandfather who built that church, people of Pentecostal and Jamaican descent would welcome you with open arms. Many people know about Pastor Barnaby's grandfather and how much he contributed to Jamaica.

Pastor Joel Barnaby is a genuinely open-minded person. He invited Pastor Tanya Edwards to a Unification Church event; she went to the conference, and they have been connected ever since. Pastor Barnaby is also the spiritual parent of his sister, Pastor Tanya Edwards. The great merit is that he is a pastor who has a generous heart and expresses himself warmly and gets things done. Pastor Barnaby's assistance helped greatly with the mobilization for the Nassau County rally several times.

Mrs. Moon gave an award to President Macky Sall of Senegal

Rather than going around the same places as much as possible, we reached out to new church congregations. I think it was possible to gradually develop new churches, especially with the presence of Pastor Barnaby. This was how GPA brothers and Japanese missionaries got together and danced various dances. It would have been unthinkable in the past, but the second generation of members danced a variety of dances. It is a little different from our time. When they were here, the banquet was gorgeous.

The people in charge of the New York and New Jersey rally gathered at the headquarters from time to time, and not only did they give us proof of the successes and failures of the rally, but they also gave us detailed information on the number of people in attendance, the number of buses, and other such matters. The meeting of the directors was led by Dr. Balcomb, Dr. Kim, and Dr. Michael Jenkins. Mr. Rendel constantly presented detailed statistics to us and told us that the mobilization was still insufficient; however, we were also being stimulated. We have five boroughs in New York, so we were constantly doing outreach. We also included New Jersey from time to time, so it was a large leadership meeting.

Work with Pastor Joel Barnaby (center)

In Queens, there is an association of churches. They have a breakfast meeting once every two months or so, and all the different Christian denominations get together there. It is also a place to advertise what kind of conventions and events our denomination is going to hold and to invite people to participate in them. We participated in this breakfast event and promoted the Nassau County Coliseum Rally. We had about 300 participants, and they mostly responded positively.

One missionary sister whose father is Nigerian and whose mother is Japanese (and her mother lives in Ehime, Japan) joined my team, and that was a big advantage. She was glad to tell people she is a child born of Nigerian and Japanese parents. The missionary's father's Nigerian birthplace and this Pastor Dominic were from the same place.

This was another miracle in some respects, and you got a big welcome from that church. This is the association of the church in Queens. People from various denominations came to the church in a friendly atmosphere. There, they received awards from the executive pastors of this organization. They had testimonies and entertainment, and I think it's a really good organization.

Speaking at the Lifeline Church

And we were fresh, too, with three new missionaries (we still get emails and Facebook messages saying how much they miss us). As the Nassau County Coliseum rally day approached, we were on an incredibly tight schedule. We had to expand our outreach, and Pastor Joel Barnaby would come to a new church, so we were able to develop relationships with some new churches this time. From time to time, our members from Queens Family Church would get together with members from Long Island church and hand out flyers about the Nassau County Coliseum rally. Then a member of Bishop Woodall saw that flyer of the convention and called her bishop. We made an appointment for the next day and made a deep connection.

Pastor Dominic has a church in a place called the Jamaica area of Queens. It's African American church. He is from the same place as my member's father that I mentioned earlier. Pastor Dominic held a three- or four-day revival meeting, and we participated in it. We visited a church in Long Island, made a friendship with the pastor there, and unexpectedly many people attended the breakfast prayer meeting that we planned.

Breakfast prayer meetings were usually held twice a month, using the New Yorker Hotel ballroom or other appropriate banquet halls in other areas. It was effective to invite people who had visited and connected with ACLC in the past, to make friendships with other pastors there, and to invite them not only to come to the rally but also to participate as members of ACLC in the future.

On November 8, 2018, the 59th True Children's Day was held at Belvedere, where everyone from New Jersey to New York gathered for the final week of the rally. Afterward, everyone went to the holy ground, where we prayed passionately to make the week a success once again. After almost everyone left, the missionaries and members from Queens stayed behind and had a testimony meeting there.

At the breakfast prayer meeting at the New Yorker Hotel on the verge of the Nassau County rally, we had over 300 people come. Various pastors shared their testimonies about how many buses they were preparing, etc., and it inspired other pastors. I think this Sunday was very important.

We finished the worship service early and divided into teams to visit 20 churches on November 11. We had to plan the schedule—we would go to this church at this time, this church after that, and then we would make up the four churches. So finally, on November 12, we mobilized members early in the morning and sent them to their respective churches. We had been to and served Pastor Boyd's church a number of times, and we had decided to send four buses there, one for me and one for each of the other GPA members.

Nassau County Coliseum had only two entrances open, and there was a long line of people waiting to get in. But once you got inside, you could hear the songs that were being sung by the 2,000-member chorus. Pastor Curtis Farrow, a renown conductor, was leading everyone, and he was training everyone on the different songs. The whole audience came together, especially in the case of "Everyone Praise," and it was exciting because they started singing and dancing.

Nassau County Coliseum Rally

During the rally, there is a holy water ceremony with representatives of around five religious groups. Linda Chang was usually always the Buddhist community representative.

Bishop Hezekiah Walker, who is a Grammy Award winner, has an amazing voice, and when he sang, the audience was captivated. I know how much respect Bishop Noel Jones is held by Christians, and many people, like Pastor Boyd, listen to his sermons on DVDs, TV, radio, and many other places. Bishop Jones is very influential.

Pastor T. L. Barrett introduced Mrs. Moon, and she told the historical background of Jesus, and that His death on the cross was not His wish but came from the disbelief of the Israelites in Him. Therefore, this time, she said, there is a mission to save America and the world through the second coming of Jesus and Christianity as one. She revealed the current mission of Christianity in a truly straightforward manner.

The rally was a great success. The atmosphere was great, and many New Yorkers and New Jerseyans were bused in. As I mentioned earlier, there was a very tight entrance system, and the lines and the number of people trying to get into the convention center, even the parking lot was filled with people. President Dunkley of Unification Church in America announced that a total of 22,800 people attended. For Queens church seventeen buses, plus 127 people by car, came to the rally. This was truly made possible with the help of Pastor Joel Barnaby. He is a true friend.

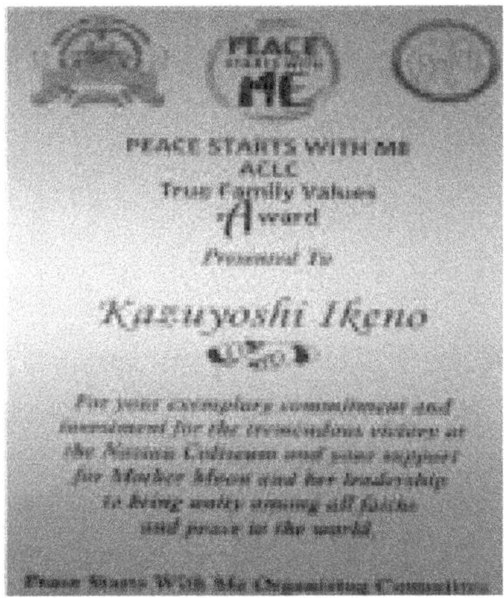

With Pastor Edwards at victory celebration and award

True Mother held a celebration after the rally. I somehow ended up sitting next to Pastor Tanya Edwards. I sincerely conveyed my appreciation to her about the ministry of Pastor Barnaby, and we had a lot of topics to talk about through him. Their parents are both pastors and a grandfather is also a pastor, so it's been going on for generations. I was impressed by the spiritual atmosphere of Pastor

Tanya Edwards and Pastor Joel Barnaby that a pure follower of Christianity can create this kind of emotional atmosphere.

President Dunkley invited the pastors to a banquet at the Manhattan Center, and I received a plaque for my service, which I was grateful for. We were able to get some amazing people involved. In the end, the rally had two Grammy winners singing and Bishop Noel Jones, a clergyman with great impact on the Christian church. Dr. Boyd was the one who made the difference this time because he sent four buses to the rally. Mrs. Moon was quite happy, and when she received the bouquets from second generation children, she really embraced and loved each child.

Then, Dr. Hak Ja Han Moon's global speaking tour continued to expand. From Zimbabwe to South Africa, Nepal to Cambodia, she gave lectures all over the world. The reason for this, which was announced to us, was that she had to search for these seven countries, even if it meant overworking herself, and that she would go to any righteous person, any saint, or any president who would welcome her. If there was a righteous person, if there was a saint, or if there was a president who would welcome her, she would go there. As I said before, it was a banquet to comfort the clergy members who contributed a lot for the event in Manhattan. Our Nassau County Coliseum rally in the United States in 2018 ended in victory.

4. Prudential Center Revival Rally and WCLC (World Christian Leadership Conference) Founding Conference (December 28, 2019)

In 2019, Dr. Hak Ja Han Moon had a busier schedule than ever, with major events and celebrations. The Blessing Ceremony was held. For example, Bishop Noel Jones called not only his own church but also various bishops he knew, and we also called our contacts to the City of Refuge Church in Los Angeles. We had a Blessing Ceremony for 3,000 pastors and congregation members at Bishop Jones' church. This was a real milestone. Then on June 1, we gathered 1,000 pastors of the ACLC in Las Vegas at the Tropicana Hotel. Mrs. Moon gave a speech to these pastors that was almost like a plea to them to unite with her and lead the world right. I was able to attend with seven pastors from both Queens and Milwaukee.

Bishop Noel Jones also spoke, and then the pastors of the main churches had a symposium. We took questions from the audience and discussed them. Bishop Woods, the bishop who supported us through persecution for about 50 years, was there. And from Queens, we brought Pastor Clifford of Pentecostal Lifeline.

The next rally was still in the process of being determined, so I joined the Wisconsin members in a blessing activity. In the midst of all this, Mrs. Moon also held the African Summit in Sao Tome and Principe, where she blessed the President and First Lady couple and the members of the National Assembly. She held the first national Blessing Ceremony. I felt that the hard work of the Ferch family, who had struggled for a long time in Sao Tome and Principe as the National Messiah from Wisconsin, had been rewarded. Therefore, this country became one of the seven nations.

In Japan, a convention of 40,000 people was held in Nagoya. And in Chicago, we had the True Family Values banquet at the Marriott Hotel, which we always do. In Europe, we had a Blessing Ceremony in Albania. In Korea, the homeland of faith, we had to establish Korean Clergy Leadership Conference (KCLC), so we sent 30 pastors from the United States to successfully complete the founding convention of KCLC. When it was decided that the founding of the World Christian Leadership Conference (WCLC) would happen at the Prudential Center "Peace Starts With Me" rally on December 28, I immediately knew that I had to go to New York or New Jersey to help.

One of our members who impressed me was Mr. Onishi. He was a little bit smaller than me, but he was able to enter into the hearts of pastors. I would think, "This pastor is not so open," but Mr. Onishi didn't think that way. He was like air. He entered into the hearts of many pastors. And the pastors, even though they were twice as tall as him, followed what he said. Pastor Saikas is his spiritual child, right? He is quite tall, twice the height of Mr. Onishi.

Mr. Onishi, unfortunately, passed away the day before he had to take the pastor to Korea. Mr. Onishi came to me in my dream and told me, "Mother's rally is being held here in New Jersey [his home base]." Thinking about that, he still wanted to help. He said, "Mr. Ikeno, please go and help as soon as possible. I will help you in the spirit world." I had this dream about three times. I said, "Mr. Onishi, I understand your regret. I will work twice as hard for you. Please cooperate with me." He asked me to work in New Jersey, and I was willing to do that.

I immediately flew to New York. However, when I stepped into the Queens Family Church for a moment, I heard that some pastors were becoming negative in various relationships. This was tough; our church members said, "We are losing the good connection with this pastor and that pastor and so on." I consulted with Dr. Kim and Bruce Gardiner, and they suggested I should go to the Prudential building in Newark, New Jersey, to pray early in the morning on Saturdays, and then help out in New Jersey. In the midst of all this, there were four Japanese missionaries, including one brother. Most of them were in the seminary of the Sun Moon University or active in purity education, and one was in law school somewhere. They came to support us, and I was very grateful to have young people with young energy and flexible minds.

Right away, I was told to hold a breakfast meeting in each borough. The Brooklyn Family Church rented a nice banquet hall called Grand Prospect Hall, and about 250 pastors, including some from Queens, attended there. It was a great venue; they have a second and third floor, and the food was amazing. Everyone cheered, and the members who were active in the Queens church got together and brought the pastors to this banquet.

At Bishop Woodall's church

At a church in Queens that occasionally asked me to conduct a Sunday service, I told them that, based on my experience in my past activities, it has become my ironclad creed that nothing succeeds unless the spirit world moves. I have been visiting churches for a long time, and the secret of success is to deny oneself. Mr. Onishi, as I mentioned earlier, was a genius at self-denial. I also said that it depends on mobilizing the spiritual world through passionate prayer.

At the same time, we didn't give much importance to offerings, but in established churches, it was important to say how much that pastor gave. We had to bring enough offerings. If you were prepared for that, externally and internally, the church would surely move. That was an important secret. My approach was that the more important the Prudential revival rally was, this was what we had do, and if we do it, we would surely succeed.

Bishop Woodall had responded to our flyer. His friend is Dr. Richard Hartley, who is founder, pastor and choir maser of Haven International Ministries in Queens. If you look on YouTube, he has several choirs. One group tours Europe, one group tours Japan, one group tours the U.S. I also saw a Japanese group singing gospel songs in English on YouTube. He is a great guy. Pastor Boyd also sent four buses last time, and Dr. Jenkins wanted Pastor Boyd to be a member of ACLC, so I had the opportunity to attend his Sunday services with him from time to time.

In Queens, there is great religious diversity. It's not just Christianity, it's also a Muslim (Islamic) mecca. It's also a mecca for Hindus. Do you know what a Sikh is? It's also the mecca of the Sikhs, the headquarters of Tenrikyo, Japanese Buddhism, Korean Buddhism, and Chinese Buddhism, all of which are in Queens. Soon we decided that we needed to have an ecumenical meeting of these different religions. Our friend, Pastor Kung, organized it, and we held it at the Queens Community Center. Around 200 people, almost all religious leaders from various fields, gathered there.

When we had conferences and meetings like this, people always came to them because they want to be welcomed. So here in Queens, you never hear anything about the Unification Church being heretical. They are tolerant about different religions.

We always had a prayer meeting on Saturdays at 7:00 AM in front of the Prudential Center. On December 14, a special prayer meeting was held at 9:00 AM, followed by a final breakfast prayer meeting at the Robert Treat Hotel. The number of participants was really large—1,000 people attended. In front of the Prudential Center, the brothers formed a circle and held a prayer meeting. After that, a banquet was held in the banquet hall of this big hotel. Pastor Barnaby here also attended, and we were able to have a reunion.

Mrs. Moon had been sending more and more goodwill to Latin America and the Caribbean Summit. Now we were on the last 40 days of 2019, and we had to go around the churches and religious organizations and make this "Peace Starts With Me" rally a great victory. More than 18,000 tickets were distributed. Mr. Rendel came out to make a report and included important statistics.

Dr. Hartley and Bishop Woodall both seemed to have been close friends since they were young. This was how we were able to introduce a famous pastor through one of the pastors. Pastor Boyd was looking very happy after receiving a thousand folded paper cranes from a Japanese missionary.

When the Prudential Center rally was approaching, each church held a prayer meeting, but the main Breakfast Prayer Meeting was important to ensure the success of the convention. At this time, about 350 pastors gathered at the Manhattan Center, and Pastor Kurtis Blow led a sort of rehearsal for the Prudential Center rally. I realized that even though I am getting older, I still need to master at least three gospel songs and gospel dances.

True Mother hit the victory gong

Finally, on December 28, 2019, the "Peace Starts With Me" rally was held at the Prudential Center. True Mother (Mrs. Hak Ja Han Moon) introduced the World Christian Clergy Leadership (WCLC) Rally of Hope for the Heavenly Unified World. She then spoke about the founding of the WCLC and the mission of the clergy. She said America was born because of the absolute faith of the Puritans who came from Europe to seek religious freedom with their lives. The foundation of their faith in God, which went beyond the starvation and death of their own families, was left as a seed by these people to be passed down to future generations.

Prudential Center rally and WCLC founding conference

God sympathized with the faith of these Puritans, and America was born. However, God did not bless the U.S. merely for its own prosperity. God blessed America as a representative of the world's humanity. That is why we must save the world. Especially at this time, people of various religions have gathered from all over the world. Therefore, you are righteous people, Mrs. Moon said. The mission of the righteous is not to think about themselves but to live for God. The most important thing is to unite with the Begotten Daughter, True Mother, because she is here and leading all fallen mankind as God's children, as True Parents' children. That is what we must do. That is the task that you, the righteous, are charged with. I was moved when I heard that.

Then True Mother (Mrs. Hak Ja Han Moon) invited 40 representatives to the podium and presented them with medals for the founding ceremony of the WCLC. It was a very moving moment, and after the ceremony, True Mother said that she cried a lot. For a long time, Christianity has persecuted us as heretics, putting Rev. Moon in jail six times. Of course, Satan, who fears us, is behind this persecution. After overcoming this persecution, the WCLC has been assigned the great task of saving the world by uniting the clergy of the world with Rev. and Mrs. Moon.

At the victory celebration, Mrs. Moon gave instructions to specific American members and leaders. Some states, she was told, had no Family Federation organization and, of course, no ACLC. She said that was not the way to go. First of all, we must establish a Family Federation and an ACLC in each of the 50 states. Then we must unite with the established churches in that area to serve and influence society, protect America from secular values, communism, and the like, and plant the same seeds that the Puritans brought to America once again.

The color scheme of Prudential Center's lights was extremely interesting, using a variety of colors, such as red for this side and blue for that side. The audience danced in various colors in response to Mrs. Moon's movements, and the 40 representatives received their awards. Mrs. Moon was so pleased that she put a lot of energy into the striking of the gong during the rally. The sound was loud. I could see how happy Mrs. Moon was with Rev. Moon in heaven. At the next victory celebration, Mrs. Moon's face was also full of joy. She also had a youthful, gorgeous, and truly beautiful expression, so much so that it was hard to believe that she had traveled all over the world.

5. Providence of the CheonBo Family Registration (2020)

Mrs. Moon received an invitation from North Korean Chairman Kim Jong Un quite some time ago. Kim Jong Un asked her many times to come as soon as possible, but True Mother said she would not go unless he agreed to three conditions.

Rev. and Mrs. Moon's grandchildren receive the Blessing

Meanwhile, this year (2020) saw the final climax of the 2020 World Summit conference as well as the anniversary of Rev. Moon's 100th birthday, the Seventh Foundation Day Festival, and the 60th Anniversary of the Holy Marriage Ceremony. These events were held at Korea International Exhibition Center (KINTEX) in Seoul and the Cheongshim World Peace Center in Korea.

The second seven-year course of the return to Canaan was also held on February 8. Then on May 8, the 60th Anniversary of the Holy Marriage Ceremony, the Heavenly Parents and the Holy Community were held to announce the new path of the Kingdom of Heaven.

My wife and I were able to attend the Cheongshim World Peace Center and, in part, the 2020 World Summit.

In this ceremony, True Mother (Mrs. Hak Ja Han Moon) performed two events. Two children of their late son, Hyo Jin Moon, received the Holy Blessing. I can only imagine how happy Mrs. Moon, Hyo Jin and Yeon Ah must have been. When I was watching this Blessing Ceremony, my heart was truly moved and I cried. While some of Mrs. Moon's children were walking their own paths against their parents, the grandchildren of Rev. and Mrs. Moon received the Blessing and walked toward their grandparents' dreams.

The 2020 World Summit was held at the same time as this Blessing Ceremony. Therefore, the internal Blessing Ceremony and the external summit conference were held at the same time. Both internally and externally, the salvation of the world was now taking concrete shape.

We are now planning to restore the U.S. by forming an online community. Long before he passed away, Rev. Moon said that the United States would be restored after the formation of 1,500 trinity communities in the 50 states. At this local center, through FAMICON, we seriously discussed the issue of how to form the Heavenly Parents Holy Community that True Mother (Mrs. Hak Ja Han Moon) talked about.

In 2020, the George Floyd incident, in which a black criminal died needlessly at the hands of the white police officers who were restraining him, revealed racial discrimination, and this, combined with the COVID-19 pandemic and a bitter presidential election, made for a truly chaotic situation in the United States. In such a situation, our hearts ached when we watched TV, and our activities were blocked at times by the pandemic. One thing that saved my heart in this situation was watching a dramatic series about Jesus Christ called, "The Chosen."

It became a valuable program that inspired us to recount the many blessings of our lives, including the Yankee Stadium rally, the Washington Monument rally, the Moscow rally, and so on. It just so happened that Dr. Shimmyo (former President of Unification Theological Seminary) and I were asked to give testimonies of our days as Japanese missionaries in the pioneer days of the United States, so we took part in it.

The program was great. The people who worked on it, from about 21 or 25 different fields, gave their testimonies. Many were now quite old, but they remembered the old days, and I appreciated all those who gave their testimonies.

Even in the midst of the COVID-19 pandemic, our movement began holding international rallies online, streaming speeches and activities through the internet, such as the One Million Rally of Hope. I think this is truly genius. When I talked to various pastors, they said we are a group with great ideas. There were several pastors who said they were not even aware of these things. With former President Donald Trump, former Vice President Mike Pence, former Vice President Dick Cheney, former Secretary of State Mike Pompeo, and former Speaker of the House Newt Gingrich participating, as well as top leaders from around the world, I think that the Rally of Hope is a groundbreaking, wonderful project through the internet.

Former U.S. House Speaker Newt Gingrich at the Summit Conference in Korea

Next, and I think this will be the last one, on October 9, 2020, a big celebration of the CheonBo family was held in Korea and all over the world at the same time. Our couple participated in the ceremony held in Chicago under the auspices of Dr. Ki Hoon Kim.

In my 57 years of church life, I have experienced many things. Financially, there were many hardships. I was also separated from my family at home for about 12 years, and I did not see my children for eight years, due to U.S. and foreign missions.

The thought of receiving the precious CheonBo designation is very moving. I wondered if this was the end of my life at the age of 78. But Dr. Yong, the FFWPU chairman of the North American Continent, said to me, "Mr. Ikeno, you will be even busier from now on."

There was a time when I had a stroke and was in despair. But Dr. Cho and the Happy Health machine saved me. When Dr. Cho told Rev. Moon, "Mr.

Ikeno was cured in a difficult place by the Happy Health machine," Rev. Moon said, "Well, I knew it would work; this machine I made conquers and cures all diseases." This was the result of his determination to create such a machine ever since he was a student at the School of Electrical Engineering at Waseda University, and it became such a happy machine.

Finally, on October 15, 2020, a global reorganization of FFWPU personnel took place. Dr. Chung Sik Yong was named president of the North American Continent and Dr. Ki Hoon Kim as president of the North American Cheong Shin Won. On November 15, Mr. Naokimi Ushiroda again became president of the American FFWPU. With the change to the new five subregion structure, the U.S. was finally ready for full-scale new start. On October 25, Dr. Yong was in charge of the first Sunday service, and from that day onward, morning devotions began at 6:00 AM. Many American brothers and sisters were able to be born again. At the Third Rally of Hope conference, Mrs. Moon emphasized that we should never forget those to whom we are indebted. Therefore, I think we will create a memorial monument to remember them.

This year (2021), Mrs. Moon will come to the U.S. again. We know how difficult it is to lead the pastors and the established churches we have cultivated so far to the Holy Blessing, especially the 40-day separation and the Three-Day Ceremony. However, it is clear that if we do this, people will receive the Holy Spirit and be changed. So, let us do it by all means and overcome this year of 2021. This was the content of Mrs. Moon's third rally.

I know this is a bit long, but it shows how attached Rev. and Mrs. Moon are to the Christian church, and how they are working together to restore the fallen humanity before God. This is what they have wished for in these long 50 years of American pioneering history—restoration of Christianity, building a defense against communism, and building ideal families. I think that is what they were hoping for. In other words, communism is Satan, right? Defense against Satan. The only way to do that is to restore Christianity once again.

Let's all work together to expand the trinity, this online Holy Community, together.

With this, I would like to conclude the First Seven-Year Path of the Return to Heavenly Cosmic Canaan. Thank you very much.

Thoughts on Receiving the Grace of CheonBo Registry

Kazuyoshi & Mieko Ikeno

I would like to express my heartfelt gratitude to Heavenly Parent and Rev. and Mrs. Moon for the precious grace of being granted the registration of CheonBo, Glorious Family of God the Parent, which is more than I can bear. Looking back now, I am deeply moved by the thought that my life has been both long and short, full of peaks and valleys and ups and downs, but that it has also been a truly joyous life.

Why did we join the Unification Church at such a young age, and what was it that we were seeking when we followed Rev. and Mrs. Moon? I believe the answer lies in the "salvation" (heavenly life) that we truly seek. We have been on overseas missions to many countries at one time or another, responding to providences issued by Rev. and Mrs. Moon, and we have struggled and suffered from the fetters caused by differences in language, culture, and customs. However, I believe that all of these experiences have been a path for each of us to grow in order to perfect our individuality.

Our Holy Blessing was the most prominent of these incidents and the most remarkable event of them all. As we started a family, we had many conflicts between husband and wife. Then children were born, and as the number of children increased, we were troubled with financial problems, education for the children, and reconciliation of providential requests and family needs. However, these difficulties were also fertilizers that promoted our growth.

In the providences, "evangelism" was consistently emphasized. Through evangelism, we can learn the feelings of our parents and grow spiritually by knowing the painful restoration of Heavenly Parent. Through evangelism, one can walk the shortest distance to the perfection of one's personality. In particular, as the Word of God says, the effect of clan messiah evangelism is that it cuts off the various bad karma of the descendants of the third to seventh generations, and purifies them spiritually. In our activities as tribal messiahs, we have always conducted our activities with this point in mind. Also, when working with our brothers and sisters, we have inspired them to do the blessing activities with sincerity because these activities are also connected to the benefits of their descendants.

My wife and I have brought 75 spiritual children (including spiritual grandchildren) who have received the Holy Blessing from Rev. and Mrs. Moon during our evangelism, and we have blessed 852 others. If there had been no pandemic, we had planned to bless 1,000 couples, but due to the coronavirus disaster that began in February 2020, we were unable to do so, and we hope to continue these activities again as soon as the pandemic is over.

Our blessing activities to date have taken many forms. First, we evangelized in Japan, our homeland, after we joined the church, and brought those people to the Blessing. We were able to bless a considerable number of members in our overseas mission fields (Russia and Belgium). On top of that, we participated in the blessing of 144,000 ministers and many pastors in Queens, New York, and Wisconsin.

My wife was a high school teacher for 20 years, so we invited some of the graduates who were already married to our home, cooked a feast, entertained them, explained the significance of the Blessing, and had them receive it, from the consecration ceremony to prayer. For those who were not yet married, we explained the significance of the Blessing Ceremony to their parents and had them receive it. I have also visited their relatives and blessed them. Through CARP activities, I have led a considerable number of people to receive the Blessing.

In addition, we secured a place at flea markets held on Saturdays and Sundays and conducted blessing activities in cooperation with brothers and sisters. In the summer, there were county festivals where we secured a place and worked together with our brothers and sisters to bless them. We also had Mexican festival, American Indian festival, and other festivals where we worked together with brothers and sisters. These activities were truly enjoyable and the people who received the blessings were truly happy.

We later attended the CheonBo registration ceremony at Chicago Family Church. When we received the plaque (number NA00008) and seal from President and Mrs. Kim, True Mother said, "On this day, you have been certified as citizens of as citizens of the God Kingdom of Heaven. Since the fall of Adam and Eve, Heavenly Parent has been waiting for this day for a long time." With these words, I realized that this is the state of so-called "salvation" that I have been seeking for 57 years—the state of having lived in Heaven's First Kingdom. I was deeply moved. When I was allowed by Heavenly Parent and Rev. and Mrs. Moon to stand in a position where there was not a cloud in my mind, my parents who are now in the spirit world, the parents of my blessed children who are in the spirit world, my daughter and her husband who died early and received the spirit world Blessing, my relatives in the spirit world, and all 430 generations of spirit world blessed ones descended, the place was glowing with light. I felt that heaven and earth were enveloped in joy with tremendous enthusiasm.

I could feel the heart of Rev. and Mrs. Moon's desire to save all mankind welling up from the bottom of my heart.

October 10, 2020

Milestones

A commemorative certificate of commendation given by Rev. and Mrs. Sun Myung Moon as we look back on our 57 years of work for the creation of the Kingdom of God.

June 13, 1976
My team (CARP) ranked first in Yankee Stadium convention attendance (10,000 people). Out of 12 people who received an award from True Parents, 10 were CARP members.
Individual Second Prize (400 people mobilized); received a gold watch and $10,000.

October 4, 1976
For the best mobilization of New York churches for the Washington Monument rally (350 buses, 15,000 people attended); received a leather-bound Bible signed by Rev. Moon with my name.

March 6, 1983
Queen's Family Church (I was the head minister at the time); received an award from Rev. Won Pil Kim for Model Home Church.

February 3, 2003
Cheon Il Guk Owners Awards

May 1, 2004

Long-term Overseas Mission Merit Award (at the Unification Church's 50th Anniversary Convention at Sun Moon University)

January 1, 2012

Meritorious Service Award

January 13, 2013

Heaven's Foundation Day of the Year, Heavenly Lunar New Year's Eve, Cheng Il Guk Foundation Day Award

October 10, 2020

CheonBo Family Registration Award

My Loving Family
—Mieko Ikeno

I was frail from an early age and had to go to the hospital for various reasons. Shortly after the war, my father was a teacher in Tianjin in Manchuria, China, and we came back to Japan in the confusion of the postwar period. I was in my mother's womb at the time and had to overcome a difficult hurdle to be born. In the midst of food shortages soon after the war, both mother and child were malnourished, and after that, my parents wondered if I would be able to bear a child even if I got married.

However, in February 1977, when I was 30 years old, Rev. and Mrs. Moon chose my husband as my eternal companion. This was the Holy Blessing of the Family Federation of World Peace and Unification (Unification Church). My husband was studying international politics at Columbia University in New York City at the time. He was a genuine Kyushu man (Southern Japan) with a big vision and was working energetically toward that dream. Since then, my husband's energy and vitality have blessed us with six children (one prematurely died) and 15 grandchildren, a blessing we never thought we would receive. My husband has been running around the world, rarely being at home, and much of the responsibility for our family's finances and our children's education fell on my shoulders.

Our six children were born in different providences, so we gave them all nicknames. One year after we started our family (June 13, 1978), our oldest daughter was born, and True Mother named her "Hanako." One day, Rev. and Mrs. Moon came all the way to Jacob House to see Hanako, and said to my husband, "I saw your child today, she looks like a man," and added, "You have a good baby." Hanako was nicknamed "New York Child" because my husband worked at a New York Church overseeing the Home Church providence. Our second daughter, Akiko, was born when I was working as a CARP under Rev. Tiger Park (Korean regional director), evangelizing on campuses all over America, so we call her "the CARP Child." Our third daughter was born while we were working home church in Queens, so that her nickname is "Home Church Child." Next, our family had a long-awaited baby boy. My husband was traveling around the country as an IOWC Commander at the time, so we nicknamed him "IOWC Child" (Eikoku was named by Rev. Won Pil Kim). Our daughter (Milei) was born in Wisconsin, where our family was finally able to live together. The International Conferences for Clergy (ICC) project was planned in the hope of contributing to the revival of Christianity in America by sending 7,000 pastors to Korea to study the Unification Principle and make pilgrimages to the Holy Land Korea. Therefore, we call her by the nickname "ICC Child."

Family picture at Milwaukee home (April 2011), while my husband was in Las Vegas

All of our children have been blessed at different times and places, and our family has rapidly grown into a large family. Perhaps the most unique Blessing Ceremony was the spirit world Blessing of our daughter Seong Ae and Yong Jung Ho, who died prematurely at a very young age. For people in this world, a Blessing Ceremony in the spirit world may seem unthinkable, but it is not so strange when we look at the principles that pervade the entire universe. Everything in the universe is based on a pairing system. Therefore, there are marriages even in the spirit world. When I lost Seong Ae, I spent three months crying because I was so sad. God sent me to Chicago with Dae Mo nim (Mrs. Kim) from Cheong

Pyeong, Korea. She told me, "Don't be so sad. Your daughter will grow up with the love of her parents, and when she comes of age, she will be blessed with a good person. So, pray every day for your daughter by candlelight."

Then suddenly in February 2002, we received a phone call from Korea, informing us that our daughter would receive the Marriage Blessing in the spirit world and that we should come to the Cheong Pyeong by February 14. My husband immediately went to Seoul, where he had a matching with Yong Jung Ho, the eldest son of Mrs. Seon Ja Jeon (of the 72 Couples Blessing). Two days later, the 400 million Couples Blessing and the Spirit World Blessing took place at the Seoul Olympic Stadium. My husband and I could not be more grateful to God and True Parents for such an amazing blessing.

The next unique Blessing I would like to mention was the International Blessing Ceremony held on December 26, 2004, at the East Garden, the residence of Rev. and Mrs. Moon, for our eldest son Eikoku and Tsukiko Sato, who attended from Japan. The Engagement and Blessing Ceremony was held at East Garden. They have since been blessed with three boys.

I married late in life, and all five of my children were born by cesarean section because natural childbirth was not possible. When the last child was born, the doctor called my husband into the delivery room and asked him to sign for the baby in case of emergency to help him cope with the difficult situation. My husband said he was moved by the sight of the bloody baby being born.

At some point, the children of True Parents' family started going their own separate ways, and suddenly, as if from out of nowhere, a huge earthquake was accompanied by a huge tsunami that swept in and swallowed up our home. This was a truly heartbreaking event. Some of my children began to walk a different path than True Parents. I couldn't stop crying, not only for my own family, but also for True Parents' heartache.

However, I cannot help but believe that when we keep our absolute faith in God and True Parents, we will be able to be a family that gathers together and shares joys as we used to do in the past. Finally, I believe that the family is a place for self-improvement, and that parents grow through their children, and children grow according to the degree of their parents' growth. I believe that if each one of us can improve the quality of our love through the family and become a person of love like Jesus and True Parents, the problems we are facing now will naturally be resolved. I believe that in the near future, all children will return to the bosom of their parents in some way due to the causality of God's lineage.

In the future, we hope that our grandchildren and great-grandchildren will receive international blessings, transcending differences in race and nationality, and that when we reach 100 years of age, all the people of the world will unite to seek God's heart and become one family under God.

285

Postscript

After writing my 79 years of personal history, I think about what Rev. Moon once said, "When the Kingdom of Heaven is established, if I can step into it just for a moment and go to the other world, I would be happy." Unfortunately, his dream did not come true and he passed away. It is not difficult to imagine how regretful it must have been for Rev. Moon. His only hope is that his spouse, Mrs. Hak Ja Han Moon, is still alive in this world and that through her efforts, God and Rev. Moon's dream of creating a heavenly kingdom will be realized. Hopefully, I too will live long enough to live in Heaven's first kingdom, even if only for a moment. That is my dream now.

I was born in an air-raid shelter in the middle of war as a tiny baby weighing 850 grams to a malnourished mother. My mother and grandparents were fond of saying that it was a miracle that I survived. The war took a heavy toll on my family. First, my uncle was killed in Leyte, Philippines. My Aunt Etsuko, an American citizen, returned with her two young children to her hometown in Japan to escape U.S. persecution against the Japanese, taking what little she had with her. The relatives who remained in the U.S. were forcibly imprisoned in Japanese internment camps in Utah and Colorado. In their home villages, some were killed in action on the Chinese mainland, while others were interned by the Soviet Union. Two different atomic bombs were dropped on Hiroshima and Nagasaki, killing 210,000 people at one time. Another 450,000 people died from the after-effects of the bombings. My own hometown was burned to the ground by incendiary bombs from U.S. B-29s. I hated this absurd war. At the same time, I wondered how we could build a peaceful world without war, especially without nuclear weapons.

Even in the 21st century, the real world is far from peaceful. The despotic dictator Vladimir Putin, who invaded the sovereign nation of Ukraine, waving his own historical views, has been threatening to use nuclear weapons when his defeat became imminent. The next nuclear war will annihilate the human race. It has been my dream for many years to see mankind living together as one big family with God at the center. But if nuclear war breaks out, that dream will be shattered. How can we create a peaceful world without nuclear weapons?

Ever since I met Rev. and Mrs. Moon (March 1971), I have been confident that if I followed them, they would surely establish the peaceful Kingdom of God. I have been working hard, dreaming of the establishment of the Kingdom of God as the scripture says, "Seek the Kingdom of God and His righteousness" (Matthew 6:33). In June 1972, I came to the United States, the country of my dreams. God founded America because of the absolute faith of the Pilgrim fathers had in God. Although the United States is now at the peak of prosperity unrivaled in the world, in recent years, it has come to be called a sickly superpower. The most important cause of America's illness is the fact that people have lost their absolute faith in God—the Creator to whom they had entrusted everything in order to seek religious freedom, and in whom they had believed would surely lead them to a new continent and help them establish the Kingdom of God on that new continent.

With the spread of materialism, people have lost their absolute faith in God. In the gap between the two, secular values have attempted to isolate the relationship between God and people. Socialism and communism also began to permeate society. These ideologies overtly deny God and Christianity. The Christian churches in this situation were taught about the threat of communism and began to campaign to turn back to God once again. Various American restoration movements have been repeated for 50 years. I have also participated in the many restoration paths that were built for the return to the United States. This is the "History of the 50th Anniversary of the American Revival," which I wrote with Rev. and Mrs. Moon. My autobiography, "My Life on Five Continents," which I wrote based on this history, is also a record of Rev. and Mrs. Moon's worldwide relief efforts.

However, just as the world restoration was nearing its climax, Rev. Moon suddenly passed away on September 3, 2012. Mrs. Moon took over all remaining projects at once and announced a roadmap that would bring us one step closer to Cheon Il Guk (Heaven on Earth). The first step was the proclamation of Cheon Il Guk Foundation Day on January 13, 2013. This proclamation announced that the first Kingdom of Heaven would be realized in the near future. The second stage was the construction of the Cheon Il Guk Sacred Temple. This feat is represented by the upcoming dedication ceremony of the Cheon Won Gung Palace in April 2025. This is similar to the palace of King Solomon, the foundation of the prosperity of the united kingdom of King David in the past. God's presence in this palace will complete the providence of heaven. The third and final stage of the proclamation is the restoration of the nation centering on God in substance and the establishment of a single heavenly kingdom. This will result in the restoration of one-third of the world to the Kingdom of Heaven. We earnestly hope that a peaceful world of one human family will come.

Lastly, I would like to mention my wife, with whom I have shared many hardships and joys, and my family, who have given me constant joy and hope. My wife has followed me silently without a word of complaint as I have changed personnel in response to the rapidly changing providence. I was deeply grateful for her. She chose to become a teacher in the U.S. to make ends meet without receiving a single penny from the church, and she raised our children well by sending them to school even though I was doing missionary work overseas. I also tried my best to pay for my overseas missionary work, but there were times when I still needed my wife's support to make up the shortfall. I sent our five children to elementary and junior high schools in Korea to learn the Korean language and filial piety culture. This ensured that they were not influenced by worldly customs when they returned to the U.S. All of my children have since gone on to study at universities and graduate schools in the U.S., received blessings, and are now working as lawyers, nurses, and in the education field. My only regret is that I did not spend more time with my children during my long, overseas missions and did not care for them as much as I should have, and unfortunately, I was not able to create a deep parent-child relationship. Therefore, I hope to spend the rest of my life not as atonement for my sins, but as a way to rebuild the relationship between parents and children, and to live happily in a three-generation sphere that includes parents, children, and grandchildren.

Finally, I would like to thank all those who have helped me to publish my autobiography. I would not have started writing my autobiography without the strong encouragement of the late Hiroshi Inose, president of the Kodan group. I would also like to thank Mr. Yukihiko Miyazawa for his efforts in recording my memoirs over a period of two and a half months. I must also thank my wife for her dedicated work in organizing the past records and creating a PowerPoint presentation, without which I would not have been able to produce a book of enormous pages. I would also like to thank Mr. Fumio Fukatsu, president of

"Good Time" publishers, for his patience in undertaking the difficult task of converting the videos into text until the autobiography was ready for publication.

November 20, 2023
Milwaukee, Wisconsin, United States of America
Kazuyoshi Ikeno

Kazuyoshi Ikeno's Timeline

Born November 20, 1944 in Sakaime, Hanazono-cho, Uto City, Kumamoto Prefecture, Japan. Eldest son of father (Kazuo) and mother (Yoshiko), with a younger sister (Reiko) and a younger brother (Kazunori)

Education: B.A. in Political Science and Economics, Waseda University; M.A. in Political Science, Waseda University; M.I.A. Columbia Graduate School, Institute of International Studies and the Institute of East Asian Studies; D.Min from St. Martin College and Seminary

Introduced to the Unification Church and Divine Principle on July 10, 1966, by a missionary of the Unification Church

Officially audited the Principle lectures at university festival in September 1966, completed 40 days of training in 1967, and pioneered the summer program

August 28, 1967, joined the Collegiate Association for the Research of Principles (CARP). Became director of the Information Bureau of the Japan CARP, and editor-in-chief of the World Student Times and Regional Director of Waseda University CARP

June 1972, Moved to the U.S. Founded CARP at Columbia University. Engaged in campaigns at Carnegie Hall, Madison Square Garden, Yankee Stadium, and Washington Monument

February 21, 1977, received Holy Blessing with Mieko Kita as part of 74 Couples Blessing in New York City. Today, the Ikeno family has six children and 15 grandchildren

November 1977, became devoted to home church under Rev. Won Pil Kim

1983, became IOWC Commander

1984, became Minnesota State Leader

1986, became Wisconsin State Leader

July 1991, left for overseas missions to Russia and China

September 1996, became National Messiah to Belgium

August 1999, became missionary to the Pantanal and Leda pioneer

March 2002, supported blessings of 144,000 clergy in the U.S.

September 3, 2012, Rev. Moon passed away

January 13, 2013 (February 22, 2013), Foundation Day

2013-2020, dedicated to the First Seven-Year Course of the Restoration of the Heavenly Cosmic Canaan

October 10, 2020, registered as CheonBo family through domestic and international messianic activities